Efficient Android Threading

Anders Göransson

Beijing · Cambridge · Farnham · Köln · Sebastopol · Tokyo

Efficient Android Threading

by Anders Göransson

Copyright © 2014 Anders Göransson. All rights reserved.

Printed in the United States of America.

Published by O'Reilly Media, Inc., 1005 Gravenstein Highway North, Sebastopol, CA 95472.

O'Reilly books may be purchased for educational, business, or sales promotional use. Online editions are also available for most titles (*http://my.safaribooksonline.com*). For more information, contact our corporate/institutional sales department: 800-998-9938 or *corporate@oreilly.com*.

Editors: Andy Oram and Rachel Roumeliotis	**Indexer:** Ellen Troutman-Zaig
Production Editor: Melanie Yarbrough	**Cover Designer:** Karen Montgomery
Copyeditor: Eliahu Sussman	**Interior Designer:** David Futato
Proofreader: Amanda Kersey	**Illustrator:** Rebecca Demarest

May 2014:   First Edition

Revision History for the First Edition:

2014-05-21:   First release

See *http://oreilly.com/catalog/errata.csp?isbn=9781449364137* for release details.

Nutshell Handbook, the Nutshell Handbook logo, and the O'Reilly logo are registered trademarks of O'Reilly Media, Inc. *Efficient Android Threading*, the cover image of mahi-mahi, and related trade dress are trademarks of O'Reilly Media, Inc.

Many of the designations used by manufacturers and sellers to distinguish their products are claimed as trademarks. Where those designations appear in this book, and O'Reilly Media, Inc. was aware of a trademark claim, the designations have been printed in caps or initial caps.

While every precaution has been taken in the preparation of this book, the publisher and author assume no responsibility for errors or omissions, or for damages resulting from the use of the information contained herein.

ISBN: 978-1-449-36413-7

[LSI]

To Anna, Fabian, and Ida.

Table of Contents

Preface. xi

1. Android Components and the Need for Multiprocessing. 1
   Android Software Stack   1
   Application Architecture   2
      Application   3
      Components   3
   Application Execution   5
      Linux Process   6
      Lifecycle   6
   Structuring Applications for Performance   9
      Creating Responsive Applications Through Threads   9
   Summary   11

Part I.   Fundamentals

2. Multithreading in Java. 15
   Thread Basics   15
      Execution   15
      Single-Threaded Application   17
      Multithreaded Application   17
   Thread Safety   19
      Intrinsic Lock and Java Monitor   20
      Synchronize Access to Shared Resources   22
      Example: Consumer and Producer   24
   Task Execution Strategies   26
      Concurrent Execution Design   27

Summary   27

3. Threads on Android. 29
    Android Application Threads   29
        UI Thread   29
        Binder Threads   30
        Background Threads   30
    The Linux Process and Threads   31
        Scheduling   34
    Summary   37

4. Thread Communication. 39
    Pipes   39
        Basic Pipe Use   40
        Example: Text Processing on a Worker Thread   42
    Shared Memory   44
        Signaling   45
    BlockingQueue   46
    Android Message Passing   47
        Example: Basic Message Passing   49
        Classes Used in Message Passing   51
        Message   55
        Looper   58
        Handler   60
        Removing Messages from the Queue   68
        Observing the Message Queue   70
    Communicating with the UI Thread   73
    Summary   74

5. Interprocess Communication. 75
    Android RPC   75
        Binder   76
    AIDL   77
        Synchronous RPC   79
        Asynchronous RPC   81
    Message Passing Using the Binder   83
        One-Way Communication   84
        Two-Way Communication   86
    Summary   87

6. Memory Management. 89
    Garbage Collection   89

Thread-Related Memory Leaks	91
Thread Execution	92
Thread Communication	98
Avoiding Memory Leaks	101
Use Static Inner Classes	101
Use Weak References	101
Stop Worker Thread Execution	102
Retain Worker Threads	102
Clean Up the Message Queue	102
Summary	103

Part II. Asynchronous Techniques

7. Managing the Lifecycle of a Basic Thread. **107**

Basics	107
Lifecycle	107
Interruptions	108
Uncaught Exceptions	110
Thread Management	112
Definition and Start	112
Retention	114
Summary	119

8. HandlerThread: A High-Level Queueing Mechanism. **121**

Fundamentals	121
Lifecycle	123
Use Cases	124
Repeated Task Execution	125
Related Tasks	125
Task Chaining	128
Conditional Task Insertion	131
Summary	131

9. Control over Thread Execution Through the Executor Framework. **133**

Executor	133
Thread Pools	136
Predefined Thread Pools	136
Custom Thread Pools	137
Designing a Thread Pool	138
Lifecycle	142
Shutting Down the Thread Pool	143

        Thread Pool Uses Cases and Pitfalls   145
    Task Management   146
        Task Representation   146
        Submitting Tasks   147
        Rejecting Tasks   151
    ExecutorCompletionService   152
    Summary   154

10. Tying a Background Task to the UI Thread with AsyncTask. **157**
    Fundamentals   157
        Creation and Start   160
        Cancellation   161
        States   162
    Implementing the AsyncTask   163
        Example: Downloading Images   164
    Background Task Execution   167
        Application Global Execution   169
        Execution Across Platform Versions   170
        Custom Execution   172
    AsyncTask Alternatives   173
        When an AsyncTask Is Trivially Implemented   173
        Background Tasks That Need a Looper   174
        Local Service   174
        Using execute(Runnable)   174
    Summary   175

11. Services. **177**
    Why Use a Service for Asynchronous Execution?   177
    Local, Remote, and Global Services   179
    Creation and Execution   181
    Lifecycle   181
    Started Service   183
        Implementing onStartCommand   184
        Options for Restarting   184
        User-Controlled Service   186
        Task-Controlled Service   190
    Bound Service   192
        Local Binding   194
    Choosing an Asynchronous Technique   197
    Summary   198

12. IntentService. **199**

Fundamentals   199
Good Ways to Use an IntentService   201
   Sequentially Ordered Tasks   201
   Asynchronous Execution in BroadcastReceiver   204
IntentService Versus Service   207
Summary   207

13. Access ContentProviders with AsyncQueryHandler. **209**
Brief Introduction to ContentProvider   209
Justification for Background Processing of a ContentProvider   211
Using the AsyncQueryHandler   212
   Example: Expanding Contact List   214
   Understanding the AsyncQueryHandler   217
   Limitations   218
Summary   218

14. Automatic Background Execution with Loaders. **219**
Loader Framework   220
   LoaderManager   221
   LoaderCallbacks   224
   AsyncTaskLoader   225
Painless Data Loading with CursorLoader   226
   Using the CursorLoader   227
   Example: Contact list   227
   Adding CRUD Support   229
Implementing Custom Loaders   233
   Loader Lifecycle   233
   Background Loading   234
   Content Management   236
   Delivering Cached Results   237
   Example: Custom File Loader   238
   Handling Multiple Loaders   241
Summary   242

15. Summary: Selecting an Asynchronous Technique. **243**
Keep It Simple   244
Thread and Resource Management   244
Message Communication for Responsiveness   245
Avoid Unexpected Task Termination   246
Easy Access to ContentProviders   247

A. Bibliography. **249**

Index.. 251

Preface

Efficient Android Threading explores how to achieve robust and reliable multithreaded Android applications. We'll look at the asynchronous mechanisms that are available in the Android SDK and determine appropriate implementations to achieve fast, responsive, and well-structured applications.

Let's face it: multithreading is required to create applications with a great user experience, but it also increases the complexity of the application and the likelihood of runtime errors. The complexity partly comes from the built-in difficulty of execution on multiple threads and from applications that aren't utilizing the Android platform efficiently.

This book aims to guide application developers to selecting an asynchronous mechanism based on an understanding of its advantages and difficulties. By using the right asynchronous mechanism at the right time, much of the complexity is transferred from the application to the platform, making the application code more maintainable and less error prone. As a rule of thumb, asynchronous execution should not induce more complexity to the code than necessary, which is achieved through a wise choice from the palette of asynchronous mechanisms in Android.

Although a high-level asynchronous mechanism can be very convenient to use, it still needs to be understood—not only used—or the application may suffer from equally difficult runtime errors, performance degradation, or memory leaks. Therefore, this book not only contains practical guidelines and examples, but also explores the underlying enablers for asynchronous execution on Android.

Audience

This book is for Java programmers who have learned the basics of Android programming. The book introduces techniques that are fundamental to writing robust and responsive applications, using standard Android libraries.

Contents of This Book

This book contains two main parts: Part I and Part II. The first part describes the foundation for threads on Android—i.e., Java, Linux, Handlers—and its impact on the application. The second part is more hands-on, looking into the asynchronous mechanisms that an application has at its disposal.

Part I describes how Java handles threads. As an Android programmer, you will sometimes use these libraries directly, and understanding their behavior is important for using the higher-level constructs in Part II correctly.

Chapter 1
> Explains how the structure of the Android runtime and how the various components of an Android application affect the use of threads and multiprocessing.

Chapter 2
> Covers the fundamentals of concurrent execution in Java.

Chapter 3
> Describes how Android handles threads and how the application threads execute in the Linux OS. It includes important topics like scheduling and control groups, as well as their impact on responsiveness.

Chapter 4
> Covers basic communication between threads, such as shared memory, signals, and the commonly used Android messages.

Chapter 5
> Shows how Android enhances the IPC mechanisms in Linux with mechanisms such as RPC and messaging.

Chapter 6
> Explains how to avoid leaks, which can cause apps to degrade the system and be uninstalled by users.

Part II covers the higher-level libraries and constructs in Android that make programming with threads safer and easier.

Chapter 7
> Describes the most basic asynchronous construction, i.e, `java.lang.Thread`, and how to handle the various states and problems that can occur.

Chapter 8
> Shows a convenient way to run tasks sequentially in the background.

Chapter 9
> Offers techniques for dealing with scheduling, errors, and other aspects of thread handling, such as thread pools.

Chapter 10

Covers the `AsyncTask`—probably the most popular asynchronous technique—and how to use it correctly to avoid its pitfalls.

Chapter 11

Covers the essential `Service` component, which is useful for functionality that you want to offer to multiple applications or to keep the application alive during background execution.

Chapter 12

Builds on the previous chapter with a discussion of a useful technique for executing off the main UI thread.

Chapter 13

A high-level mechanism that simplifies fast asynchronous access to content providers.

Chapter 14

Discover how the UI can be updated with loaders, where new data is delivered asynchronously whenever the content changes.

Chapter 15

Given all the techniques described throughout this book, how do you choose the right one for your app? This chapter offers guidelines for making this choice.

Conventions Used in this Book

The following typographical conventions are used in this book:

Italic

Used for emphasis, new terms, URLs, commands and utilities, and file and directory names.

`Constant width`

Indicates variables, functions, types, objects, and other programming constructs.

`Constant width italic`

Indicates place-holders in code or commands that should be replaced by appropriate values.

This element signifies a tip, suggestion, or a general note.

This element indicates a trap or pitfall to watch out for, typically something that isn't immediately obvious.

Using Code Examples

Supplemental material (code examples, exercises, etc.) is available for download at *https://github.com/andersgoransson/eatbookexamples*.

This book is here to help you get your job done. In general, you may use the code in this book in your programs and documentation. You do not need to contact us for permission unless you are reproducing a significant portion of the code. For example, writing a program that uses several chunks of code from this book does not require permission. Selling or distributing a CD-ROM of examples from O'Reilly books does require permission. Answering a question by citing this book and quoting example code does not require permission. Incorporating a significant amount of example code from this book into your product's documentation does require permission.

We appreciate attribution. An attribution usually includes the title, author, publisher, and ISBN.

If you believe that your use of code examples falls outside of fair use or the permission given above, feel free to contact us at *permissions@oreilly.com*.

Examples will be maintained at: *git@github.com*:andersgoransson/eatbookexamples.git

Safari® Books Online

 Safari Books Online is an on-demand digital library that delivers expert content in both book and video form from the world's leading authors in technology and business.

Technology professionals, software developers, web designers, and business and creative professionals use Safari Books Online as their primary resource for research, problem solving, learning, and certification training.

Safari Books Online offers a range of product mixes and pricing programs for organizations, government agencies, and individuals. Subscribers have access to thousands of books, training videos, and prepublication manuscripts in one fully searchable database from publishers like O'Reilly Media, Prentice Hall Professional, Addison-Wesley Professional, Microsoft Press, Sams, Que, Peachpit Press, Focal Press, Cisco Press, John Wiley & Sons, Syngress, Morgan Kaufmann, IBM Redbooks, Packt, Adobe Press, FT Press, Apress, Manning, New Riders, McGraw-Hill, Jones & Bartlett, Course Technology, and dozens more. For more information about Safari Books Online, please visit us online.

How to Contact Us

Please address comments and questions concerning this book to the publisher:

O'Reilly Media, Inc.
1005 Gravenstein Highway North
Sebastopol, CA 95472
800-998-9938 (in the United States or Canada)
707-829-0515 (international or local)
707-829-0104 (fax)

We have a web page for this book, where we list errata, examples, and any additional information. You can access this page at *http://bit.ly/efficient-android-threading*.

To comment or ask technical questions about this book, send email to *bookques tions@oreilly.com*.

For more information about our books, courses, conferences, and news, see our website at *http://bit.ly/efficient-android-threading*.

Find us on Facebook: *http://facebook.com/oreilly*

Follow us on Twitter: *http://twitter.com/oreillymedia*

Watch us on YouTube: *http://www.youtube.com/oreillymedia*

Acknowledgements

The writing of a book may often be seen as a lonely task, but that only holds for the late-night hours when you just want to get that last paragraph written before you absolutely have to get some sleep. In truth, the writing is surrounded by people who made the book possible.

First of all, I would like to thank Rachel Roumeliotis at O'Reilly for approaching me with an idea to write a book and helping out with all the initial steps in the writing process. In fact, all the people at O'Reilly whom I've had the pleasure to work with have shown great professionalism and helpfulness throughout the writing of this book, which made it easy for me to focus on the writing. In particular, I would like to thank editor Andy Oram, who has played a key role in making this book a reality. He has patiently worked with me on this project, always challenging my drafts and providing invaluable feedback.

Just like writing complex software, the writing of a book includes a lot of bugs along the way, and every chapter undergoes a bugfixing and stabilization period before a final release. I've had the best of help to pinpoint problems in the drafts by technical reviewers Jeff Six and Ian Darwin, who have provided numerous comments that ranged from missing commas to coding errors and structural improvements. Thanks a lot!

A book can't be written without a supportive family. Thanks for putting up with my late-night working hours. Truth be told, I hold it as unlikely that this book will ever be read by you; nevertheless, I hope it will be a part of your future bookshelf...

CHAPTER 1

Android Components and the Need for Multiprocessing

Before we immerse ourselves in the world of threading, we will start with an introduction to the Android platform, the application architecture, and the application's execution. This chapter provides a baseline of knowledge required for an effective discussion of threading in the rest of the book, but a complete information on the Android platform can be found in the official documentation (*https://developer.android.com*) or in most of the numerous Android programming books on the market.

Android Software Stack

Applications run on top of a software stack that is based on a Linux kernel, native C/C++ libraries, and a runtime that executes the application code (Figure 1-1).

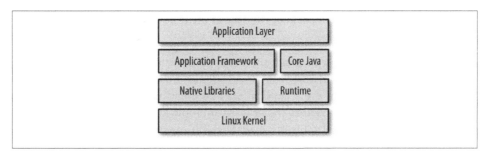

Figure 1-1. Android software stack

The major building blocks of the Android software stack are:

Applications

Android applications that are implemented in Java. They utilize both Java and Android framework libraries.

Core Java

The core Java libraries used by applications and the application framework. It is not a fully compliant Java SE or ME implementation, but a subset of the retired Apache Harmony (*http://harmony.apache.org*) implementation, based on Java 5. It provides the fundamental Java threading mechanisms: the `java.lang.Thread` class and `java.util.concurrent` package.

Application framework

The Android classes that handle the window system, UI toolkit, resources, and so on—basically everything that is required to write an Android application in Java. The framework defines and manages the lifecycles of the Android components and their intercommunication. Furthermore, it defines a set of Android-specific asynchronous mechanisms that applications can utilize to simplify the thread management: `HandlerThread`, `AsyncTask`, `IntentService`, `AsyncQueryHandler`, and `Loaders`. All these mechanisms will be described in this book.

Native libraries

C/C++ libraries that handle graphics, media, database, fonts, OpenGL, etc. Java applications normally don't interact directly with the native libraries because the Application framework provides Java wrappers for the native code.

Runtime

Sandboxed runtime environment that executes compiled Android application code in a virtual machine, with an internal byte code representation. Every application executes in its own runtime, either Dalvik or ART (Android Runtime). The latter was added in KitKat (API level 19) as an optional runtime that can be enabled by the user, but Dalvik is the default runtime at the time of writing.

Linux kernel

Underlying operating system that allows applications to use the hardware functions of the device: sound, network, camera, etc. It also manages processes and threads. A process is started for every application, and every process holds a runtime with a running application. Within the process, multiple threads can execute the application code. The kernel splits the available CPU execution time for processes and their threads through *scheduling*.

Application Architecture

The cornerstones of an application are the `Application` object and the Android components: `Activity`, `Service`, `BroadcastReceiver`, and `ContentProvider`.

Application

The representation of an executing application in Java is the `android.app.Applica` `tion` object, which is instantiated upon application start and destroyed when the application stops (i.e., an instance of the `Application` class lasts for the lifetime of the Linux process of the application). When the process is terminated and restarted, a new `Application` instance is created.

Components

The fundamental pieces of an Android application are the components managed by the runtime: `Activity`, `Service`, `BroadcastReceiver`, and `ContentProvider`. The configuration and interaction of these components define the application's behavior. These entities have different responsibilities and lifecycles, but they all represent application entry points, where the application can be started. Once a component is started, it can trigger another component, and so on, throughout the application's lifecycle. A component is trigged to start with an `Intent`, either within the application or between applications. The `Intent` specifies actions for the receiver to act upon—for instance, sending an email or taking a photograph—and can also provide data from the sender to the receiver. An `Intent` can be explicit or implicit:

Explicit `Intent`
> Defines the fully classified name of the component, which is known within the application at compile time.

Implicit `Intent`
> A runtime binding to a component that has defined a set of characteristics in an `IntentFilter`. If the `Intent` matches the characteristics of a component's `Intent` `Filter`, the component can be started.

Components and their lifecycles are Android-specific terminologies, and they are not directly matched by the underlying Java objects. A Java object can outlive its component, and the runtime can contain multiple Java objects related to the same live component. This is a source of confusion, and as we will see in Chapter 6, it poses a risk for memory leaks.

An application implements a component by subclassing it, and all components in an application must be registered in the *AndroidManifest.xml* file.

Activity

An `Activity` is a screen—almost always taking up the device's full screen—shown to the user. It displays information, handles user input, and so on. It contains the UI components—buttons, texts, images, and so forth—shown on the screen and holds an object reference to the view hierarchy with all the `View` instances. Hence, the memory footprint of an `Activity` can grow large.

When the user navigates between screens, `Activity` instances form a stack. Navigation to a new screen pushes an `Activity` to the stack, whereas backward navigation causes a corresponding pop.

In Figure 1-2, the user has started an initial `Activity` A and navigated to B while A was finished, then on to C and D. A, B, and C are full-screen, but D covers only a part of the display. Thus, A is destroyed, B is totally obscured, C is partly shown, and D is fully shown at the top of the stack. Hence, D has focus and receives user input. The position in the stack determines the state of each `Activity`:

- Active in the foreground: D
- Paused and partly visible: C
- Stopped and invisible: B
- Inactive and destroyed: A

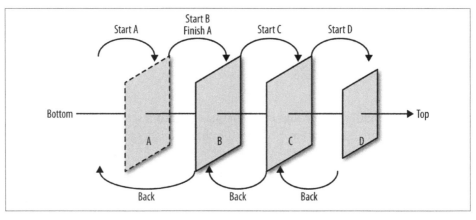

Figure 1-2. Activity stack

The state of an application's topmost `Activity` has an impact on the application's system priority—also known as *process rank*—which in turn affects both the chances of terminating an application ("Application termination" on page 7) and the scheduled execution time of the application threads (Chapter 3).

An `Activity` lifecycle ends either when the user navigates back—for example, presses the back button—or when the `Activity` explicitly calls `finish()`.

Service

A `Service` can execute invisibly in the background without direct user interaction. It is typically used to offload execution from other components, when the operations can outlive their lifetime. A `Service` can be executed in either a *started* or a *bound* mode:

Started `Service`

The `Service` is started with a call to `Context.startService(Intent)` with an explicit or implicit `Intent`. It terminates when `Context.stopService(Intent)` is called.

Bound `Service`

Multiple components can bind to a `Service` through `Context.bindService(Intent, ServiceConnection, int)` with explicit or implicit `Intent` parameters. After the binding, a component can interact with the `Service` through the `ServiceConnection` interface, and it unbinds from the `Service` through `Context.unbindService(ServiceConnection)`. When the last component unbinds from the `Service`, it is destroyed.

ContentProvider

An application that wants to share substantial amounts of data within or between applications can utilize a `ContentProvider`. It can provide access to any data source, but it is most commonly used in collaboration with SQLite databases, which are always private to an application. With the help of a `ContentProvider`, an application can publish that data to applications that execute in remote processes.

BroadcastReceiver

This component has a very restricted function: it listens for intents sent from within the application, remote applications, or the platform. It filters incoming intents to determine which ones are sent to the `BroadcastReceiver`. A `BroadcastReceiver` should be registered dynamically when you want to start listening for intents, and unregistered when it stops listening. If it is statically registered in the `AndroidManifest`, it listens for intents while the application is installed. Thus, the `BroadcastReceiver` can start its associated application if an `Intent` matches the filter.

Application Execution

Android is a multiuser, multitasking system that can run multiple applications at the same time and let the user switch between applications without noticing a significant delay. The Linux kernel handles the multitasking, and application execution is based on Linux processes.

Linux Process

Linux assigns every user a unique user ID, basically a number tracked by the OS to keep the users apart. Every user has access to private resources protected by permissions, and no user (except *root*, the super user, which does not concern us here) can access another user's private resources. Thus, sandboxes are created to isolate users. In Android, every application package has a unique user ID; for example, an application in Android corresponds to a unique user in Linux and cannot access other applications' resources.

What Android adds to each process is a runtime execution environment, such as the Dalvik virtual machine, for each instance of an application. Figure 1-3 shows the relationship between the Linux process model, the VM, and the application.

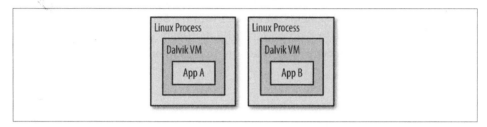

Figure 1-3. Applications execute in different processes and VMs

By default, applications and processes have a one-to-one relationship, but if required, it is possible for an application to run in several processes, or for several applications to run in the same process.

Lifecycle

The application lifecycle is encapsulated within its Linux process, which, in Java, maps to the `android.app.Application` class. The `Application` object for each app starts when the runtime calls its `onCreate()` method. Ideally, the app terminates with a call by the runtime to its `onTerminate()`, but an application cannot rely upon this. The underlying Linux process may have been killed before the runtime had a chance to call `onTerminate()`. The `Application` object is the first component to be instantiated in a process and the last to be destroyed.

Application start

An application is started when one of its components is initiated for execution. Any component can be the entry point for the application, and once the first component is triggered to start, a Linux process is started—unless it is already running—leading to the following startup sequence:

1. Start Linux process.

2. Create runtime.

3. Create `Application` instance.

4. Create the entry point component for the application.

Setting up a new Linux process and the runtime is not an instantaneous operation. It can degrade performance and have a noticeable impact on the user experience. Thus, the system tries to shorten the startup time for Android applications by starting a special process called *Zygote* on system boot. Zygote has the entire set of core libraries preloaded. New application processes are forked from the Zygote process without copying the core libraries, which are shared across all applications.

Application termination

A process is created at the start of the application and finishes when the system wants to free up resources. Because a user may request an application at any later time, the runtime avoids destroying all its resources until the number of live applications leads to an actual shortage of resources across the system. Hence, an application isn't automatically terminated even when all of its components have been destroyed.

When the system is low on resources, it's up to the runtime to decide which process should be killed. To make this decision, the system imposes a ranking on each process depending on the application's visibility and the components that are currently executing. In the following ranking, the bottom-ranked processes are forced to quit before the higher-ranked ones. With the highest first, the process ranks are:

Foreground
> Application has a visible component in front, `Service` is bound to an `Activity` in front in a remote process, or `BroadcastReceiver` is running.

Visible
> Application has a visible component but is partly obscured.

Service
> Service is executing in the background and is not tied to a visible component.

Background
> A nonvisible `Activity`. This is the process level that contains most applications.

Empty
> A process without active components. Empty processes are kept around to improve startup times, but they are the first to be terminated when the system reclaims resources.

In practice, the ranking system ensures that no visible applications will be terminated by the platform when it runs out of resources.

Lifecycles of Two Interacting Applications

This example illustrates the lifecycles of two processes, P1 and P2, that interact in a typical way (Figure 1-4). P1 is a client application that invokes a `Service` in P2, a server application. The client process, P1, starts when it is triggered by a broadcasted `Intent`. At startup, the process starts both a `BroadcastReceiver` and the `Application` instance. After a while, an `Activity` is started, and during all of this time, P1 has the highest possible process rank: Foreground.

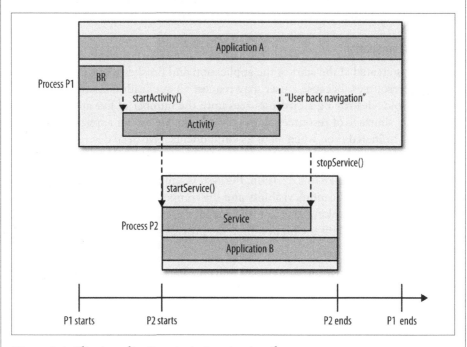

Figure 1-4. Client application starts `Service` in other process

The `Activity` offloads work to a `Service` that runs in process P2, which starts the `Service` and the associated `Application` instance. Therefore, the application has split the work into two different processes. The P1 `Activity` can terminate while the P2 `Service` keeps running.

Once all components have finished—the user has navigated back from the `Activity` in P1, and the `Service` in P2 is asked by some other process or the runtime to stop—both processes are ranked as empty, making them plausible candidates for termination by the system when it requires resources.

A detailed list of the process ranks during the execution appears in Table 1-1.

Table 1-1. Process rank transitions

Application state	P1 process rank	P2 process rank
P1 starts with `BroadcastReceiver` entry point	Foreground	N/A
P1 starts Activity	Foreground	N/A
P1 starts `Service` entry point in P2	Foreground	Foreground
P1 Activity is destroyed	Empty	Service
P2 Service is stopped	Empty	Empty

It should be noted that there is a difference between the actual application lifecycle—defined by the Linux process—and the perceived application lifecycle. The system can have multiple application processes running even while the user perceives them as terminated. The empty processes are lingering—if system resources permit it—to shorten the startup time on restarts.

Structuring Applications for Performance

Android devices are multiprocessor systems that can run multiple operations simultaneously, but it is up to each application to ensure that operations can be partitioned and executed concurrently to optimize application performance. If the application doesn't enable partitioned operations but prefers to run everything as one long operation, it can exploit only one CPU, leading to suboptimal performance. Unpartitioned operations must run *synchronously*, whereas partitioned operations can run *asynchronously*. With asynchronous operations, the system can share the execution among multiple CPUs and therefore increase throughput.

An application with multiple independent tasks should be structured to utilize asynchronous execution. One approach is to split application execution into several processes, because those can run concurrently. However, every process allocates memory for its own substantial resources, so the execution of an application in multiple processes will use more memory than an application in one process. Furthermore, starting and communicating between processes is slow, and not an efficient way of achieving asynchronous execution. Multiple processes may still be a valid design, but that decision should be independent of performance. To achieve higher throughput and better performance, an application should utilize multiple threads within each process.

Creating Responsive Applications Through Threads

An application can utilize asynchronous execution on multiple CPU's with high throughput, but that doesn't guarantee a responsive application. Responsiveness is the way the user perceives the application during interaction: that the UI responds quickly to button clicks, smooth animations, etc. Basically, performance from the perspective of the user experienced is determined by how fast the application can update the UI components. The responsibility for updating the UI components lies with the *UI thread*, which is the only thread the system allows to update UI components.[1]

To make the application responsive, it should ensure that no long-running tasks are executed on the UI thread. If they do, all the other execution on that thread will be delayed. Typically, the first symptom of executing long-running tasks on the UI thread is that the UI becomes unresponsive because it is not allowed to update the screen or accept user button presses properly. If the application delays the UI thread too long, typically 5-10 seconds, the runtime displays an "Application Not Responding" (ANR) dialog to the user, giving her an option to close the application. Clearly, you want to avoid this. In fact, the runtime prohibits certain time-consuming operations, such as network downloads, from running on the UI thread.

So, long operations should be handled on a background thread. Long-running tasks typically include:

- Network communication
- Reading or writing to a file
- Creating, deleting, and updating elements in databases
- Reading or writing to `SharedPreferences`
- Image processing
- Text parsing

What Is a Long Task?

There is no fixed definition of a long task or a clear indication when a task should execute on a background thread, but as soon as a user perceives a lagging UI—for example, slow button feedback and stuttering animations—it is a signal that the task is too long to run on the UI thread. Typically, animations are a lot more sensitive to competing tasks on the UI thread than button clicks, because the human brain is a bit vague about when a screen touch actually happened. Hence, let us do some coarse reasoning with animations as the most demanding use case.

Animations are updated in an event loop where every event updates the animation with one frame, i.e., one drawing cycle. The more drawing cycles that can be executed per time frame, the better the animation is perceived. If the goal is to do 60 drawing cycles per second—a.k.a. frames per second (fps)—every frame has to render within 16 ms. If

---

1. Also known as the *main thread*, but throughout this book we stick to the convention of calling it the "UI thread."

another task is running on the UI thread simultaneously, both the drawing cycle and the secondary task have to finish within 16 ms to avoid a stuttering animation. Consequently, a task may require less than 16 ms execution time and still be considered long.

The example and calculations are coarse and meant as an indication of how an application's responsiveness can be affected not only by network connections that last for several seconds, but also tasks that at first glance look harmless. Bottlenecks in your application can hide anywhere.

Threads in Android applications are as fundamental as any of the component building blocks. All Android components and system callbacks—unless denoted otherwise—run on the UI thread and should use background threads when executing longer tasks.

Summary

An Android application runs on top of a Linux OS in a Dalvik runtime, which is contained in a Linux process. Android applies a process-ranking system that priorities the importance of each running application to ensure that it is only the least prioritized applications that are terminated. To increase performance, an application should split operations among several threads so that the code is executed concurrently. Every Linux process contains a specific thread that is responsible for updating the UI. All long operations should be kept off the UI thread and executed on other threads.

PART I
Fundamentals

This part of the book covers the building blocks for asynchronous processing provided by Linux, Java, and Android. You should understand how these work, the trade-offs involved in using the various techniques, and what risks they introduce. This understanding will give you the basis for using the techniques described in Part II.

CHAPTER 2

Multithreading in Java

Every Android application should adhere to the multithreaded programming model built in to the Java language. With multithreading comes improvements to performance and responsiveness that are required for a great user experience, but it is accompanied by increased complexities:

- Handling the concurrent programming model in Java
- Keeping data consistency in a multithreaded environment
- Setting up task execution strategies

Thread Basics

Software programming is all about instructing the hardware to perform an action (e.g., show images on a monitor, store data on the filesystem, etc.). The instructions are defined by the application code that the CPU processes in an ordered sequence, which is the high-level definition of a *thread*. From an application perspective, a thread is execution along a code path of Java statements that are performed sequentially. A code path that is sequentially executed on a thread is referred to as a *task*, a unit of work that coherently executes on one thread. A thread can either execute one or multiple tasks in sequence.

Execution

A thread in an Android application is represented by `java.lang.Thread`. It is the most basic execution environment in Android that executes tasks when it starts and terminates when the task is finished or there are no more tasks to execute; the alive time of the thread is determined by the length of the task. `Thread` supports execution of tasks that are implementions of the `java.lang.Runnable` interface. An implementation defines the task in the `run` method:

```
private class MyTask implements Runnable {
    public void run() {
        int i = 0; // Stored on the thread local stack.
    }
}
```

All the local variables in the method calls from within a `run()` method—direct or indirect—will be stored on the local memory stack of the thread. The task's execution is started by instantiating and starting a `Thread`:

```
Thread myThread = new Thread(new MyTask());
myThread.start();
```

On the operating system level, the thread has both an instruction and a stack pointer. The instruction pointer references the next instruction to be processed, and the stack pointer references a private memory area—not available to other threads—where thread-local data is stored. Thread local data is typically variable literals that are defined in the Java methods of the application.

A CPU can process instructions from one thread at a time, but a system normally has multiple threads that require processing at the same time, such as a system with multiple simultaneously running applications. For the user to perceive that applications can run in parallel, the CPU has to share its processing time between the application threads. The sharing of a CPU's processing time is handled by a *scheduler*. That determines what thread the CPU should process and for how long. The scheduling strategy can be implemented in various ways, but it is mainly based on the thread *priority*: a high-priority thread gets the CPU allocation before a low-priority thread, which gives more execution time to high-priority threads. Thread priority in Java can be set between 1 (lowest) and 10 (highest), but—unless explicitly set—the normal priority is 5:

```
myThread.setPriority(8);
```

If, however, the scheduling is only priority based, the low-priority threads may not get enough processing time carry out the job it was intended for—known as *starvation*. Hence, schedulers also take the processing time of the threads into account when changing to a new thread. A thread change is known as *context switch*. A context switch starts by storing the state of the executing thread so that the execution can be resumed at a later point, whereafter that thread has to wait. The scheduler then restores another waiting thread for processing.

Two concurrently running threads—executed by a single processor—are split into execution intervals, as Figure 2-1 shows:

```
Thread T1 = new Thread(new MyTask());
T1.start();
```

```
Thread T2 = new Thread(new MyTask());
T2.start();
```

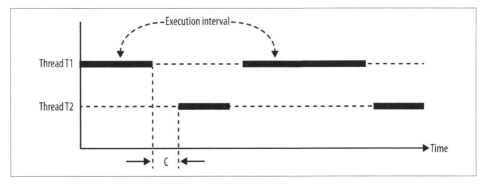

Figure 2-1. Two threads executing on one CPU. The context switch is denoted C.

Every scheduling point includes a context switch, where the operating system has to use the CPU to carry out the switch. One such context switch is noted as C in the figure.

Single-Threaded Application

Each application has at least one thread that defines the code path of execution. If no more threads are created, all of the code will be processed along the same code path, and an instruction has to wait for all preceding intructions to finish before it can be processed.

The single-threaded execution is a simple programming model with deterministic execution order, but most often it is not a sufficient approach because instructions may be postponed significantly by preceding instructions, even if the latter instruction is not depending on the preceding instructions. For example, a user who presses a button on the device should get immediate visual feedback that the button is pressed; but in a single-threaded environment, the UI event can be delayed until preceding instructions have finished execution, which degrades both performance and responsiveness. To solve this, an application needs to split the execution into multiple code paths, i.e., threads.

Multithreaded Application

With multiple threads, the application code can be split into several code paths so that operations are perceived to be executing concurrently. If the number of executing threads exceeds the number of processors, true concurrency can not be achieved, but the scheduler switches rapidly between threads to be processed so that every code path is split into execution intervals that are processed in a sequence.

Multithreading is a must-have, but the improved performance comes at a cost—increased complexity, increased memory consumption, nondeterministic order of execution—that the application has to manage.

Increased resource consumption

Threads come with an overhead in terms of memory and processor usage. Each thread allocates a private memory area that is mainly used to store method local variables and parameters during the execution of the method. The private memory area is allocated when the thread is created and deallocated once the thread terminates (i.e., as long as the thread is active, it holds on to system resources—even if it is idle or blocked).

The processor entails overhead for the setup and teardown of threads and to store and restore threads in context switches. The more threads it executes, the more context switches may occur and deteriorate performance.

Increased complexity

Analyzing the execution of a single-threaded application is relatively simple because the order of execution is known. In multithreaded applications, it is a lot more difficult to analyze how the program is executed and in which order the code is processed. The execution order is indeterministic between threads, as it is not known beforehand how the scheduler will allocate execution time to the threads. Hence, multiple threads introduce uncertainty into execution. Not only does this indeterminacy make it much harder to debug errors in the code, but the necessity of coordinating threads poses a risk of introducing new errors.

Data inconsistency

A new set of problems arise in multithreaded programs when the order of resource access is nondeterministic. If two or more threads use a shared resource, it is not known in which order the threads will reach and process the resource. For example, if threads t1 and t2 try to modify the member variable sharedResource, the access order is indeterminate—it may either be incremented or decremented first:

```
public class RaceCondition {

    int sharedResource = 0;

    public void startTwoThreads() {
        Thread t1 = new Thread(new Runnable() {
            @Override
            public void run() {
                sharedResource++;
            }
        });
        t1.start();
```

```
        Thread t2 = new Thread(new Runnable() {
            @Override
            public void run() {
                sharedResource--;
            }
        });
        t2.start();
    }
}
```

The `sharedResource` is exposed to a *race condition*, which can occur because the ordering of the code execution can differ from every execution; it cannot be guaranteed that thread `t1` always comes before thread `t2`. In this case, it is not only the ordering that is troublesome, but also the fact that the incrementer and decrementer operations are multiple byte code instructions—read, modify, and write. Context switches can occur between the byte-code instructions, leaving the end result of `sharedResource` dependent on the order of execution: it can be either 0, -1 or 1. The first result occurs if the first thread manages to write the value before the second thread reads it, whereas the two latter results occur if both threads first read the initial value 0, making the last written value determine the end result.

Because context switches can occur while one thread is executing a part of the code that should not be interrupted, it is necessary to create *atomic regions* of code instructions that are always executed in sequence without interleaving of other threads. If a thread executes in an atomic region, other threads will be *blocked* until no other thread executes in the atomic region. Hence, an atomic region in Java is said to be *mutually exclusive* because it allows access to only one thread. An atomic region can be created in various ways (see "Intrinsic Lock and Java Monitor" on page 20), but the most fundamental synchronization mechanism is the *synchronized* keyword:

```
synchronized (this) {
    sharedResource++;
}
```

If every access to the shared resource is synchronized, the data cannot be inconsistent in spite of multithreaded access. Many of the threading mechanisms discussed in this book were designed to reduce the risk of such errors.

Thread Safety

Giving multiple threads access to the same object is a great way for threads to communicate quickly—one thread writes, another thread reads—but it threatens correctness. Multiple threads can execute the same instance of an object simultaneously, causing concurrent access to the state in shared memory. That imposes a risk of threads either seeing the value of the state before it has been updated or corrupting the value.

Thread safety is achieved when an object always maintains the correct state when accessed by multiple threads. This is achieved by synchronizing the object's state so that the access to the state is controlled. Synchronization should be applied to code that reads or writes any variable that otherwise could be accessed by one thread while being changed by another thread. Such areas of code are called *critical sections* and must be executed atomically—i.e., by only by one thread at the time. Synchronization is achieved by using a locking mechanism that checks whether there currently is a thread executing in a critical section. If so, all the other threads trying to enter the critical section will block until the thread is finished executing the critical section.

 If a shared resource is accessible from multiple threads and the state is mutable—i.e., the value can be changed during the lifetime of the resource—every access to the resource needs to be guarded by the same lock.

In short, locks guarantee atomic execution of the regions they lock. Locking mechanisms in Android include:

- Object intrinsic lock
  — The synchronized keyword
- Explicit locks
  — java.util.concurrent.locks.ReentrantLock
  — java.util.concurrent.locks.ReentrantReadWriteLock

Intrinsic Lock and Java Monitor

The synchronized keyword operates on the intrinsic lock that is implicitly available in every Java object. The intrinsic lock is mutually exclusive, meaning that thread execution in the critical section is exclusive to one thread. Other threads that try to access a critical region—while being occupied—are blocked and cannot continue executing until the lock has been released. The intrinsic lock acts as a *monitor* (see Figure 2-2). The Java monitor can be modeled with three states:

Blocked
> Threads that are suspended while they wait for the monitor to be released by another thread.

Executing
> The one and only thread that owns the monitor and is currently running the code in the critical section.

Waiting

Threads that have voluntarely given up ownership of the monitor before it has reached the end of the critical section. The threads are waiting to be signalled before they can take ownership again.

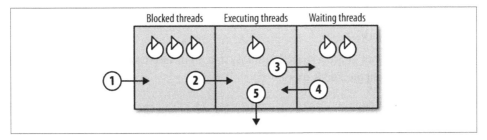

Figure 2-2. Java monitor

A thread transitions between the monitor states when it reaches and executes a code block protected by the intrinsic lock:

1. *Enter the monitor.* A thread tries to access a section that is guarded by an intrinsic lock. It enters the monitor, but if the lock is already acquired by another thread, it is suspended.

2. *Acquire the lock.* If there is no other thread that owns the monitor, a blocked thread can take ownership and execute in the critical section. If there is more than one blocked thread, the scheduler selects which thread to execute. There is no FIFO ordering among the blocked threads; in other words, the first thread to enter the monitor is not necessarily the first one to be selected for execution.

3. *Release the lock and wait.* The thread suspends itself through `Object.wait()` because it wants to wait for a condition to be fulfilled before it continues to execute.

4. *Acquire the lock after signal.* Waiting threads are signalled from another thread through `Object.notify()` or `Object.notifyAll()` and can take ownership of the monitor again if selected by the scheduler. However, the waiting threads have no precedence over potentially blocked threads that also want to own the monitor.

5. *Release the lock and exit the monitor.* At the end of a critical section, the thread exits the monitor and leaves room for another thread to take ownership.

The transitions map to a synchronized code block accordingly:

```
synchronized (this) { // (1)
    // Execute code (2)
    wait(); // (3)
    // Execute code (4)
} // (5)
```

Synchronize Access to Shared Resources

A shared mutable state that can be accessed and altered by multiple threads requires a synchronization strategy to keep the data consistent during the concurrent execution. The strategy involves choosing the right kind of lock for the situation and setting the scope for the critical section.

Using the intrinsic lock

An intrinsic lock can guard a shared mutable state in different ways, depending on how the keyword `synchronized` is used:

- Method level that operates on the intrinsic lock of the enclosing object instance:

```
synchronized void changeState() {
    sharedResource++;
}
```

- Block-level that operates on the intrinsic lock of the enclosing object instance:

```
void changeState() {
    synchronized(this) {
        sharedResource++;
    }
}
```

- Block-level with other objects intrinsic lock:

```
private final Object mLock = new Object();

void changeState() {
    synchronized(mLock) {
        sharedResource++;
    }
}
```

- Method-level that operates on the intrinsic lock of the enclosing class instance:

```
synchronized static void changeState() {
    staticSharedResource++;
}
```

- Block-level that operates on the intrinsic lock of the enclosing class instance:

```
static void changeState() {
    synchronized(this.getClass()) {
        staticSharedResource++;
    }
}
```

A reference to the `this` object in block-level synchronization uses the same intrinsic lock as method-level synchronization. But by using this syntax, you can control the precise block of code covered by the critical section and therefore reduce it to cover only the code that actually concerns the state you want to protect. It's bad practice to create larger atomic areas than necessary, since that may block other threads when not necessary, leading to slower execution across the application.

Synchronizing on other objects' intrinsic locks enables the use of multiple locks within a class. An application should strive to protect each independent state with a lock of its own. Hence, if a class has more than one independent state, performance is improved by using several locks.

 The synchronized keyword can operate in different intrinsic locks. Keep in mind that synchronization on static methods operates on the intrinsic lock of the class object and not the instance object.

Using explicit locking mechanisms

If a more advanced locking strategy is needed, ReentrantLock or ReentrantReadWri teLock classes can be used instead of the synchronized keyword. Critical sections are protected by explicitly locking and unlocking regions in the code:

```
int sharedResource;
private ReentrantLock mLock = new ReentrantLock();

public void changeState() {
    mLock.lock();
    try {
        sharedResource++;
    }
    finally {
        mLock.unlock();
    }
}
```

The synchronized keyword and ReentrantLock have the same semantics: they both block all threads trying to execute a critical section if another thread has already entered that region. This is a defensive strategy that assumes that all concurrent accesses are problematic, but it is not harmful for multiple threads to read a shared variable simultaneously. Hence, synchronized and ReentrantLock can be overprotective.

The ReentrantReadWriteLock lets reading threads execute concurrently but still blocks readers versus writers and writers versus other writers:

```
int sharedResource;
private ReentrantReadWriteLock mLock = new ReentrantReadWriteLock();

public void changeState() {
    mLock.writeLock().lock();
    try {
            sharedResource++;
```

```
            }
            finally {
                    mLock.writeLock().unlock();
            }
    }

    public int readState() {
            mLock.readLock().lock();
            try {
                    return sharedResource;
            }
            finally {
                    mLock.readLock().unlock();
            }
    }
```

The ReentrantReadWriteLock is relatively complex, which leads to a performance penalty because the evaluation required to determine whether a thread should be allowed to execute or be blocked is longer than with synchronized and ReentrantLock. Hence, there is a trade-off between the performance gain from letting multiple threads read shared resources simultaneously and the performance loss from evaluation complexity. The typical good use case for ReentrantReadWriteLock is when there are many reading threads and few writing threads.

Example: Consumer and Producer

A common use case with collaborating threads is the *consumer-producer pattern*—i.e., one thread that produces data and one thread that consumes the data. The threads collaborate through a list that is shared between them. When the list is not full, the producer thread adds items to the list, whereas the consumer thread removes items while the list is not empty. If the list is full, the producing thread should block, and if the list is empty, the consuming thread is blocked.

The ConsumerProducer class contains a shared resource LinkedList and two methods: produce() to add items and consume to remove items:

```
public class ConsumerProducer {

    private LinkedList<Integer> list = new LinkedList<Integer>();
    private final int LIMIT = 10;
    private Object lock = new Object();

    public void produce() throws InterruptedException {

        int value = 0;

        while (true) {
            synchronized (lock) {
                while(list.size() == LIMIT) {
```

```
                    lock.wait();
                }
                list.add(value++);
                lock.notify();
            }
        }
    }

    public void consume() throws InterruptedException {

        while (true) {
            synchronized (lock) {
                while(list.size() == 0) {
                    lock.wait();
                }
                int value = list.removeFirst();
                lock.notify();
            }
        }
    }
}
```

Both produce and consume use the same intrinsic lock for guarding the shared list. Threads that try to access the list are blocked as long another thread owns the monitor, but producing threads give up execution—i.e., wait() if the list is full—and consuming threads if the list is empty.

When items are either added or removed from the list, the monitor is signalled—i.e., notify() is called—so that waiting threads can execute again. The consumer threads signal producer threads and vice versa.

The following code shows two threads that execute the producing and consuming operations:

```
final ConsumerProducer cp = new ConsumerProducer();

Thread t1 = new Thread(new Runnable() {
    @Override
    public void run() {
        try {
            cp.produce();
        } catch (InterruptedException e) {
            e.printStackTrace();
        }
    }
}).start();

Thread t2 = new Thread(new Runnable() {
    @Override
    public void run() {
        try {
            cp.consume();
```

```
        } catch (InterruptedException e) {
            e.printStackTrace();
        }
    }
}).start();
```

Task Execution Strategies

To make sure that multiple threads are used properly to create responsive applications, applications should be designed with thread creation and task execution in mind. Two suboptimal designs and extremes are:

One thread for all tasks
> All tasks are executed on the same thread. The result is often an unresponsive application that fails to use available processors.

One thread per task
> Tasks are always executed on a new thread that is started and terminated for every task. If the tasks are frequently created and have short lifetimes, the overhead of thread creation and teardown can degrade performance.

Although these extremes should be avoided, they both represent variants of sequential and concurrent execution at the extreme:

Sequential execution
> Tasks are executed in a sequence that requires one task to finish before the next is processed. Thus, the execution interval of the tasks does not overlap. Advantages of this design are:

> - It is inherently thread safe.
> - Can be executed on one thread, which consumes less memory than multiple threads.

>   Disadvantages include:

> - Low throughput.
> - The start of each task's execution depends on previously executed tasks. The start may either be delayed or possibly not executed at all.

Concurrent execution
> Task are executed in parallel and interleaved. The advantage is better CPU utilization, whereas the disadvantage is that the design is not inherently thread-safe, so synchronization may be required.

An effective multithreaded design utilizes execution environments with both sequential and concurrent execution; the choice depends on the tasks. Isolated and independent tasks can execute concurrently to increase throughput, but tasks that require an ordering or share a common resource without synchronization should be executed sequentially.

Concurrent Execution Design

Concurrent execution can be implemented in many ways, so design has to consider how to manage the number of executing threads and their relationships. Basic principles include:

- Favoring reuse of threads instead of always creating new threads, so that the frequency of creation and teardown of resources can be reduced.

- Not using more threads than required. The more threads that are used, the more memory and processor time is consumed.

Summary

Android applications should be multithreaded to improve performance on both single and multiprocessor platforms. Threads can share execution on a single processor or utilize true concurrency when multiple processors are available. The increased performance comes at a cost of increased complexity, as well as a responsibility to guard resources shared among threads and to preserve data consistency.

CHAPTER 3

Threads on Android

Every Android application is started with numerous threads that are bundled with the Linux process and the Dalvik VM to manage its internal execution. But the application is exposed to system threads, like the UI and binder threads, and creates background threads of its own. In this chapter, we'll get under the hood of threading on the Android platform, examining the following:

- Differences and similarities between UI, binder, and background threads
- Linux thread coupling
- How thread scheduling is affected by the application process rank
- Running Linux threads

Android Application Threads

All application threads are based on the native `pthreads` in Linux with a `Thread` representation in Java, but the platform still assigns special properties to threads that make them differ. From an application perspective, the thread types are UI, binder, and background threads.

UI Thread

The UI thread is started on application start and stays alive during the lifetime of the Linux process. The UI thread is the main thread of the application, used for executing Android components and updating the UI elements on the screen. If the platform detects that UI updates are attempted from any other thread, it will promptly notify the application by throwing a `CalledFromWrongThreadException`. This harsh platform behavior is required because the Android UI Toolkit is not thread safe, so the runtime allows access to the UI elements from one thread only.

UI elements in Android are often defined as instance fields of activities, so they constitute a part of the object's state. However, access to those elements doesn't require synchronization because UI elements can be accessed only from the UI thread. In other words, the runtime enforces a single-threaded environment for UI elements, so they are not susceptible to concurrency problems.

The UI thread is a sequential event handler thread that can execute events sent from any other thread in the platform. The events are handled serially and are queued if the UI thread is occupied with processing a previous event. Any event can be posted to the UI thread, but if events are sent that do not explicitly require the UI thread for execution, the UI-critical events may have to wait in the queue before being processed and before responsiveness is decreased.

"Android Message Passing" on page 47 describes event handling in detail.

Binder Threads

Binder threads are used for communicating between threads in different processes. Each process maintains a set of threads, called a *thread pool*, that is never terminated or recreated, but can run tasks at the request of another thread in the process. These threads handle incoming requests from other processes, including system services, intents, content providers, and services. When needed, a new binder thread will be created to handle the incoming request. In most cases, an application does not have to be concerned about binder threads because the platform normally transforms the requests to use the UI thread first. The exception is when the application offers a Service that can be bound from other processes via an AIDL interface. Binder threads are discussed more thoroughly in Chapter 5.

Background Threads

All the threads that an application explicitly creates are background threads. This means that they have no predefined purpose, but are empty execution environments waiting to execute any task. The background threads are descendants of the UI thread, so they inherit the UI thread properties, such as its priority. By default, a newly created process doesn't contain any background threads. It is always up to the application itself to create them when needed.

 The second part of this book, Part II, is all about creating background threads.

A background thread created here in the application would look like this in the *ps -t* output. The last field is the name. The thread name, by default, ends with the number assigned by the runtime to the thread as its ID:

```
u0_a72 4283 4257 320304 34540 ffffffff 00000000 S Thread-12412
```

In the application, the use cases for the UI thread and worker threads are quite different, but in Linux they are both plain native threads and are handled equally. The constraints on the UI thread—that it should handle all UI updates—are enforced by the Window Manager in the Application Framework and not by Linux.

The Linux Process and Threads

The execution of long operations on background threads on Android can be handled in many ways, but no matter how the application implements the execution mechanism, the threads, in the end, are always the same on the operating system level. The Android platform is a Linux-based OS, and every application is executed as a Linux application in the OS. Both the Android application and its threads adhere to the Linux execution environment. As we will see, knowledge of the Linux environment helps us not only to grasp and investigate the application execution, but also to improve our applications' performance.

Each running application has an underlying Linux process, forked from the prestarted Zygote process, which has the following properties:

User ID (UID)
A process has a unique user identifier that represents a user on a Linux system. Linux is a multiuser system, and on Android, each application represents a user in this system. When the application is installed, it is assigned a user ID.

Process identifier (PID)
A unique identifier for the process.

Parent process identifier (PPID)
After system startup, each process is created from another process. The running system forms a tree hierarchy of the running processes. Hence, each application process has a parent process. For Android, the parent of all processes is the Zygote.

Stack
Local function pointers and variables.

Heap
The address space allocated to a process. The address space is kept private to a process and can't be accessed by other processes.

Finding Application Process Information

The process information of a running application is retrieved by the *ps* (process status) command, which you can call from the ADB shell. The Android *ps* command retrieves process information just as it would on any Linux distribution. However, the set of options is different than the traditional Linux version of *ps*:

-t

Shows thread information in the processes.

-x

Shows time spent in user code (utime) and system code (stime) in "jiffies," which typically is units of 10 ms.

-p

Shows priorities.

-P

Shows scheduling policy, normally indicating whether the application is executing in the foreground or background.

-c

Shows which CPU is executing the process.

name|pid

Filter on the application's name or process ID. Only the last defined value is used.

You can also filter through the *grep* command. For instance, executing the *ps* command for a com.eat application[1] process would look like this:

```
$ adb shell ps | grep com.eat
USER      PID   PPID  VSIZE  RSS   WCHAN    PS        NAME
u0_a72    4257  144   320304 34540 ffffffff 00000000 S com.eat
```

From this output, we can extract the following interesting properties of the com.eat application:

- UID: u0_a72

- PID: 4257

- PPID: 144 (process number of the parent, which in the case of an Android application is always the Zygote)

---

1. I have used the string EAT to create a namespace for applications in this book. The string is an acronym of the book's title.

Another way of retrieving process and thread information is with DDMS[2] in the Android tools.

All the threads that an application creates and starts are native Linux threads, a.k.a. *pthreads*, because they were defined in a POSIX standard. The threads belong to the process where they were created, and the parent of each thread is the process. Threads and processes are very much alike, with the difference between them coming in the sharing of resources. The process is an isolated execution of a program in a sandboxed environment compared to other processes, whereas the threads share the resources within a process. An important distinction between processes and threads is that processes don't share address space with each other, but threads share the address space within a process. This memory sharing makes it a lot faster to communicate between threads than between processes, which require remote procedure calls that take up more overhead. Thread communication is covered in Chapter 4 and process communication in Chapter 5.

When a process starts, a single thread is automatically created for that process. A process always contains at least one thread to handle its execution. In Android, the thread created automatically in a process is the one we've already seen as the UI thread.

Let's take a look at the threads created in a process for an Android application with the package name com.eat:

```
$ adb shell ps -t | grep u0_a72
USER      PID    PPID   VSIZE  RSS    WCHAN    PS         NAME
u0_a72    4257   144    320304 34540  ffffffff 00000000 S com.eat
u0_a72    4259   4257   320304 34540  ffffffff 00000000 S GC
u0_a72    4262   4257   320304 34540  ffffffff 00000000 S Signal Catcher
u0_a72    4263   4257   320304 34540  ffffffff 00000000 S JDWP
u0_a72    4264   4257   320304 34540  ffffffff 00000000 S Compiler
u0_a72    4265   4257   320304 34540  ffffffff 00000000 S ReferenceQueueDemon
u0_a72    4266   4257   320304 34540  ffffffff 00000000 S FinalizerDaemon
u0_a72    4267   4257   320304 34540  ffffffff 00000000 S FinalizerWatchdogDaemon
u0_a72    4268   4257   320304 34540  ffffffff 00000000 S Binder_1
u0_a72    4269   4257   320304 34540  ffffffff 00000000 S Binder_2
```

On application start, no fewer than 10 threads are started in our process. The first thread —named com.eat—is started by default when the application launches. Hence, that is the UI thread of the application. All the other threads are spawned from the UI thread, which is seen on the parent process ID (PPID) of the other threads. Their PPID corresponds to the process ID (PID) of the UI thread.

2. Dalvik Debug Monitor Service (*http://developer.android.com/tools/debugging/ddms.html*)

Most of the threads are Dalvik internal threads, and we don't have to worry about them from an application perspective. They handle garbage collection, debug connections, finalizers, etc. Let's focus on the threads we need to pay attention to:

```
u0_a72    4257  144   320304 34540 ffffffff 00000000 S com.eat
u0_a72    4268  4257  320304 34540 ffffffff 00000000 S Binder_1
u0_a72    4269  4257  320304 34540 ffffffff 00000000 S Binder_2
```

Scheduling

Linux treats threads and not processes as the fundamental unit for execution. Hence, scheduling on Android concerns threads and not processes. Scheduling allocates execution time for threads on a processor. Each thread that is executing in an application is competing with all of the other threads in the application for execution time. The scheduler decides which thread should execute and for how long it should be allowed to execute before it picks a new thread to execute and a context switch occurs. A scheduler picks the next thread to execute depending on some thread properties, which are different for each scheduler type, although the thread priority is the most important one. In Android, the application threads are scheduled by the standard scheduler in the Linux kernel and not by the Dalvik virtual machine. In practice, this means that the threads in our application are competing not only directly with each other for execution time, but also against all threads in all the other applications.

The Linux kernel scheduler is known as a *completely fair scheduler* (CFS). It is "fair" in the sense that it tries to balance the execution of tasks not only based on the priority of the thread but also by tracking the amount of execution time[3] that has been given to a thread. If a thread has previously had low access to the processor, it will be allowed to execute before higher-prioritized threads. If a thread doesn't use the allocated time to execute, the CFS will ensure that the priority is lowered so that it will get less execution time in the future.

The platform mainly has two ways of affecting the thread scheduling:

Priority
    Change the Linux thread priority.

Control group
    Change the Android-specific control group.

Priority

All threads in an application are associated with a priority that indicates to the scheduler which thread it should allocate execution time to on every context switch. On Linux, the thread priority is called *niceness* or *nice value*, which basically is an indication of

---

3. The CFS calls this the *virtual runtime* of a thread.

how nice a certain thread should behave toward other threads. Hence, a low niceness corresponds to a high priority. In Android, a Linux thread has niceness values in the range of -20 (most prioritized) to 19 (least prioritized), with a default niceness of 0. A thread inherits its priority from the thread where it is started and keeps it unless it's explicitly changed by the application.

An application can change priority of threads from two classes:

`java.lang.Thread`

```
    setPriority(int priority);
```

Sets the new priority based on the Java priority values from 0 (least prioritized) to 10 (most prioritized).

`android.os.Process`

```
    Process.setThreadPriority(int priority); // Calling thread.
    Process.setThreadPriority(int threadId, int priority); // Thread with
                                                           // specific id.
```

Sets the new priority using Linux niceness, i.e. -20 to 19.

Java Priority Versus Linux Niceness

`Thread.setPriority()` is platform independent. It represents an abstraction of the underlying platform-specific thread priorities. The abstract priority values correspond to Linux niceness values according to the following table:

Thread.setPriority(int)	Linux niceness
1 (Thread.MIN_PRIORITY)	19
2	16
3	13
4	10
5 (Thread.NORM_PRIORITY)	0
6	-2
7	-4
8	-5
9	-6
10 (Thread.MAX_PRIORITY)	-8

The mapping of Java priorities is an implementation detail and may vary depending on platform version. The niceness mapping values in the table are from Jelly Bean.

Control groups

Android not only relies on the regular Linux CFS for thread scheduling, but also imposes thread control groups[4] on all threads. The thread control groups are Linux containers that are used to manage the allocation of processor time for all threads in one container. All threads created in an application belong to one of the thread control groups.

Android defines multiple control groups, but the most important ones for applications are the Foreground Group and Background Group. The Android platform defines execution constraints so that the threads in the different control groups are allocated different amounts of execution time on the processor. Threads in the Foreground Group are allocated a lot more execution time than threads in the Background Group,[5] and Android utilizes this to ensure that visible applications on the screen get more processor allocation than applications that are not visible on the screen. The visibility on the screen relates to the process levels (see "The Linux Process and Threads" on page 31), as illustrated in Figure 3-1.

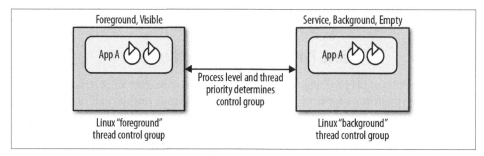

Figure 3-1. Thread control groups

If an application runs at the Foreground or Visible process level, the threads created by that application will belong to the Foreground Group and receive most of the total processing time, while the remaining time will be divided among the threads in the other applications. A *ps* command issued on a foreground thread shows something like this (note the appearance of the fg group):

```
$ adb shell ps -P | grep u0_a72
u0_a72    4257  144   320304 34504 fg  ffffffff 00000000 S com.eat
```

If the user moves an application to the background, such as by pressing the Home button, all the threads in that application will switch the control group to the Background Group and will receive less processor allocation. *ps* shows something like, with the application in the bg group:

---

4. *cgroups* in Linux.

5. The threads in the Background Group can't get more than ~5-10% execution time altogether.

```
$ adb shell ps -P | grep u0_a72
u0_a72    4257  144   318700 32164 bg  ffffffff 00000000 S com.eat
```

When the application is seen on the screen again, the threads move back to the Fore-ground Group. This moving of threads between control groups is done as soon as the application become visible or invisible. The use of control groups increases the performance of the applications seen on the screen and reduces the risk of background applications disturbing the applications actually seen by the user, hence improving the user experience.

Although the control groups ensure that background applications interfere as little as possible with the performance of visible applications, an application can still create many threads that compete with the UI thread. The threads created by the application by default have the same priority and control group membership as the UI thread, so they compete on equal terms for processor allocation. Hence, an application that creates a lot of background threads may reduce the performance of the UI thread even though the intention is the opposite. To solve this, it's possible to decouple background threads from the control group where the application threads execute by default. This decoupling is ensured by setting the priority of the background threads low enough so that they always belong to the Background Group, even though the application is visible.

 Lowering the priority of a thread with `Process.setThreadPriori` `ty(Process.THREAD_PRIORITY_BACKGROUND)` will not only reduce the priority but also ensure that this thread is decoupled from the process level of the application and always put in the Background Group.

Summary

All thread types in Android—UI, binder, and background—are Linux Posix threads. An application has a UI thread and binder threads when the process is started, but the application has to create background threads itself. All Android components execute on the UI thread by default, but long-running tasks should be executed on background threads to avoid slow UI rendering and the risk for ANRs. The UI thread is the most important thread, but it gets no special scheduling advantage compared to the other threads—the scheduler is unaware of which thread is the UI thread. Instead, it is up to the application to not let the background threads interfere more than necessary with the UI thread—typically by lowering the priority and letting the less important background threads execute in the background control group.

CHAPTER 4

Thread Communication

In multithreaded appplications, tasks can run in parallel and collaborate to produce a result. Hence, threads have to be able to communicate to enable true asynchronous processing. In Android, the importance of thread communication is emphasized in the platform-specific handler/looper mechanism that is the focus in this chapter, together with the traditional Java techniques. The chapter covers:

- Passing data through a one-way data pipe
- Shared memory communication
- Implementing a consumer-producer pattern with `BlockingQueue`
- Operations on message queues
- Sending tasks back to the UI Thread

Pipes

Pipes are a part of the `java.io` package. That is, they are general Java functionality and not Android specific. A pipe provides a way for two threads, within the same process, to connect and establish a one-way data channel. A producer thread writes data to the pipe, whereas a consumer thread reads data from the pipe.

 The Java pipe is comparable to the Unix and Linux pipe operator (the | shell character) that is used to redirect the output from one command to the input for another command. The pipe operator works across processes in Linux, but Java pipes work across threads in the virtual machine, for example, within a process.

The pipe itself is a circular buffer allocated in memory, available only to the two connected threads. No other threads can access the data. Hence, thread safety—discussed in "Thread Safety" on page 19—is ensured. The pipe is also one-directional, permitting just one thread to write and the other to read (Figure 4-1).

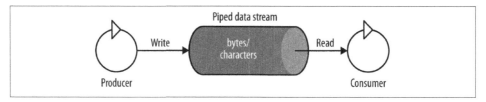

Figure 4-1. Thread communication with pipes

Pipes are typically used when you have two long-running tasks and one has to offload data to another continuously. Pipes make it easy to decouple tasks to several threads, instead of having only one thread handle many tasks. When one task has produced a result on a thread, it pipes the result on to the next thread that processes the data further. The gain comes from clean code separation and concurrent execution. Pipes can be used between worker threads and to offload work from the UI thread, which you want to keep light to preserve a responsive user experience.

A pipe can transfer either binary or character data. Binary data transfer is represented by PipedOutputStream (in the producer) and PipedInputStream (in the consumer), whereas character data transfer is represented by PipedWriter (in the producer) and PipedReader (in the consumer). Apart from the data transfer type, the two pipes have similar functionality. The lifetime of the pipe starts when either the writer or the reader thread establishes a connection, and it ends when the connection is closed.

Basic Pipe Use

The fundamental pipe life cycle can be summarized in three steps: setup, data transfer (which can be repeated as long as the two threads want to exchange data), and disconnection. The following examples are created with PipedWriter/PipedReader, but the same steps work with PipedOutputStream/PipedInputStream.

1. Set up the connection:

   ```
   PipedReader r = new PipedReader();
   PipedWriter w = new PipedWriter();
   w.connect(r);
   ```

   Here, the connection is established by the writer connecting to the reader. The connection could just as well be established from the reader. Several constructors also implicitly set up a pipe. The default buffer size is 1024 but is configurable from the consumer side of the pipe, as shown later:

```
int BUFFER_SIZE_IN_CHARS = 1024 * 4;
PipedReader r = new PipedReader(BUFFER_SIZE_IN_CHARS);
PipedWriter w = new PipedWriter(r);
```

2. Pass the reader to a processing thread:

```
Thread t = new MyReaderThread(r);
t.start();
```

After the reader thread starts, it is ready to receive data from the writer.

3. Transfer data:

```
// Producer thread: Write single character or array of characters
w.write('A');

// Consumer thread: Read the data
int result = r.read();
```

Communication adheres to the consumer-producer pattern with a blocking mechanism. If the pipe is full, the write() method will block until enough data has been read, and consequently removed from the pipe, to leave room for the data the writer is trying to add. The read() method blocks whenever there is no data to read from the pipe. It's worth noticing that the read() method returns the character as an integer value to ensure that enough space is available to handle various encoding with different sizes. You can cast the integer value back to a character.

In practice, a better approach would look like this:

```
// Producer thread: Flush the pipe after a write.
w.write('A');
w.flush();

// Consumer thread: Read the data in a loop.
int i;
while((i = reader.read()) != -1){
    char c = (char) i;
    // Handle received data
}
```

Calling flush() after a write to the pipe notifies the consumer thread that new data is available. This is useful from a performance perspective, because when the buffer is empty, the PipedReader uses a blocking call to wait() with one-second timeout. Hence, if the flush() call is omitted, the consumer thread may delay the reading of data up to one second. By calling flush(), the producer cuts short the wait in the consumer thread and allows data processing to continue immediately.

4. Close the connection.

When the communication phase is finished, the pipe should be disconnected:

```
// Producer thread: Close the writer.
w.close();
```

```
// Consumer thread: Close the reader.
r.close();
```

If the writer and reader are connected, it's enough to close only one of them. If the writer is closed, the pipe is disconnected but the data in the buffer can still be read. If the reader is closed, the buffer is cleared.

Example: Text Processing on a Worker Thread

This next example illustrates how pipes can process text that a user enters in an Edit Text. To keep the UI thread responsive, each character entered by the user is passed to a worker thread, which presumably handles some time-consuming processing:

```java
public class PipeExampleActivity extends Activity {

    private static final String TAG = "PipeExampleActivity";
    private EditText editText;

    PipedReader r;
    PipedWriter w;

    private Thread workerThread;

    public void onCreate(Bundle savedInstanceState) {
        super.onCreate(savedInstanceState);

        r = new PipedReader();
        w = new PipedWriter();

        try {
            w.connect(r);
        } catch (IOException e) {
            e.printStackTrace();
        }

        setContentView(R.layout.activity_pipe);
        editText = (EditText) findViewById(R.id.edit_text);
        editText.addTextChangedListener(new TextWatcher() {
            @Override
            public void beforeTextChanged(CharSequence charSequence, int start,
                                          int count, int after) {
            }

            @Override
            public void onTextChanged(CharSequence charSequence, int start,
                                      int before, int count) {
                try {
                    // Only handle addition of characters
                    if(count > before) {
                        // Write the last entered character to the pipe
```

```
                    w.write(charSequence.subSequence(before, count).
                            toString());
                }
            } catch (IOException e) {
                e.printStackTrace();
            }
        }

        @Override
        public void afterTextChanged(Editable editable) {
        }
    });

    workerThread = new Thread(new TextHandlerTask(r));
    workerThread.start();
}

@Override
protected void onDestroy() {
    super.onDestroy();
    workerThread.interrupt();
    try {
        r.close();
        w.close();
    } catch (IOException e) {
    }
}

private static class TextHandlerTask implements Runnable {
    private final PipedReader reader;

    public TextHandlerTask(PipedReader reader){
        this.reader = reader;
    }
    @Override
    public void run() {
        while(Thread.currentThread().isInterrupted()){
            try {
                int i;
                while((i = reader.read()) != -1){
                    char c = (char) i;
                    //ADD TEXT PROCESSING LOGIC HERE
                    Log.d(TAG, "char = " + c);
                }

            } catch (IOException e) {
                e.printStackTrace();
            }
        }
    }
}
}
```

When the `PipeExampleActivity` is created, it will show an `EditText` box, which has a listener (`TextWatcher`) for changes in the content. Whenever a new character is added in the `EditText`, the character will be written to the pipe and read in the `TextHandler` `Task`. The consumer task is an infinite loop that reads a character from the pipe as soon as there is anything to read. The inner while-loop will block when calling `read()` if the pipe is empty.

 Be careful when involving the UI thread with pipes, due to the possible blocking of calls if the pipe is either full (producer blocks on its `write()` call) or empty (consumer blocks on its `read()` call).

Shared Memory

Shared memory (using the memory area known in programming as the *heap*) is a common way to pass information between threads. All threads in an application can access the same address space within the process. Hence, if one thread writes a value on a variable in the shared memory, it can be read by all the other threads, as shown in Figure 4-2.

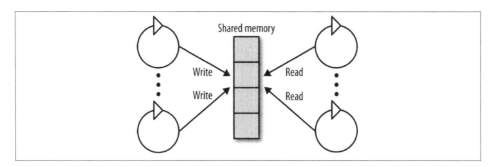

Figure 4-2. Thread communication with shared memory

If a thread stores data as a local variable, no other thread can see it. By storing it in shared memory, it can use the variables for communication and share work with other threads. Objects are stored in the shared memory if they are scoped as one of the following:

- Instance member variables
- Class member variables
- Objects declared in methods

The reference of an object is stored locally on the thread's stack, but the object itself is stored in shared memory. The object is accessible from multiple threads only if the method publishes the reference outside the method scope, for example, by passing the reference to another object's method. Threads communicate through shared memory by defining instance and class fields that are accessible from multiple threads.

Signaling

While threads are communicating through the state variables on the shared memory, they could poll the state value to fetch changes to the state. But a more efficient mechanism is the Java library's built-in signaling mechanism that lets a thread notify other threads of changes in the state. The signaling mechanism varies depending on the synchronization type (see Table 4-1).

Table 4-1. Thread signaling

	synchronized	ReentrantLock	ReentrantReadWriteLock
Blocking call, waiting for a state	Object.wait() Object.wait(timeout)	Condition.await() Condition.await(timeout)	Condition.await() Condition.await(timeout)
Signal blocked threads	Object.notify() Object.notifyAll()	Condition.signal() Condition.signalAll()	Condition.signal() Condition.signalAll()

When a thread cannot continue execution until another thread reaches a specific state, it calls wait()/wait(timeout) or the equivalents await()/await(timeout), depending on the synchronization used. The timeout parameters indicate how long the calling thread should wait before continuing the execution.

When another thread has changed the state, it signals the change with notify()/notifyAll() or the equivalents signal()/signalAll(). Upon a signal, the waiting thread continues execution. The calls thus support two different design patterns that use conditions: the notify() or signal() version wakes one thread, chosen at random, whereas the notifyAll() or signalAll() version wakes all threads waiting on the signal.

Because multiple threads could receive the signal and one could enter the critical section before the others wake, receiving the signal does not guarantee that the correct state is achieved. A waiting thread should apply a design pattern where it checks that the wanted condition is fulfilled before executing further. For example, if the shared state is protected with synchronization on the intrinsic lock, check the condition before calling wait():

```
synchronized(this) {
    while(isConditionFulfilled == false) {
        wait();
    }
    // When the execution reaches this point,
    // the state is correct.
}
```

This pattern checks whether the condition predicate is fulfilled. If not, the thread blocks by calling wait(). When another thread notifies on the monitor and the waiting thread wakes up, it checks again whether the condition has been fulfilled and, if not, it blocks again, waiting for a new signal.

 A very common Android use case is to create a worker thread from the UI thread and let the worker thread produce a result to be used by some UI element, so the UI thread should wait for the result. However, the UI thread should not wait for a signal from a background thread, as it may block the UI thread. Instead, use the Android message passing mechanism discussed later.

BlockingQueue

Thread signaling is a low-level, highly configurable mechanism that can be adapted to fit many use cases, but it may also be considered as the most error-prone technique. Therefore, the Java platform builds high-level abstractions upon the thread signaling mechanism to solve one-directional handoff of arbitrary objects between threads. The abstraction is often called "solving the producer-consumer synchronization problem." The problem consists of use cases where there can be threads producing content (producer threads) and threads consuming content (consumer threads). The producers hand off messages for the consumers to process. The intermediator between the threads is a queue with blocking behavior, i.e., `java.util.concurrent.BlockingQueue` (see Figure 4-3).

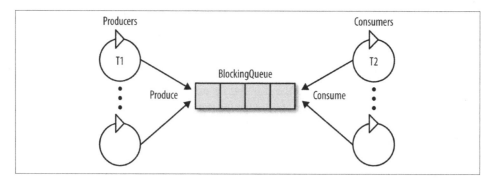

Figure 4-3. Thread communication with `BlockingQueue`

The `BlockingQueue` acts as the coordinator between the producer and consumer threads, wrapping a list implementation together with thread signaling. The list contains a configurable number of elements that the producing threads fill with arbitrary data messages. On the other side, the consumer threads extract the messages in the order that they were enqueued and then process them. Coordination between the producers and consumers is necessary if they get out of sync, for example, if the producers hand off more messages than the consumers can handle. So BlockingQueue uses thread conditions to ensure that producers cannot enqueue new messages if the BlockingQueue list is full, and that consumers know when there are messages to fetch. Synchronization between the threads can be achieved with thread signaling, as "Example: Consumer and Producer" on page 24 shows. But the BlockingQueue both blocks threads and signals the important state changes—i.e., the list is not full and the list is not empty.

The consumer-producer pattern implemented with the LinkedBlockingQueue-implementation is easily implemented by adding messages to the queue with put(), and removing them with take(), where put() blocks the caller if the queue is full, and take() blocks the caller if the queue is empty:

```
public class ConsumerProducer {

    private final int LIMIT = 10;
    private BlockingQueue<Integer> blockingQueue =
        new LinkedBlockingQueue<Integer>(LIMIT);

    public void produce() throws InterruptedException {
        int value = 0;

        while (true) {
            blockingQueue.put(value++);
        }
    }

    public void consume() throws InterruptedException {
        while (true) {
            int value = blockingQueue.take();
        }
    }
}
```

Android Message Passing

So far, the thread communication options discussed have been regular Java, available in any Java application. The mechanisms—pipes, shared memory, and blocking queues—apply to Android applications but impose problems for the UI thread because of their tendency to block. The UI thread responsiveness is at risk when using mechanisms with blocking behavior, because that may occasionally hang the thread.

The most common thread communication use case in Android is between the UI thread and worker threads. Hence, the Android platform defines its own message passing mechanism for communication between threads. The UI thread can offload long tasks by sending data messages to be processed on background threads. The message passing mechanism is a nonblocking consumer-producer pattern, where neither the producer thread nor the consumer thread will block during the message handoff.

The message handling mechanism is fundamental in the Android platform and the API is located in the `android.os` package, with a set of classes shown in Figure 4-4 that implement the functionality.

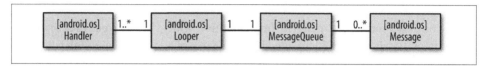

Figure 4-4. API overview

`android.os.Looper`
> A message dispatcher associated with the one and only consumer thread.

`android.os.Handler`
> Consumer thread message processor, and the interface for a producer thread to insert messages into the queue. A `Looper` can have many associated handlers, but they all insert messages into the same queue.

`android.os.MessageQueue`
> Unbounded linked list of messages to be processed on the consumer thread. Every `Looper`—and `Thread`—has at most one `MessageQueue`.

`android.os.Message`
> Message to be executed on the consumer thread.

Messages are inserted by producer threads and processed by the consumer thread, as illustrated in Figure 4-5.

1. Insert: The producer thread inserts messages in the queue by using the `Handler` connected to the consumer thread, as shown in "Handler" on page 60.

2. Retrieve: The `Looper`, discussed in "Looper" on page 58, runs in the consumer thread and retrieves messages from the queue in a sequential order.

3. Dispatch: The handlers are responsible for processing the messages on the consumer thread. A thread may have multiple `Handler` instances for processing messages; the `Looper` ensures that messages are dispatched to the correct `Handler`.

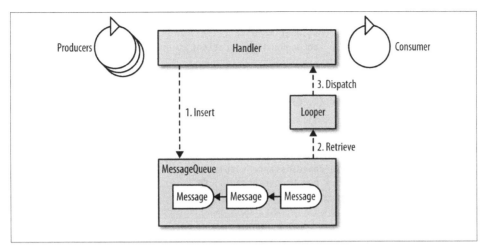

Figure 4-5. Overview of the message-passing mechanism between multiple producer threads and one consumer thread. Every message refers to to the next message in the queue, here indicated by a left-pointing arrow.

Example: Basic Message Passing

Before we dissect the components in detail, let's look at a fundamental message passing example to get us acquainted with the code setup.

The following code implements what is probably one of the most common use cases. The user presses a button on the screen that could trigger a long operation, such as a network operation. To avoid stalling the rendering of the UI, the long operation, represented here by a dummy doLongRunningOperation() method, has to be executed on a worker thread. Hence, the setup is merely one producer thread (the UI thread) and one consumer thread (LooperThread).

Our code sets up a message queue. It handles the button click as usual in the on Click() callback, which executes on the UI thread. In our implementation, the callback inserts a dummy message into the message queue. For sake of brevity, layouts and UI components have been left out of the example code:

```
public class LooperActivity extends Activity {

    LooperThread mLooperThread;

    private static class LooperThread extends Thread { ❶

        public Handler mHandler;

        public void run() {
            Looper.prepare(); ❷
            mHandler = new Handler() { ❸
```

```
                    public void handleMessage(Message msg) { ❹
                        if(msg.what == 0) {
                            doLongRunningOperation();
                        }
                    }
                };
                Looper.loop(); ❺
                }
        }

        public void onCreate(Bundle savedInstanceState) {
            super.onCreate(savedInstanceState);
            mLooperThread = new LooperThread(); ❻
            mLooperThread.start();
        }

        public void onClick(View v) {
            if (mLooperThread.mHandler != null) {❼
                Message msg = mLooperThread.mHandler.obtainMessage(0); ❽
                        mLooperThread.mHandler.sendMessage(msg); ❾
            }
        }

        private void doLongRunningOperation() {
            // Add long running operation here.
        }

        protected void onDestroy() {
            mLooperThread.mHandler.getLooper().quit(); ❿
        }
    }
```

❶ Definition of the worker thread, acting as a consumer of the message queue.

❷ Associate a Looper—and implicitly a MessageQueue—with the thread.

❸ Set up a Handler to be used by the producer for inserting messages in the queue.
    Here we use the default constructor so it will bind to the Looper of the current
    thread. Hence, this Handler can created only after Looper.prepare(), or it will
    have nothing to bind to.

❹ Callback that runs when the message has been dispatched to the worker thread.
    It checks the what parameter and then executes the long operation.

❺ Start dispatching messages from the message queue to the consumer thread.
    This is a blocking call, so the worker thread will not finish.

❻ Start the worker thread, so that it is ready to process messages.

❼ There is race condition between the setup of mHandler on a background thread
    and this usage on the UI thread. Hence, validate that mHandler is available.

❽ Initialize a Message-object with the what argument arbitrarily set to 0.

❾   Insert the message in the queue.

❿   Terminate the background thread. The call to `Looper.quit()` stops the dispatching of messages and releases `Looper.loop()` from blocking so the `run` method can finish, leading to the termination of the thread.

Classes Used in Message Passing

Let's take a more detailed look now at the specific components of message passing and their use.

MessageQueue

The message queue is represented by the `android.os.MessageQueue` class. It is built with linked messages, constituting an unbound one-directional linked list. Producer threads insert messages that will later be dispatched to the consumer. The messages are sorted based on timestamps. The pending message with the lowest timestamp value is first in line for dispatch to the consumer. However, a message is dispatched only if the timestamp value is less than the current time. If not, the dispatch will wait until the current time has passed the timestamp value.

Figure 4-6 illustrates a message queue with three pending messages, sorted with timestamps where t1 < t2 < t3. Only one message has passed the dispatch barrier, which is the current time. Messages eligible for dispatch have a timestamp value less than the current time (represented by "Now" in the figure).

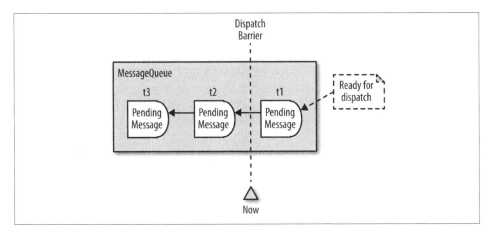

Figure 4-6. Pending messages in the queue. The rightmost message is first in queue to be processed. The message arrows denote references to the next message in the queue.

If no message has passed the dispatch barrier when the Looper is ready to retrieve the next message, the consumer thread blocks. Execution is resumed as soon as a message passes the dispatch barrier.

The producers can insert new messages in the queue at any time and on any position in the queue. The insert position in the queue is based on the timestamp value. If a new message has the lowest timestamp value compared to the pending messages in the queue, it will occupy the first position in the queue, which is next to be dispatched. Insertions always conform to the timestamp sorting order. Message insertion is discussed further in "Handler" on page 60.

MessageQueue.IdleHandler

If there is no message to process, a consumer thread has some idle time. For instance, Figure 4-7 illustrates a time slot where the consumer thread is idle. By default, the consumer thread simply waits for new messages during idle time; but instead of waiting, the thread can be utilized to execute other tasks during these idle slots. This feature can be utilized to let noncritical tasks postpone their execution until no other messages are competing for execution time.

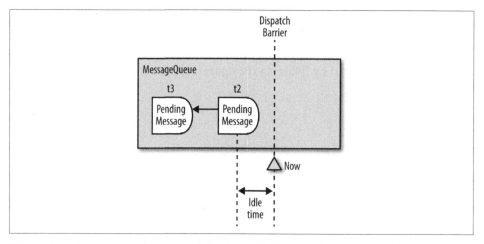

Figure 4-7. If no message has passed the dispatch barrier, there is a time slot that can be utilized for execution before the next pending message needs to be executed

When a pending message has been dispatched, and no other message has passed the dispatch barrier, a time slot occurs where the consumer thread can be utilized for execution of other tasks. An application gets hold of this time slot with the android.os.MessageQueue.IdleHandler-interface, a listener that generates callbacks when the consumer thread is idle. The listener is attached to the MessageQueue and detached from it through the following calls:

```
// Get the message queue of the current thread.
MessageQueue mq = Looper.myQueue();
// Create and register an idle listener.
MessageQueue.IdleHandler idleHandler = new MessageQueue.IdleHandler();
mq.addIdleHandler(idleHandler)
// Unregister an idle listener.
mq.removeIdleHandler(idleHandler)
```

The idle handler interface consists of one callback method only:

```
interface IdleHandler {
    boolean queueIdle();
}
```

When the message queue detects idle time for the consumer thread, it invokes `queueI` `dle()` on all registered `IdleHandler`-instances. It is up to the application to implement the callback responsibly. You should usually avoid long-running tasks because they will delay pending messages during the time they run.

The implementation of `queueIdle()` must return a Boolean value with the following meanings:

true
> The idle handler is kept active; it will continue to receive callbacks for successive idle time slots.

false
> The idle handler is inactive; it will not receive anymore callbacks for successive idle time slots. This is the same thing as removing the listener through `Message` `Queue.removeIdleHandler()`.

Example: Using IdleHandler to terminate an unused thread

All registered `IdleHandler`s to a `MessageQueue` are invoked when a thread has idle slots, where it waits for new messages to process. The idle slots can occur before the first message, between messages, and after the last message. If multiple content producers should process data sequentially on a consumer thread, the `IdleHandler` can be used to terminate the consumer thread when all messages are processed so that the unused thread does not linger in memory. With the `IdleHandler`, it is not necessary to keep track of the last inserted message to know when the thread can be terminated.

 This use case applies only when the producing threads insert messages in the `MessageQueue` without delay, so that the consumer thread is never idle until the last message is inserted.

The ConsumeAndQuitThread method shows the structure of a consuming thread with Looper and MessageQueue that terminates the thread when there are no more messages to process:

```java
public class ConsumeAndQuitThread extends Thread
    implements MessageQueue.IdleHandler {

    private static final String THREAD_NAME = "ConsumeAndQuitThread";

    public Handler mConsumerHandler;
    private boolean mIsFirstIdle = true;

    public ConsumeAndQuitThread() {
        super(THREAD_NAME);
    }

    @Override
    public void run() {
        Looper.prepare();
        mConsumerHandler = new Handler() {
            @Override
            public void handleMessage(Message msg) {
                // Consume data
            }
        };
        Looper.myQueue().addIdleHandler(this);❶
        Looper.loop();
    }


    @Override
    public boolean queueIdle() {
        if (mIsFirstIdle) { ❷
            mIsFirstIdle = false;
            return true; ❸
        }
        mConsumerHandler.getLooper().quit(); ❹
        return false;
    }

    public void enqueueData(int i) {
        mConsumerHandler.sendEmptyMessage(i);
    }
}
```

❶ Register the IdleHandler on the background thread when it is started and the Looper is prepared so that the MessageQueue is set up.

❷ Let the first queueIdle invocation pass, since it occurs before the first message is received.

❸ Return true on the first invocation so that the IdleHandler still is registered.

❹ Terminate the thread.

The message insertion is done from multiple threads concurrently, with a simulated randomness of the insertion time:

```
final ConsumeAndQuitThread consumeAndQuitThread = new ConsumeAndQuitThread();
consumeAndQuitThread.start();

for (int i = 0; i < 10; i++) {
    new Thread(new Runnable() {
        @Override
        public void run() {
            for (int i = 0; i < 10; i++) {
                SystemClock.sleep(new Random().nextInt(10));
                consumeAndQuitThread.enqueueData(i);
            }
        }
    }).start();
```

Message

Each item on the MessageQueue is of the android.os.Message class. This is a container object carrying either a data item or a task, never both. Data is processed by the consumer thread, whereas a task is simply executed when it is dequeued and you have no other processing to do:

The message knows its recipient processor—i.e., Handler—and can enqueue itself through Message.sendToTarget():

```
Message m = Message.obtain(handler, runnable);
m.sendToTarget();
```

As we will see in "Handler" on page 60, the handler is most commonly used for message enqueuing, as it offers more flexibility with regard to message insertion.

Data message

The data set has multiple parameters that can be handed off to the consumer thread, as shown in Table 4-2.

Table 4-2. Message parameters

Parameter name	Type	Usage
what	int	Message identifier. Communicates intention of the message.
arg1, arg2	int	Simple data values to handle the common use case of handing over integers. If a maximum of two integer values are to be passed to the consumer, these parameters are more efficient than allocating a Bundle, as explained under the data parameter.
obj	Object	Arbitrary object. If the object is handed off to a thread in another process, it has to implement Parcelable.
data	Bundle	Container of arbitrary data values.
replyTo	Messenger	Reference to Handler in some other process. Enables interprocess message communication, as described in "Two-Way Communication" on page 86.
callback	Runnable	Task to execute on a thread. This is an internal instance field that holds the Runnable object from the Handler.post methods in "Handler" on page 60.

Task message

The task is represented by a `java.lang.Runnable` object to be executed on the consumer thread. Task messages cannot contain any data beyond the task itself.

A `MessageQueue` can contain any combination of data and task messages. The consumer thread processes them in a sequential manner, independent of the type. If a message is a data message, the consumer processes the data. Task messages are handled by letting the `Runnable` execute on the consumer thread, but the consumer thread does not receive a message to be processed in `Handler.handleMessage(Message)`, as it does with data messages.

The lifecycle of a message is simple: the producer creates the message, and eventually it is processed by the consumer. This description suffices for most use cases, but when a problem arises, a deeper understanding of message handling is invaluable. Let us take a look into what actually happens with the message during its lifecycle, which can be split up into four principal states shown in Figure 4-8. The runtime stores message objects in an application-wide pool to enable the reuse of previous messages; this avoids the overhead of creating new instances for every handoff. The message object execution time is normally very short, and many messages are processed per time unit.

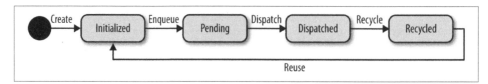

Figure 4-8. Message lifecycle states

The state transfers are partly controlled by the application and partly by the platform. Note that the states are not observable, and an application cannot follow the changes from one state to another (although there are ways to follow the movement of messages, explained in "Observing the Message Queue" on page 70). Therefore, an application should not make any assumptions about the current state when handling a message.

Initialized

In the initialized state, a message object with mutable state has been created and, if it is a data message, populated with data. The application is responsible for creating the message object using one of the following calls. They take an object from the object pool:

- Explicit object construction:

  ```
  Message m  = new Message();
  ```

- Factory methods:

  — Empty message:

  ```
  Message m = Message.obtain();
  ```

  — Data message:

  ```
  Message m = Message.obtain(Handler h);
  Message m = Message.obtain(Handler h, int what);
  Message m = Message.obtain(Handler h, int what, Object o);
  Message m = Message.obtain(Handler h, int what, int arg1, int arg2);
  Message m = Message.obtain(Handler h, int what, int arg1, int arg2,
                             Object o);
  ```

  — Task message:

  ```
  Message m = Message.obtain(Handler h, Runnable task);
  ```

  — Copy constructor:

  ```
  Message m = Message.obtain(Message originalMsg);
  ```

Pending

The message has been inserted into the queue by the producer thread, and it is waiting to be dispatched to the consumer thread.

Dispatched

In this state, the Looper has retrieved and removed the message from the queue. The message has been dispatched to the consumer thread and is currently being processed. There is no application API for this operation because the dispatch is controlled by the Looper, without the influence of the application. When the Looper dispatches a message, it checks the delivery information of the message and delivers the message to the correct recipient. Once dispatched, the message is executed on the consumer thread.

Recycled

At this point in the lifecycle, the message state is cleared and the instance is returned to the message pool. The Looper handles the recycling of the message when it has finished executing on the consumer thread. Recycling of messages is handled by the runtime and should not be done explicitly by the application.

 Once a message is inserted in the queue, the content should not be altered. In theory, it is valid to change the content before the message is dispatched. However, because the state is not observable, the message may be processed by the consumer thread while the producer tries to change the data, raising thread safety concerns. It would be even worse if the message has been recycled, because it then has been returned to the message pool and possibly used by another producer to pass data in another queue.

Looper

The android.os.Looper class handles the dispatch of messages in the queue to the associated handler. All messages that have passed the dispatch barrier, as illustrated in Figure 4-6, are eligible for dispatch by the Looper. As long as the queue has messages eligible for dispatch, the Looper will ensure that the consumer thread receives the messages. When no messages have passed the dispatch barrier, the consumer thread will block until a message has passed the dispatch barrier.

The consumer thread does not interact with the message queue directly to retrieve the messages. Instead, a message queue is added to the thread when the Looper has been attached. The Looper manages the message queue and facilitates the dispatch of messages to the consumer thread.

By default, only the UI thread has a Looper; threads created in the application need to get a Looper associated explicitly. When the Looper is created for a thread, it is connected to a message queue. The Looper acts as the intermediator between the queue and the thread. The setup is done in the run method of the thread:

```
class ConsumerThread extends Thread {
    @Override
    public void run() {
        Looper.prepare(); ❶

        // Handler creation omitted.

        Looper.loop(); ❷
```

```
        }
    }
```

❶   The first step is to create the `Looper`, which is done with the static `prepare()` method; it will create a message queue and associate it with the current thread. At this point, the message queue is ready for insertion of messages, but they are not dispatched to the consumer thread.

❷   Start handling messages in the message queue. This is a blocking method that ensures the `run()` method is not finished; while `run()` blocks, the `Looper` dispatches messages to the consumer thread for processing.

A thread can have only one associated `Looper`; a runtime error will occur if the application tries to set up a second one. Consequently, a thread can have only one message queue, meaning that messages sent by multiple producer threads are processed sequentially on the consumer thread. Hence, the currently executing message will postpone subsequent messages until it has been processed. Messages with long execution times shall not be used if they can delay other important tasks in the queue.

Looper termination

The `Looper` is requested to stop processing messages with either `quit` or `quitSafely`: `quit()` stops the looper from dispatching any more messages from the queue; all pending messages in the queue, including those that have passed the dispatch barrier, will be discarded. `quitSafely`, on the other hand, only discards the messages that have not passed the dispatch barrier. Pending messages that are eligible for dispatch will be processed before the `Looper` is terminated.

 `quitSafely` was added in API level 18 (Jelly Bean 4.3). Previous API levels only support `quit`.

Terminating a `Looper` does not terminate the thread; it merely exits `Looper.loop()` and lets the thread resume running in the method that invoked the `loop` call. But you cannot start the old `Looper` or a new one, so the thread can no longer enqueue or handle messages. If you call `Looper.prepare()`, it will throw `RuntimeException` because the thread already has an attached `Looper`. If you call `Looper.loop()`, it will block, but no messages will be dispatched from the queue.

The UI thread Looper

The UI thread is the only thread with an associated Looper by default. It is a regular thread, like any other thread created by the application itself, but the Looper is associated with the thread[1] before the application components are initialized.

There are a few practical differences between the UI thread Looper and other application thread loopers:

- It is accessible from everywhere, through the Looper.getMainLooper() method.
- It cannot be terminated. Looper.quit() throws RuntimeException.
- The runtime associates a Looper to the UI thread by Looper.prepareMainLooper(). This can be done only once per application. Thus, trying to attach the main looper to another thread will throw an exception.

Handler

So far, the focus has been on the internals of Android thread communication, but an application mostly interacts with the android.os.Handler class. It is a two-sided API that both handles the insertion of messages into the queue and the message processing. As indicated in Figure 4-5, it is invoked from both the producer and consumer thread typically used for:

- Creating messages
- Inserting messages into the queue
- Processing messages on the consumer thread
- Managing messages in the queue

Setup

While carrying out its responsibilities, the Handler interacts with the Looper, message queue, and message. As Figure 4-4 illustrates, the only direct instance relation is to the Looper, which is used to connect to the MessageQueue. Without a Looper, handlers cannot function; they cannot couple with a queue to insert messages, and consequently they will not receive any messages to process. Hence, a Handler instance is already bound to a Looper instance at construction time:

- Constructors without an explicit Looper bind to the Looper of the current thread:

---

1. The UI thread is managed by the platform internal class android.app.ActivityThread.

```
new Handler();
new Handler(Handler.Callback)
```

- Constructors with an explicit Looper bind to that Looper:

```
new Handler(Looper);
new Handler(Looper, Handler.Callback);
```

If the constructors without an explicit Looper are called on a thread without a Looper (i.e., it has not called Looper.prepare()), there is nothing handlers can bind to, leading to a RuntimeException. Once a handler is bound to a Looper, the binding is final.

A thread can have multiple handlers; messages from them coexist in the queue but are dispatched to the correct Handler instance, as shown in Figure 4-9.

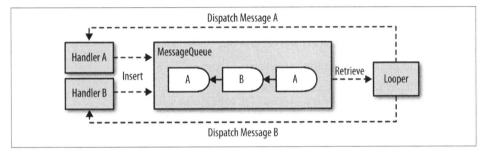

Figure 4-9. Multiple handlers using one Looper. *The handler inserting a message is the same handler that processes the message.*

   Multiple handlers will not enable concurrent execution. The messages are still in the same queue and are processed sequentially.

Message creation

For simplicity, the Handler class offers wrapper functions for the factory methods shown in "Initialized" on page 57 to create objects of the Message class:

```
Message obtainMessage(int what, int arg1, int arg2)
Message obtainMessage()
Message obtainMessage(int what, int arg1, int arg2, Object obj)
Message obtainMessage(int what)
Message obtainMessage(int what, Object obj)
```

The message obtained from a Handler is retrieved from the message pool and implicitly connected to the Handler instance that requested it. This connection enables the Looper to dispatch each message to the correct Handler.

Message insertion

The Handler inserts messages in the message queue in various ways depending on the message type. Task messages are inserted through methods that are prefixed *post*, whereas data insertion methods are prefixed *send*:

- Add a task to the message queue:

  ```
  boolean post(Runnable r)f
  boolean postAtFrontOfQueue(Runnable r)
  boolean postAtTime(Runnable r, Object token, long uptimeMillis)
  boolean postAtTime(Runnable r, long uptimeMillis)
  boolean postDelayed(Runnable r, long delayMillis)
  ```

- Add a data object to the message queue:

  ```
  boolean sendMessage(Message msg)
  boolean sendMessageAtFrontOfQueue(Message msg)
  boolean sendMessageAtTime(Message msg, long uptimeMillis)
  boolean sendMessageDelayed(Message msg, long delayMillis)
  ```

- Add simple data object to the message queue:

  ```
  boolean sendEmptyMessage(int what)
  boolean sendEmptyMessageAtTime(int what, long uptimeMillis)
  boolean sendEmptyMessageDelayed(int what, long delayMillis)
  ```

All insertion methods put a new Message object in the queue, even though the application does not create the Message object explicitly. The objects, such as Runnable in a task post and what in a send, are wrapped into Message objects, because those are the only data types allowed in the queue.

Every message inserted in the queue comes with a time parameter indicating the time when the message is eligible for dispatch to the consumer thread. The sorting is based on the time parameter, and it is the only way an application can affect the dispatch order:

default
   Immediately eligible for dispatch.

at_front
   This message is eligible for dispatch at time 0. Hence, it will be the next dispatched message, unless another is inserted at the front before this one is processed.

delay
   The amount of time after which this message is eligible for dispatch.

uptime
   The absolute time at which this message is eligible for dispatch.

Even though explicit delays or uptimes can be specified, the time required to process each message is still indeterminate. It depends both on whatever existing messages need to be processed first and the operating system scheduling.

Inserting a message in the queue is not failsafe. Some common errors that can occur are listed in Table 4-3.

Table 4-3. Message insertion errors

Failure	Error response	Typical application problem
Message has no Handler.	RuntimeException	Message was created from a Message.obtain() method without a specified Handler.
Message has already been dispatched and is being processed.	RuntimeException	The same message instance was inserted twice.
Looper has exited.	Return false	Message is inserted after Looper.quit() has been called.

 The dispatchMessage method of the Handler class is used by the Looper to dispatch messages to the consumer thread. If used by the application directly, the message will be processed immediately on the calling thread and not the consumer thread.

Example: Two-way message passing

The HandlerExampleActivity simulates a long-running operation that is started when the user clicks a button. The long-running task is executed on a background thread; meanwhile, the UI displays a progress bar that is removed when the background thread reports the result back to the UI thread.

First, the setup of the Activity:

```
public class HandlerExampleActivity extends Activity {

    private final static int SHOW_PROGRESS_BAR = 1;
    private final static int HIDE_PROGRESS_BAR = 0;
    private BackgroundThread mBackgroundThread;

    private TextView mText;
    private Button mButton;
    private ProgressBar mProgressBar;

    @Override
    public void onCreate(Bundle savedInstanceState) {
        super.onCreate(savedInstanceState);
        setContentView(R.layout.activity_handler_example);

        mBackgroundThread = new BackgroundThread();
        mBackgroundThread.start();❶
```

```
    mText = (TextView) findViewById(R.id.text);
    mProgressBar = (ProgressBar) findViewById(R.id.progress);
    mButton = (Button) findViewById(R.id.button);
    mButton.setOnClickListener(new OnClickListener() {
        @Override
        public void onClick(View v) {
            mBackgroundThread.doWork(); ❷
        }
    });
}

@Override
protected void onDestroy() {
    super.onDestroy();
    mBackgroundThread.exit();❸
}

// ... The rest of the Activity is defined further down

}
```

❶ A background thread with a message queue is started when the HandlerExam pleActivity is created. It handles tasks from the UI thread.

❷ When the user clicks a button, a new task is sent to the background thread. As the tasks will be executed sequentially on the background thread, multiple button clicks may lead to queueing of tasks before they are processed.

❸ The background thread is stopped when the HandlerExampleActivity is destroyed.

BackgroundThread is used to offload tasks from the UI thread. It runs—and can receive messages—during the lifetime of the HandlerExampleActivity. It does not expose its internal Handler; instead it wraps all accesses to the Handler in public methods doW ork and exit:

```
private class BackgroundThread extends Thread {

    private Handler mBackgroundHandler;

    public void run() { ❶
        Looper.prepare();
        mBackgroundHandler = new Handler(); ❷
        Looper.loop();
    }

    public void doWork() {
        mBackgroundHandler.post(new Runnable() { ❸
            @Override
            public void run() {
                Message uiMsg = mUiHandler.obtainMessage(
```

```
                    SHOW_PROGRESS_BAR, 0, 0, null); ❹

            mUiHandler.sendMessage(uiMsg); ❺

            Random r = new Random();
            int randomInt = r.nextInt(5000);
            SystemClock.sleep(randomInt); ❻

            uiMsg = mUiHandler.obtainMessage(
                HIDE_PROGRESS_BAR, randomInt, 0, null); ❼
                mUiHandler.sendMessage(uiMsg); ❽
        }
    });
    }

    public void exit() { ❾
        mBackgroundHandler.getLooper().quit();
    }
}
```

❶ Associate a Looper with the thread.

❷ The Handler processes only Runnables. Hence, it is not required to implement
    Handler.handleMessage.

❸ Post a long task to be executed in the background.

❹ Create a Message object that contains only a what argument with a command—
    SHOW_PROGRESS_BAR—to the UI thread so that it can show the progress bar.

❺ Send the start message to the UI thread.

❻ Simulate a long task of random length, that produces some data randomInt.

❼ Create a Message object with the result randomInt, that is passed in the arg1
    parameter. The what parameter contains a command—HIDE_PROGRESS_BAR—
    to remove the progress bar.

❽ The message with the end result that both informs the UI thread that the task
    is finished and delivers a result.

❾ Quit the Looper so that the thread can finish.

The UI thread defines its own Handler that can receive commands to control the progress bar and update the UI with results from the background thread:

```
private final Handler mUiHandler = new Handler() {
    public void handleMessage(Message msg) {

        switch(msg.what) {
            case SHOW_PROGRESS_BAR: ❶
                mProgressBar.setVisibility(View.VISIBLE);
                break;
            case HIDE_PROGRESS_BAR: ❷
```

```
                   mText.setText(String.valueOf(msg.arg1));
                   mProgressBar.setVisibility(View.INVISIBLE);
                   break;
            }
        }
    };
```

❶   Show the progress bar.

❷   Hide the progress bar and update the `TextView` with the produced result.

Message processing

Messages dispatched by the `Looper` are processed by the `Handler` on the consumer thread. The message type determines the processing:

Task messages

> Task messages contain only a `Runnable` and no data. Hence, the processing to be executed is defined in the `run` method of the `Runnable`, which is executed automatically on the consumer thread, without invoking `Handler.handleMessage()`.

Data messages

> When the message contains data, the `Handler` is the receiver of the data and is responsible for its processing. The consumer thread processes the data by overriding the `Handler.handleMessage(Message msg)` method. There are two ways to do this, described in the text that follows.

One way to define `handleMessage` is to do it as part of creating a `Handler`. The method should be defined as soon as the message queue is available (after `Looper.prepare()` is called) but before the message retrieval starts (before `Looper.loop()` is called).

A template follows for setting up the handling of data messages:

```
class ConsumerThread extends Thread {
    Handler mHandler;
    @Override
    public void run() {
        Looper.prepare();
        mHandler = new Handler() {
            public void handleMessage(Message msg) {
                // Process data message here
            }
        };)
        Looper.loop();
    }
}
```

In this code, the `Handler` is defined as an anonymous inner class, but it could as well have been defined as a regular or inner class.

A convenient alternative to extending the Handler class is to use the Handler.Call back interface, which defines a handleMessage method with an additional return parameter not in Handler.handleMessage():

```
public interface Callback {
    public boolean handleMessage(Message msg);
}
```

With the Callback interface, it is not necessary to extend the Handler class. Instead, the Callback implementation can be passed to the Handler constructor, and it will then receive the dispatched messages for processing:

```
public class HandlerCallbackActivity extends Activity implements Handler.Callback {
    Handler mUiHandler;

    @Override
    public void onCreate(Bundle savedInstanceState) {
        super.onCreate(savedInstanceState);
        mUiHandler = new Handler(this);
    }

    @Override
    public boolean handleMessage(Message message) {
        // Process messages
        return true;
    }
}
```

Callback.handleMessage should return true if the message is handled, which guarantees that no further processing of the message is done. If, however, false is returned, the message is passed on to the Handler.handleMessage method for further processing. Note that the Callback does not override Handler.handleMessage. Instead, it adds a message preprocessor that is invoked before the Handlers own method. The Call back preprocessor can intercept and change messages before the Handler receives them. The following code shows the principle for intercepting messages with the Callback:

```
public class HandlerCallbackActivity extends Activity implements Handler.Callback {❶

    @Override
    public boolean handleMessage(Message msg) { ❷
        switch (msg.what) {
            case 1:
                msg.what = 11;
                return true;
            default:
                msg.what = 22;
                return false;
        }
    }

    // Invoked on button click
```

```
    public void onHandlerCallback(View v) {
        Handler handler = new Handler(this) {
            @Override
            public void handleMessage(Message msg) {
                // Process message ❸
            }
        };
        handler.sendEmptyMessage(1); ❹
        handler.sendEmptyMessage(2); ❺
    }
}
```

❶   The `HandlerCallbackActivity` implements the `Callback` interface to intercept
    messages.

❷   The `Callback` implementation intercepts messages. If `msg.what` is 1, it returns
    `true`—the message is handled. Otherwise, it changes the value of `msg.what` to
    22 and returns `false`—the message is not handled, so it is passed on to the
    `Handler` implementation of `handleMessage`.

❸   Process messages in the second `Handler`.

❹   Insert a message with `msg.what == 1`. The message is intercepted by the `Call`
    back as it returns `true`.

❺   Insert a message with `msg.what == 2`. The message is changed by the `Call`
    back and passed on to the `Handler` that prints `Secondary Handler - msg = 22`.

Removing Messages from the Queue

After enqueuing a message, the producer can invoke a method of the `Handler` class to
remove the message, so long as it has not been dequeued by the `Looper`. Sometimes an
application may want to clean the message queue by removing all messages, which is
possible, but most often a more fine-grained approach is desired: an application wants
to target only a subset of the messages. For that, it needs to be able to identify the correct
messages. Therefore, messages can be identified from certain properties, as shown in
Table 4-4.

Table 4-4. Message identifiers

Identifier type	Description	Messages to which it applies
Handler	Message receiver	Both task and data messages
Object	Message tag	Both task and data messages
Integer	`what` parameter of message	Data messages
Runnable	Task to be executed	Task messages

The handler identifier is mandatory for every message, because a message always knows
what `Handler` it will be dispatched to. This requirement implicitly restricts each Han

---

dler to removing only messages belonging to that Handler. It is not possible for a Handler to remove messages in the queue that were inserted by another Handler.

The methods available in the Handler class for managing the message queue are:

- Remove a task from the message: queue.

```
removeCallbacks(Runnable r)
removeCallbacks(Runnable r, Object token)
```

- Remove a data message from the message queue:

```
removeMessages(int what)
removeMessages(int what, Object object)
```

- Remove tasks and data messages from the message queue:

```
removeCallbacksAndMessages(Object token)
```

The Object identifier is used in both the data and task message. Hence, it can be assigned to messages as a kind of tag, allowing you later to remove related messages that you have tagged with the same Object.

For instance, the following excerpt inserts two messages in the queue to make it possible to remove them later based on the tag:

```
Object tag = new Object(); ❶

Handler handler = new Handler()
    public void handleMessage(Message msg) {
        // Process message
        Log.d("Example", "Processing message");
    }
};

Message message = handler.obtainMessage(0, tag); ❷
handler.sendMessage(message);

handler.postAtTime(new Runnable() { ❸
    public void run() {
        // Left empty for brevity
    }
}, tag, SystemClock.uptimeMillis());

handler.removeCallbacksAndMessages(tag); ❹
```

❶ The message tag identifier, common to both the task and data message.

❷ The object in a Message instance is used both as data container and implicitly defined message tag.

❸ Post a task message with an explicitly defined message tag.

❹ Remove all messages with the tag.

As indicated before, you have no way to find out whether a message was dispatched and handled before you issue a call to remove it. Once the message is dispatched, the producer thread that enqueued it cannot stop its task from executing or its data from being processed.

Observing the Message Queue

It is possible to observe pending messages and the dispatching of messages from a Looper to the associated handlers. The Android platform offers two observing mechanisms. Let us take a look at them by example.

The first example shows how it is possible to log the current snapshot of pending messages in the queue.

Taking a snapshot of the current message queue

This example creates a worker thread when the Activity is created. When the user presses a button, causing onClick to be called, six messages are added to the queue in different ways. Afterward we observe the state of the message queue:

```
public class MQDebugActivity extends Activity {

    private static final String TAG = "EAT";
    Handler mWorkerHandler;

    public void onCreate(Bundle savedInstanceState) {
        super.onCreate(savedInstanceState);
        setContentView(R.layout.activity_mqdebug);

        Thread t = new Thread() {
            @Override
            public void run() {
                Looper.prepare();
                mWorkerHandler = new Handler() {
                    @Override
                    public void handleMessage(Message msg) {
                        Log.d(TAG, "handleMessage - what = " + msg.what);
                    }
                };
                Looper.loop();
            }
        };
        t.start();
    }

    // Called on button click, i.e. from the UI thread.
    public void onClick(View v) {
        mWorkerHandler.sendEmptyMessageDelayed(1, 2000);
        mWorkerHandler.sendEmptyMessage(2);
        mWorkerHandler.obtainMessage(3, 0, 0, new Object()).sendToTarget();
```

```
        mWorkerHandler.sendEmptyMessageDelayed(4, 300);
        mWorkerHandler.postDelayed(new Runnable() {
            @Override
            public void run() {
                Log.d(TAG, "Execute");
            }
        }, 400);
        mWorkerHandler.sendEmptyMessage(5);

        mWorkerHandler.dump(new LogPrinter(Log.DEBUG, TAG), "");
    }
}
```

Six messages, with the parameters shown in Figure 4-10, are added to the queue.

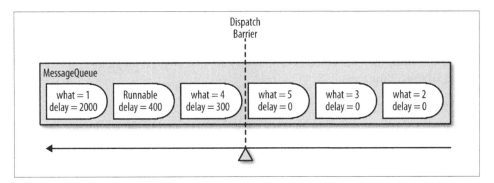

Figure 4-10. Added messages in the queue

Right after the messages are added to the queue, a snapshot is printed to the log. Only pending messages are observed. Hence, the number of messages actually observed depends on how many messages have already been dispatched to the handler. Three of the messages are added without a delay, which makes them eligible for dispatch at the time of the snapshot.

A typical run of the preceding code produces the following log:

```
49.397: handleMessage - what = 2
49.397: handleMessage - what = 3
49.397: handleMessage - what = 5
49.397: Handler (com.eat.MQDebugActivity$1$1) {412cb3d8} @ 5994288
49.407: Looper{412cb070}
49.407:     mRun=true
49.407:     mThread=Thread[Thread-111,5,main]
49.407:     mQueue=android.os.MessageQueue@412cb090
49.407:         Message 0: { what=4 when=+293ms }
49.407:         Message 1: { what=0 when=+394ms }
49.407:         Message 2: { what=1 when=+1s990ms }
49.407:         (Total messages: 3)
49.707: handleMessage - what = 4
```

```
49.808: Execute
51.407: handleMessage - what = 1
```

The snapshot of the message queue shows that the messages with what parameters (0, 1, and 4) are pending in the queue. These are the messages added to the queue with a dispatch delay, whereas the others without a dispatch delay apparently have been dispatched already. This is a reasonable result because the handler processing is very short —just a print to the log.

The snapshot also shows how much time is left before each message in the queue will pass the dispatch barrier. For instance, the next message to pass the barrier is Message 0 (what= 4) in 293 ms. Messages still pending in the queue but eligible for dispatch will have a negative time indication in the log—e.g., if when is less than zero.

Tracing the message queue processing

The message processing information can be printed to the log. Message queue logging is enabled from the Looper class. The following call enables logging on the message queue of the calling thread:

```
Looper.myLooper().setMessageLogging(new LogPrinter(Log.DEBUG, TAG));
```

Let's look at an example of tracing a message that is posted to the UI thread:

```
mHandler.post(new Runnable() {
    @Override
    public void run() {
        Log.d(TAG, "Executing Runnable");
    }
});

mHandler.sendEmptyMessage(42);
```

The example posts two events to the message queue: first a Runnable followed by an empty message. As expected, with the sequential execution in mind, the Runnable is processed first, and consequently, is the first to be logged:

```
>>>>> Dispatching to Handler (android.os.Handler) {4111ef40}
      com.eat.MessageTracingActivity$1@41130820: 0
Executing Runnable
<<<<< Finished to Handler (android.os.Handler) {4111ef40}
      com.eat.MessageTracingActivity$1@41130820
```

The trace prints the start and end of the event identified by three properties:

Handler instance
    android.os.Handler 4111ef40

Task instance
    com.eat.MessageTracingActivity$1@41130820

The what *parameter*

0 (Runnable tasks do not carry a what parameter)

Similarly, the trace of an message with the what parameter set to 42 prints the message argument but not any Runnable instance:

```
>>>>> Dispatching to Handler (android.os.Handler) {4111ef40} null: 42
<<<<< Finished to Handler (android.os.Handler) {4111ef40} null
```

Combining the two techniques of message queue snapshots and dispatch tracing allows the application to observe message passing in detail.

Communicating with the UI Thread

The UI thread is the only thread in an application that has an associated Looper by default, which is associated on the thread before the first Android component is started. The UI thread can be a consumer, to which other threads can pass messages. It's important to send only short-lived tasks to the UI thread. The UI thread is application global and processes both Android component and system messages sequentially. Hence, long-lived tasks will have a global impact across the application.

Messages are passed to the UI thread through its Looper that is accessible globally in the application from all threads with Looper.getMainLooper():

```
Runnable task = new Runnable() {...};
new Handler(Looper.getMainLooper()).post(task);
```

Independent of the posting thread, the message is inserted in the queue of the UI thread. If it is the UI thread that posts the message to itself, the message can be processed at the earliest after the current message is done:

```
// Method called on UI thread.
private void postFromUiThreadToUiThread() {
    new Handler().post(new Runnable() { ... });

    // The code at this point is part of a message being processed
    // and is executed before the posted message.

}
```

However, a task message that is posted from the UI thread to itself can bypass the message passing and execute immediately within the currently processed message on the UI thread with the convenience method Activity.runOnUiThread(Runnable):

```
// Method called on UI thread.
private void postFromUiThreadToUiThread() {
    runOnUiThread(new Runnable() { ... });

    // The code at this point is executed after the message.
```

```
    }
```

If it is called outside the UI thread, the message is inserted in the queue. The `runO nUiThread` method can only be executed from an `Activity` instance, but the same behavior can be implemented by tracking the ID of the UI thread, for example, with a convenience method `customRunOnUiThread` in an `Application` subclass. The `custom RunOnUiThread` inserts a message in the queue like the following example:

```
public class EatApplication extends Application {
    private long mUiThreadId;
    private Handler mUiHandler;

    @Override
    public void onCreate() {
        super.onCreate();
        mUiThreadId = Thread.currentThread().getId();
        mUiHandler = new Handler();
    }

    public void customRunOnUiThread(Runnable action) {
        if (Thread.currentThread().getId() != mUiThreadId) {
            mUiHandler.post(action);
        } else {
            action.run();
        }
    }
}
```

Summary

Android applications have access to the regular Java thread communication techniques, which suit worker-thread communication well. However, they rarely fit the use case when one of the threads is the UI thread, which is the most common case. Android message passing is used extensively throughout applications, either explicitly or implicitly, through various wrapping techniques that are discussed in the second part of this book.

CHAPTER 5

Interprocess Communication

Android application threads most often communicate within a process, sharing the process's memory, as discussed in Chapter 4. However, communication across process boundaries—i.e., *interprocess communication* (IPC)—is supported by the Android platform through the *binder framework*, which manages the data transactions when there is no shared memory area between the threads.

The most common IPC use cases are handled by high-level components in Android, such as intents, system services, and content providers. They can be used by an application without it having to know whether it communicates within the process or between processes. Sometimes, however, it is necessary for an application to define a more explicit communication model and be more involved in the actual communication. This chapter covers how threads communicate across process boundaries, which includes:

- Synchronous and asynchronous remote procedure calls (RPCs)
- Message communication through `Messenger`
- Returning data with `ResultReceiver`

Android RPC

IPC is managed by the Linux OS, which supports several IPC techniques: signals, pipes, message queues, semaphores, and shared memory. In Android's modified Linux kernel, the Linux IPC techniques have been replaced[1] by the binder framework, which enables an RPC mechanism between processes; a client process can call remote methods in a server process as if the methods were executed locally. Hence, data can be passed to the server process, executed on a thread, and return a result value to the calling thread. The

---

1. See the NDK documentation in the *ndk/docs/system/libc/SYSV-IPC.html* file in your Android SDK directory.

RPC method call itself is trivial, but the underlying RPC mechanism consists of the following steps:

- Method and data decomposition, also known as *marshalling*
- Transferring the marshalled information to the remote process
- Recomposing the information in the remote process, also known as *unmarshalling*
- Transferring return values back to the originating process

The Android application framework and core libraries abstract out the process communication with the binder framework and the Android Interface Definition Language (AIDL).

Binder

The binder enables applications to transfer both functions and data—method calls—between threads running in different processes. The server process defines a remote interface supported by the android.os.Binder class, and threads in a client process can access the remote interface through this remote object.

A remote procedure call that transfers both a function and data is called a *transaction*; the client process calls the transact method, and the server process receives the call in the onTransact method (Figure 5-1).

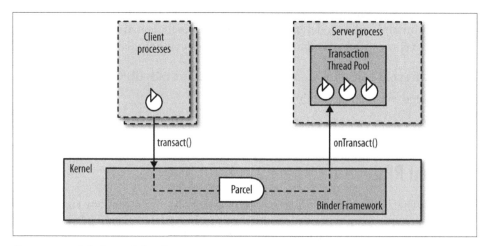

Figure 5-1. IPC through binder

The client thread calling transact is blocked by default until onTransact has finished executing on the remote thread. Transaction data consists of android.os.Parcel objects, which are optimized to be sent across processes via the Binder. Arguments and return values are transferred as `Parcel` objects. These can contain literal arguments or custom objects that implement `android.os.Parcelable`—an interface that defines marshalling and unmarshalling of data in a more efficient way than a `Serializable`.

The `onTransact` method is executed on a thread from a pool of binder threads, discussed in "Binder Threads" on page 30. This pool exists only to handle incoming requests from other processes. It has a maximum of 16 threads,[2] so 16 remote calls can be handled concurrently in every process. This requires the implementations of the calls to ensure thread safety.

IPC can be bidirectional. The server process can issue a transaction to the client process and reverse the flow: the former server process becomes the client and executes a transaction on another binder implemented in the former client process, whose own binder threads handle the processing. Hence, a two-way communication mechanism between two processes can be established. As we will see, this mechanism is important to enable asynchronous RPC.

 If the server process starts a transaction, calling `transact` to send a request to the client process while executing `onTransact`, the client process will not receive the incoming request on a binder thread, but on the thread waiting for the first transaction to finish.

Binders also support asynchronous transactions, which you can specify by setting `IBinder.FLAG_ONEWAY`. With that flag set, the client thread will call `transact` and return immediately. A binder will continue calling `onTransact` on the binder thread in the server process, but cannot return any data synchronously to the client thread.

AIDL

When a process wants to expose functionality for other processes to access, it has to define the communication contract. Basically, the server defines an interface of methods that clients can call. The simplest and most common way to describe the interface in the Android Interface Definition Language (AIDL)—defined in an *.aidl*.file. Compilation of the AIDL file generates Java code that supports IPC.[3] Android applications interact with the generated Java code, but the applications only need to be aware of the interface. The procedure for defining the communication contract is shown in Figure 5-2.

---

2. The number of threads is a platform implementation detail and may change.

3. See the *platform-tools/aidl* file in the Android SDK directory for information about the compiler.

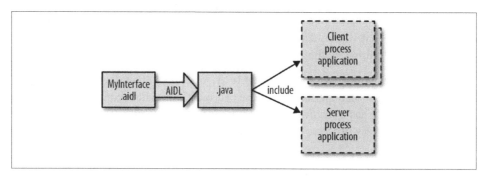

Figure 5-2. Construction of the remote communication interface

The generated Java interface is included in all the client applications and in the server application. The interface file defines two inner classes, Proxy and Stub, that handle all the marshalling and unmarshalling of the data, as well as the transaction itself. Hence, the creation of AIDL automatically generates Java code that wraps the binder framework and sets up the communication contract.

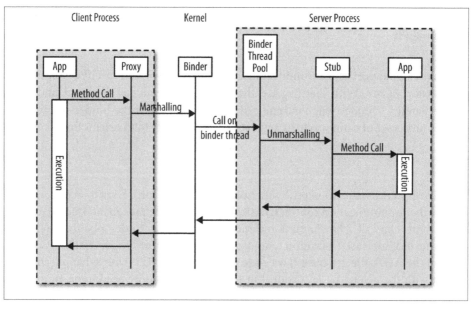

Figure 5-3. Remote procedure calls over AIDL and the generated Proxy and Stub classes

As Figure 5-3 shows, the client proxy and the server stub manage the RPC on behalf of the two applications, allowing clients to invoke methods locally, although executed in a server process (more precisely, on binder threads belonging to a thread pool in the server). The server has to support simultaneous method invocations from multiple client processes and threads—i.e., to ensure that the execution is thread safe.

Synchronous RPC

Although remote method calls are executed concurrently in the server process, the calling thread in the client process will experience it as a synchronous, or blocking, call. The calling thread will resume execution when the remote execution on the binder thread has finished, and possibly has returned a value to the client.

Let us illustrate synchronous RPC, and its implications, with a conceptual code example that only returns the thread name in the remote process:

The first step is to define the interface—the communication contract—in an *.aidl* file. The interface description contains method definitions that a client process can invoke in a server process:

```
interface ISynchronous {
    String getThreadNameFast();
    String getThreadNameSlow(long sleep);
    String getThreadNameBlocking();
    String getThreadNameUnblock();
}
```

The Java interface with `Proxy` and `Stub` inner classes is generated from the *aidl* tool, and the server process overrides the `Stub` class to implement the functionality to be supported:

```
private final ISynchronous.Stub mBinder = new ISynchronous.Stub() {

    CountDownLatch mLatch = new CountDownLatch(1);

    @Override
    public String getThreadNameFast() throws RemoteException {
        return Thread.currentThread().getName();
    }

    @Override
    public String getThreadNameSlow(long sleep) throws RemoteException {
        // Simulate a slow call
        SystemClock.sleep(sleep);
        return Thread.currentThread().getName();
    }

    @Override
    public String getThreadNameBlocking() throws RemoteException {
        mLatch.await();
        return Thread.currentThread().getName();
    }

    @Override
```

```
        public String getThreadNameUnblock() throws RemoteException {
            mLatch.countDown();
            return Thread.currentThread().getName();
        }
    };
```

The method implementations all return the name of the execution thread in the server process, but after various delays. `getThreadNameFast` returns immediately, whereas `getThreadNameSlow` sleeps for a duration defined by the client, and `getThreadName` `Blocking` blocks by waiting for a `CountDownLatch` to be decremented. The decrement has to be done from another thread by calling `getThreadNameUnblock`.

A client process with access to the binder object of the server process can retrieve the `Proxy` implementation and invoke the methods that will be executed remotely:

```
ISynchronous mISynchronous = ISynchronous.Stub.asInterface(binder);
String remoteThreadName = mISynchronous.getThreadNameFast();
Log.d(TAG, "result = " + remoteThreadName);
```

The result of the remote call is printed as *result = Binder_1*; i.e., the execution occured on a binder thread in the remote process, as expected.

The `Proxy`, implementing the `ISynchronous` interface, is used to call the remote methods on binder threads. So let us look at a few ways to use RPC:

Invoking short-lived operations remotely

Calls to `mISynchronous.getThreadNameFast()` return as fast as the runtime can handle the communication, and the calling client threads will block only briefly. Concurrent calls from one or multiple clients will utilize multiple binder threads if necessary, but since the implementation returns quickly, binder threads can be reused efficiently.

Invoking long-lived operations remotely

Calls to `mISynchronous.getThreadNameSlow(long sleep)` execute for a configurable duration before returning a value to the client. The calling client thread will block for equally long until a return value can be retrieved.

Every client call occupies one binder thread for a long time. Consequently, multiple calls may strain the binder thread pool so that it runs out of threads. In that case, the next thread that invokes one of these remote methods will get that transaction put on a binder queue and has to wait for the execution to start until there is an available binder thread.

Invoking blocking methods

Blocking binder threads—as `mISynchronous.getThreadNameBlocking` illustrates —also block the client threads until the remote method can finish. If multiple client threads invoke blocking methods in the server process concurrently, the binder thread pool may run out of threads, preventing other client threads from getting results from remote calls. If the server process has no more available binder threads due to blocking, there are no more binder threads available to wake up the blocked threads. The server then has to rely on its own internal threads to handle the wake up; otherwise, the server will never handle any more incoming calls, and all the client threads that are waiting for the return of the server method will block forever.

Blocked Java threads are usually interruptible, meaning that another thread can interrupt a currently blocked thread in an attempt to let it finish the execution. However, threads in a client process have no direct access to the threads in the server process, so they cannot interrupt the remote threads. Furthermore, client threads that are waiting for a synchronous RPC to return cannot catch and handle an interruption.

Invoking methods with shared state

AIDL enables client processes to execute methods in the server process concurrently. The normal rules for concurrent execution apply: thread safety is the responsibility of the interface implementation. In the example code shown for our server, `mISynchronous.getThreadNameBlocking` and `mISynchronous.getThread NameUnblock` share a `CountDownLatch`, but there is nothing protecting it from being accessed from multiple threads simultaneously. Hence, a client cannot rely on `get ThreadNameBlocking` to remain blocked until it has called `getThreadNameUn block` itself. Another client may already have done this call.

 A client should not assume that a certain synchronous remote method invocation is short-lived, and thus safe to call from the UI thread. A server process implementation may change over time and have a negative impact on the UI thread's responsiveness. Consequently, use client-worker threads to make remote method calls, unless the remote method execution is known and under your control.

Asynchronous RPC

The strength of synchronous RPC lies in its simplicity: it is easy both to understand and to implement. The simplicity, however, comes at a cost, because the calling threads are blocked. This, of course, also applies to process-local calls, but often the execution of remote calls is done in code unknown to the client developer. The amount of time that calling threads spend blocked may differ as the remote implementation changes. Hence, synchronous remote calls may have unpredictable impacts on your applications' responsiveness. Impacts on the UI thread are commonly avoided by executing all remote calls in worker threads, running asynchronously with the UI thread. However, if the server thread is blocked, the client thread will also block indeterminately, keeping the thread and all its object references alive. This risks memory leaks, as we will see in Chapter 6.

Enter asynchronous RPC! Instead of letting the client implement its own asynchronous policy, every remote method call can be defined to execute asynchronously. The client thread initiates a transaction with asynchronous RPC and returns immediately. The binder gives the transaction to the server process and closes the connection from the client to the server.

Asynchronous methods must return void, and must not have arguments declared out or inout. To retrieve results, the implementation will use a callback.

Asynchronous RPC is defined in AIDL with the oneway keyword. It can be applied at either the interface level or on an individual method:

Asynchronous interface
    All methods are executed asynchronously:

```
oneway interface IAsynchronousInterface {
    void method1();
    void method2();
}
```

Asynchronous method
    The method is executed asynchronously:

```
interface IAsynchronousInterface {
    oneway void method1();
    void method2();
}
```

The simplest form of asynchronous RPC defines a callback interface in the method call. The callback is a reverse RPC, such as a call from the server to the client. Thus, the callback interface is also defined in AIDL.

The following AIDL shows a simple example of asynchronous RPC, where the remote interface is defined by one method that contains a callback interface:

```
interface IAsynchronous1 {
    oneway void getThreadNameSlow(IAsynchronousCallback callback);
}
```

The implementation of the remote interface in the server process follows. At the end of the method, the result is returned in the callback method:

```
IAsynchronous1.Stub mIAsynchronous1 = new IAsynchronous1.Stub() {
    @Override
    public void getThreadNameSlow(IAsynchronousCallback callback)
        throws RemoteException {
        // Simulate a slow call
        String threadName = Thread.currentThread().getName();
        SystemClock.sleep(10000);
        callback.handleResult(threadName);
    }
};
```

The callback interface is declared in AIDL as follows:

```
interface IAsynchronousCallback {
    void handleResult(String name);
}
```

And the implementation of the callback interface in the client process handles the result:

```
private IAsynchronousCallback.Stub mCallback = new IAsynchronousCallback.Stub() {

    @Override
    public void handleResult(String remoteThreadName) throws RemoteException {
        // Handle the callback
        Log.d(TAG, "remoteThreadName = " + name);
        Log.d(TAG, "currentThreadName = " + Thread.currentThread().getName());
    }
}
```

Note that both thread names—remote and current—are printed as "Binder_1", but they belong to different binder threads, from the client and server process, respectively. The asynchronous callback will be received on a binder thread. Hence, the callback implementation should ensure thread safety if it shares data with other threads in the client process.

Message Passing Using the Binder

As we have seen in "Android Message Passing" on page 47, the Android platform provides a flexible kind of interthread communication through message passing. However, it requires that the threads execute in the same process, because the Message objects are located in the memory shared by the threads. If the threads execute in different processes, they do not have any common memory for sharing messages; instead, the messages have to be passed across process boundaries, using the binder framework. For this purpose, you can use the android.os.Messenger class to send messages to a dedicated Handler in a remote process. The Messenger utilizes the binder framework both to pass a Messenger reference to a client process and to send Message objects. The Handler is not sent across processes; instead, the Messenger acts as the intermediary.

Figure 5-4 shows the elements of message passing between processes. A Message can be sent to a thread in another process with the Messenger, but the sending process (the client) has to retrieve a Messenger reference from the receiving process (server). There are two steps:

1. Pass a Messenger reference to client processes.

2. Send a message to server process. Once the client has the Messenger reference, this step can be repeated as often as desired.

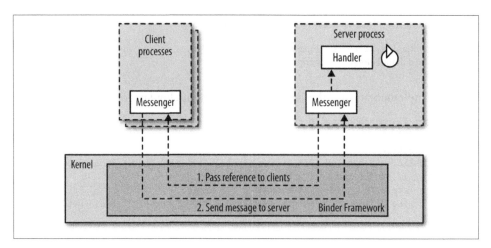

Figure 5-4. Interprocess communication with Messenger

One-Way Communication

In the following example, a `Service` executes in the server process and communicates with an `Activity` in the client process. Hence, the `Service` implements a `Messenger` and passes it to the `Activity`, which in return can pass `Message` objects to the `Service`. First let's look into the `Service`:

```
public class WorkerThreadService extends Service {

    WorkerThread mWorkerThread;
    Messenger mWorkerMessenger;

    @Override
    public void onCreate() {
        super.onCreate();
        mWorkerThread.start(); ❶
    }

    /**
     * Worker thread has prepared a looper and handler.
     **/
    private void onWorkerPrepared() {
        mWorkerMessenger = new Messenger(mWorkerThread.mWorkerHandler); ❷
    }

    public IBinder onBind(Intent intent) { ❸
        return mWorkerMessenger.getBinder();
    }

    @Override
    public void onDestroy() {
        super.onDestroy();
```

```
        mWorkerThread.quit();
    }

    private class WorkerThread extends Thread {

        Handler mWorkerHandler;

        @Override
        public void run() {
            Looper.prepare();
            mWorkerHandler = new Handler() {
                @Override
                public void handleMessage(Message msg) { ❹
                    // Implement message processing
                }
            };
            onWorkerPrepared();
            Looper.loop();
        }

        public void quit() {
            mWorkerHandler.getLooper().quit();
        }
    }
}
```

❶ The messages are handled on a worker thread, which is started upon Service creation. All binding clients will use the same worker thread.

❷ A Handler to the worker thread is connected to the Messenger upon construction. This Handler will process incoming messages from client processes.

❸ A binding client receives the IBinder object of the Messenger, so that the client can communicate with the associated Handler in the Service.

❹ Process incoming messages.

On the client side, an Activity binds to the Service in the server process and sends messages:

```
public class MessengerOnewayActivity extends Activity {

    private boolean mBound = false;
    private Messenger mRemoteService = null;

    private ServiceConnection mRemoteConnection = new ServiceConnection() {

        public void onServiceConnected(ComponentName className, IBinder service) {
            mRemoteService = new Messenger(service); ❶
            mBound = true;
        }
```

```
            public void onServiceDisconnected(ComponentName className) {
                mRemoteService = null;
                mBound = false;
            }
        };

        public void onCreate(Bundle savedInstanceState) {
            super.onCreate(savedInstanceState);
            Intent intent = new Intent("com.wifill.eatservice.ACTION_BIND");
            bindService(intent, mRemoteConnection, Context.BIND_AUTO_CREATE); ❷
        }

        public void onSendClick(View v) {
            if (mBound) {
                mRemoteService.send(Message.obtain(null, 2, 0, 0)); ❸
            }
        }
    }
```

❶ Create a `Messenger` instance from the binder that was passed from the server.

❷ Bind to the remote service.

❸ Send a `Message` when the button is clicked.

Two-Way Communication

A `Message` passed across processes keeps a reference to a `Messenger` in the originating process in the `Message.replyTo` argument, which is one of the data types that a Message can carry (refer back to Table 4-2). This reference can be used to create a two-way communication mechanism between two threads in different processes.

The following code example illustrates two-way communication between an `Activity` and a `Service` executing in different processes. The `Activity` sends a `Message`, with a `replyTo` argument, to a remote `Service`:

```
    public void onSendClick(View v) {
        if (mBound) {
            try {
                Message msg = Message.obtain(null, 1, 0, 0);
                msg.replyTo = new Messenger(new Handler() { ❶
                    @Override
                    public void handleMessage(Message msg) {
                        Log.d(TAG, "Message sent back - msg.what = " + msg.what);
                    }
                });
                mRemoteService.send(msg);
            } catch (RemoteException e) {
                Log.e(TAG, e.getMessage());
            }
```

```
        }
    }
```

❶ Create a `Messenger` that is passed to the remote service. The `Messenger` holds a `Handler` reference to the current thread that executes messages from other processes.

The `Service` receives the `Message` and sends a new `Message` back to the `Activity`:

```
public void run() {
    Looper.prepare();
    mWorkerHandler = new Handler() {
        @Override
        public void handleMessage(Message msg) {
            switch (msg.what) {
                case 1:
                    try {
                        msg.replyTo.send(Message.obtain(null, msg.what, 0, 0));
                    } catch (RemoteException e) {
                        Log.e(TAG, e.getMessage());
                    }
                    break;
            }
        }
    };
    onWorkerPrepared();
    Looper.loop();
}
```

 The `Messenger` is coupled with a `Handler` that processes messages on the thread it belongs to. Hence, task execution is sequential by design, compared to AIDL that can execute tasks concurrently on binder threads.

Summary

Most of the interprocess communication in an application is handled behind the scenes by high-level components. But where needed, you can drop down to the low-level mechanisms of the binder: RPC and `Messenger`. RPC is preferred if you want to improve performance by handling incoming requests concurrently. If not, `Messenger` is an easier approach to implement, but its execution is single threaded.

Chapter 11 will go into detail about the `Service` component that can be accessed through IPC.

CHAPTER 6

Memory Management

Memory leaks can be extremely detrimental to your app strategy because they not only lead to app crashes but also affect the performance of the whole device and will deteriorate performance. A good deal of this chapter is devoted to background, because to prevent leaks, you need to understand how Android can have them in general, and specifically how threads and thread communication can cause them. The chapter does, however, offer strategies for managing the risk of memory leaks involved with threading through correct design and lifecycle handling.

Memory leaks can occur on different occasions for each of the asynchronous techniques used on Android and described in Part II. So this chapter takes a general approach, and specific practical measures will be discussed when each of the asynchronous techniques is explained in detail.

Garbage Collection

The Dalvik VM is a memory-managed system that frequently reclaims allocated memory with the garbage collector (GC) from the shared memory, known as the *heap*, when it grows too large. Each process—and consequently each application—has its own VM and its own garbage collector. In spite of this, an application can fill up the heap with allocated objects that cannot be reclaimed in time, which causes memory leaks.

 A memory leak is sometimes strictly defined as memory allocated by the application that is not used anymore but never identified by the GC as memory that can be reclaimed. Hence, the memory is occupied until the application process is terminated. A wider definition would also include memory allocated for too long a time, essentially hogging memory. Throughout this book, we use the wider definition of memory leak, because allocating memory longer than required may lead to memory exhaustion.

An application continuously creates new objects during its lifetime, and the objects are created on the heap irrespective of the scope—i.e., whether instance fields or local variables are allocated. When an object is not used anymore, the GC removes the object from the heap, freeing up the memory for new allocations. The GC can reclaim the memory when an object or its parents have no more strong references[1] to it. As long as an object is referenced, it is considered to be *reachable* and not eligible for garbage collection. But once it becomes *unreachable*, the GC can finalize the object and reclaim the memory. If objects are reachable without being used anymore, the GC cannot reclaim the allocated memory. Ultimately, this leakage can lead to the exhaustion of the application heap, causing termination of the process and a notification to the application through a `java.lang.OutOfMemoryError`.

Up until Gingerbread, garbage collection on Android executed sequentially with the application, such as application execution halted while memory was being reclaimed. This could lead to sudden hiccups in the UI rendering, reducing the user experience. As of Honeycomb, the GC executes concurrently on its own thread, not halting the application threads.

The Dalvik GC uses a very common two-step mechanism called *mark and sweep*. The mark step traverses the object trees and marks all objects that are not referenced by any other objects as *unused*. Unused objects become eligible for garbage collection, and the sweep step deallocates all the marked objects. An object is said to be unused if it is unreachable from any of the application's *garbage collection roots*, which are Java objects acting as starting points for the traversal of the object trees. GC roots themselves are not considered unused or eligible for garbage collection, even though no other application object references them.

A small example of an object tree appears in Figure 6-1. It leads to the following dependency chain:

1. GC root A→A1→A2
2. GC root B→B1→B2→B3→B4
3. GC root B→B1→B2→B4

All A and B objects are linked to a GC root and will not be considered unused because all of them are referenced by other objects and connected to a GC root. Each of the C objects has a reference to it (from the other C object), but since neither of them connects to a GC root, they are considered to be an island of objects that can be removed. An object is unreachable once the last reference to it is removed, or (as in the case of the C

---

1. The default object reference is a strong reference, but references can also have weaker semantics, as mentioned in "Avoiding Memory Leaks" on page 101. Refer to the java.lang.ref documentation (*https://developer.android.com/reference/java/lang/ref/package-summary.html*) for an overview of reference types.

objects in Figure 6-1) if none of the remaining references have any connection to a GC root.

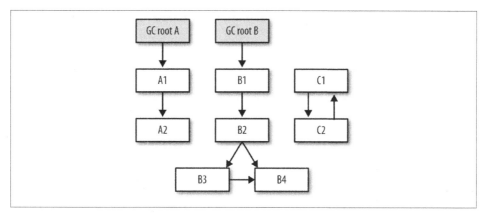

Figure 6-1. Objects traversed during the mark step of the garbage collector

Any object that is accessible from outside the heap is considered to be a GC root. This includes static objects, local objects on the stack, and threads. Thus, objects directly or indirectly referenced from a thread will be reachable during the execution of the thread.

Thread-Related Memory Leaks

Application threads potentially pose a risk for memory leaks because they can hinder the garbage collector from reclaiming memory while they execute; it is only when a thread has finished the execution that its objects can be deallocated from the heap.

The application threads are the UI thread, binder threads, and worker threads, as described in "Android Application Threads" on page 29. The latter two thread types can be started and terminated during the application's execution. Consequently, they release their object references upon termination, making the objects unreachable if they are not reachable from another GC root. The time during which these threads are alive determines the risk of a memory leak.

There are two important characteristics of memory leaks in regard to threads:

Potential risk
> The risk for a memory leak increases with the time a thread is alive and keeps object references. Short-lived thread instances are seldom a cause for memory leaks, but threads that are long-lived due to running long tasks, processing messages, blocking, etc., can keep references to objects that may not be required anymore, as illustrated in "The lifecycle mismatch" on page 95.

Leak size

An application that occasionally leaks a small amount of memory will probably work fine for most of the time and the leakage will pass by unnoticed. But if the leak size is large—e.g., bitmaps, view hierarchies, etc.—a few leaks may be enough to exhaust the application's heap.

In conclusion, an application shall be implemented with a low risk for memory and with the goal of keeping potential leaks as small as possible. With these two characteristics in mind, the next sections will get more into detail about threads and memory leaks on Android.

Thread Execution

An application that executes a task on a worker thread utilizes `Thread` and `Runnable` instances. As illustrated in Figure 6-2, both are involved in the creation of objects that obstruct garbage collection.

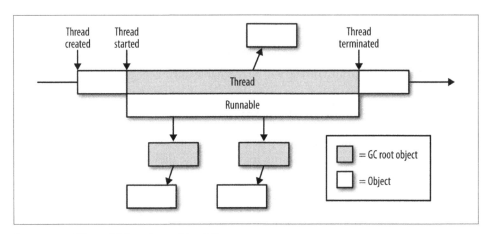

Figure 6-2. Thread lifecycle and its GC roots

The lifecycle of worker thread execution basically constitutes three steps:

1. Create a thread object.

   A `Thread` object is instantiated.

2. Start thread execution.

   The thread is started and the `Runnable` is executed.

3. Thread terminated.

   The `Runnable` has finished execution.

When the thread is executing, as during step 2, the `Thread` object itself becomes a GC root, and all objects it references are reachable. Similarly, all objects directly referenced from an executing `Runnable` are GC roots. Hence, while a thread executes, both the `Thread` and the `Runnable` instance can hold references to other objects that cannot be reclaimed until the thread terminates.

Objects created in a method are eligible for garbage collection when the method returns, unless the method returns the object to its caller so that it can be referenced from other methods.

 Threads that execute for a long time or are blocked pose a risk for memory leaks because they hold on to objects that will be linked to GC roots. Consequently, those objects cannot be garbage collected.

Let us illustrate the object tree for a couple of simple thread definition examples.

Inner classes

Inner classes are members of the enclosing object, like the outer class, and have access to all the other members of the outer class. Hence, the inner class implicitly has a reference to the outer class (see Figure 6-3). Consequently, threads defined as inner classes keep references to the outer class, which will never be marked for garbage collection as long as the thread is executing. In the following example, any objects in the `Outer` class must be left in memory, along with objects in the inner `SampleThread` class, as long as that thread is running.

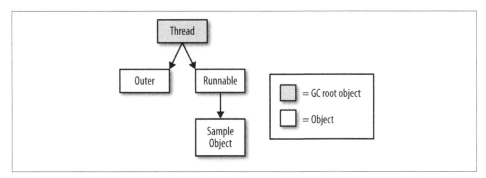

Figure 6-3. Object dependency tree with inner class thread

```
public class Outer {

    public void sampleMethod() {
        SampleThread sampleThread = new SampleThread();
```

```
        sampleThread.start();
    }

    private class SampleThread extends Thread {
        public void run() {
            Object sampleObject = new Object();
            // Do execution
        }
    }
}
```

Threads defined as local classes and anonymous inner classes have the same relations to the outer class as inner classes, keeping the outer class reachable from a GC root during execution.

Static inner classes

Static inner classes are members of the class instance of the enclosing object. Threads defined in a static inner class therefore keep references to the class of the outer object, but *not* to the outer object itself (Figure 6-4). Therefore, the outer object can be garbage collected once other references to it disappear. This rule, applies, for instance, in the following code.

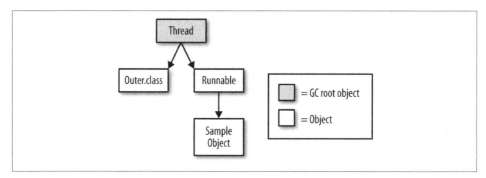

Figure 6-4. Object dependency tree with static inner class thread

```
public class Outer {

    public void sampleMethod() {
        SampleThread sampleThread = new SampleThread();
        sampleThread.start();
    }

    private static class SampleThread extends Thread {
        public void run() {
            Object sampleObject = new Object();

            // Do execution
```

```
        }
      }
    }
```

However, on most occasions, the programmer wants to separate the execution environment (`Thread`) from the task (`Runnable`). If you create a new `Runnable` as an inner class, it will hold a reference to the outer class during the execution, even if it is run by a static inner class. Code such as the following produces the situation in Figure 6-5.

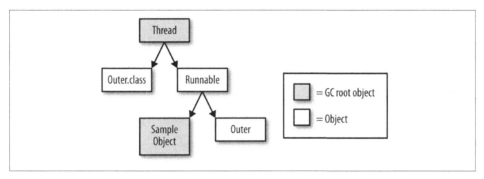

Figure 6-5. Object dependency tree with static inner class thread executing an external `Runnable`

```
public class Outer {

    public void sampleMethod() {

        SampleThread sampleThread = new SampleThread(new Runnable() {
            @Override
            public void run() {
                Object sampleObject = new Object();
                // Do execution
            }
        });
        sampleThread.start();
    }

    private static class SampleThread extends Thread {
        public SampleThread(Runnable runnable) {
            super(runnable);
        }
    }
}
```

The lifecycle mismatch

A fundamental reason for leakage on Android is the lifecycle mismatch between components, objects, and threads. Objects are allocated on the heap, can be eligible for garbage collection, and are kept in memory when they are referenced by threads. In Android, however, it is not only the lifecycle of the object that the application has to handle, but also the lifecycle of its components. All components—`Activity`, `Service`, `BroadcastReceiver`, and `ContentProvider`—have their own lifecycles that do not comply with their objects' lifecycles.

Leaking `Activity` objects is the most serious—and probably the most common—component leak. An `Activity` holds references, for instance, to the view hierarchy that may contain a lot of heap allocations. Figure 6-6 illustrates the component and object lifecycles of an `Activity`.

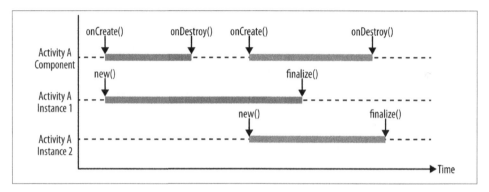

Figure 6-6. Lifecycles of Activity component and instance

The creation of an `Activity` component—i.e., `onCreate()` is called—leads to the construction of an `Activity` Java object. During the entire lifetime of the `Activity` component—from `onCreate()` to `onDestroy()`—the underlying Java object is of course in use. When the `Activity` object is finished or destroyed by the system, the component lifecycle ends with a call to `onDestroy`, which can happen for multiple reasons:

- The user presses the back button. This implicitly finishes the `Activity`.
- The `Activity` explicitly calls `finish()`.
- The system has determined that the application process, where the `Activity` executes, can be killed to spare system resources.
- A configuration change occurs, for example, if the device is rotated, which destroys the `Activity` component and creates a new one.

When the `Activity` component has finished, the `Activity` object may still remain on the heap. It is the garbage collector that determines when the `Activity` object can be removed. If any references to the `Activity` object linger after the component is destroyed, the object remains on the heap and is not eligible for garbage collection. As

Figure 6-6 illustrates, multiple `Activity` objects for the same `Activity` component can coexist on the heap. In the figure, the component runs its course and is destroyed, but the first `Activity` object (Activity A) remains in memory for some time longer. In the meantime, Activity B starts, causing the component's object to be recreated. Activity B also remains in memory for some time after the component is destroyed. Activity A and B are of no use without the component, and can be considered a memory leak if they remain in memory for a long time.

Worker threads may impose a memory leak in the application, because threads can continue to execute in the background even after the component is destroyed. Thus, Figure 6-7 illustrates how an `Activity` object lingers on the heap long after the component has finished its lifetime. The reason is that Activity A started a worker thread that is still executing in the background. Having been created by the `Activity`, the thread references the `Activity` object.

During back-and-forth navigation to an `Activity`, as well as configuration changes, new component lifecycles are initiated, and thus a new `Activity` object for every lifecycle. If threads are automatically started upon creation, every new lifecycle can create a thread with a reference to the `Activity` object—and its view hierarchy, too. This poses a risk for problematic memory leaks if the `Activity` recreation cycle is shorter than the lifetime of the threads.

 Automatically started threads pose a higher memory leakage risk than user started threads, as configuration changes and user navigation can yield many concurrent threads with `Activity` object references.

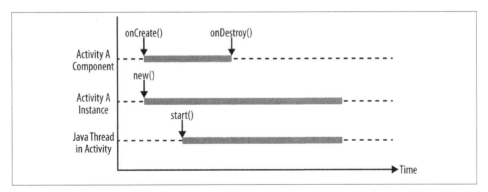

Figure 6-7. Activity lifecycle with executing thread

Thread Communication

Thread execution is a potential source for memory leaks, and so is the message passing mechanism between threads. These leaks can happen whether the executor is the UI thread or another thread created by the application. For a thread to receive a `Message` object from another thread, it needs to have a `MessageQueue` to hold pending messages, a `Looper` to dispatch the messages, and a `Handler` to execute the messages, as explained in "Android Message Passing" on page 47. Most of these objects are referenced only from the producer thread and therefore can be garbage collected when it exits, but `Handler` is a candidate for memory leaks because it is referenced from the consumer thread through a chain of objects, as shown in Figure 6-8. The `Handler` instance and the objects it references cannot be deallocated until the thread terminates.

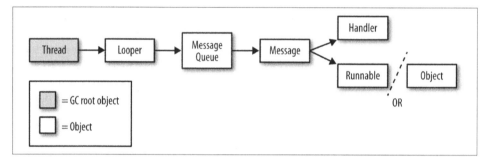

Figure 6-8. A thread that can receive messages, and the referenced objects

While the consumer thread executes, all the direct or indirect referenced objects are still reachable from a GC root and are ineligible for garbage collection. The `Message` instance, passed between the threads, holds references to a `Handler` and either to data (`Object`) or to a task (`Runnable`) (refer to Table 4-2). From the creation through the recycling of a `Message`, it holds a `Handler` reference to the consumer thread. While the message is pending in the message queue or executed on the thread, it is ineligible for garbage collection. Furthermore, the `Handler` and the `Object` or `Runnable`, together with all their implicit and explicit references, are still reachable from the GC root.

The definition of `Thread` and `Runnable` as seen in "Thread Execution" on page 92 can increase the memory leak, and that also applies to `Handler` and `Runnable` during thread communication. We will look at two code examples to illustrate problems involving these two objects: when sending a data message and when posting a `Runnable`.

Sending a data message

Data messages can be passed in various ways; the chosen implementation determines both the risk for, and the size of, a memory leak. The following code example illustrates the implementation pitfalls. The example contains an Outer class with a Handler to process messages. The Handler is connected to the thread that creates the Outer class:

```
public class Outer {

    Handler mHandler = new Handler() {
        public void handleMessage(Message msg) {
            // Handle message
        }
    };

    public void doSend() {
        Message message = mHandler.obtainMessage();
        message.obj = new SampleObject();
        mHandler.sendMessageDelayed(message, 60 * 1000);
    }
}
```

Figure 6-9 illustrates the object reference tree in the executing thread, from the time the Message has been sent to the message queue till the time it is recycled, i.e., after the Handler has processed it. The reference chain has been shortened for brevity to cover just the key objects we want to trace.

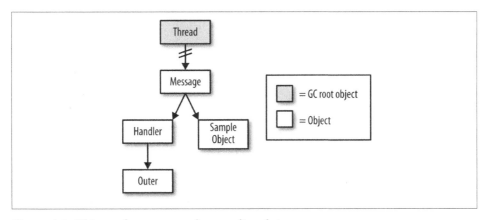

Figure 6-9. Object reference tree when sending data message

The code example violates both memory leak characteristics: it lets a thread hold references to more objects than necessary, and it keeps the references reachable for a long time. We will look shortly at how to avoid these problems.

Posting a task message

Posting a Runnable, to be executed on a consumer Thread with a Looper, raises the same concerns as sending a Message but with an additional extra Outer class reference to watch out for:

```
public class Outer {

    Handler mHandler = new Handler() {
        public void handleMessage(Message msg) {
            // Handle message
        }
    };

    public void doPost() {
        mHandler.post(new Runnable() {
            public void run() {
                // Long running task
            }
        });
    }
}
```

This simple code example posts a Runnable to a thread that calls doPost. Both the Handler and Runnable instances refer to the Outer class and increase the size of a potential memory leak, as shown in Figure 6-10.

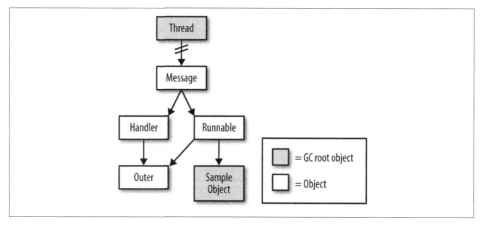

Figure 6-10. Object reference tree when posting task message

The risk for a memory leak increases with the length of the task. Short-lived tasks are better in avoiding the risk.

 Once a Message object is added to the message queue, the Message is indirectly referenced from the consumer thread. The longer the Message is pending, is in the queue, or does a lengthy execution on the receiving thread, the higher the risk is for a memory leak.

Avoiding Memory Leaks

As noted earlier, most memory leaks involving threads are caused by objects lingering in memory longer than required. Threads and handlers can—unintentionally—keep objects reachable from a thread GC root even when they are not used anymore. Let us look at how to avoid—or mitigate—these memory leaks.

Use Static Inner Classes

Local classes, inner classes, and anonymous inner classes all hold implicit references to the outer class they are declared in. Hence, they can leak not only their own objects, but also those referenced from the outer class. Typically, an `Activity` and its view hierarchy can cause a major leak through the outer class reference.

Instead of using nested classes with outer class references, it is preferred to use static inner classes because they reference only the global class object and not the instance object. This just mitigates the leak, because all explicit references to other instance objects from the static inner class are still live while the thread executes.

Use Weak References

As we have seen, static inner classes do not have access to instance fields of the outer class. This can be a limitation if an application would like to execute a task on a worker thread and access or update an instance field of the outer instance. For this need, `java.lang.ref.WeakReference` comes to the rescue:

```
public class Outer {
    private int mField;
    private static class SampleThread extends Thread {

        private final WeakReference<Outer> mOuter;

        SampleThread(Outer outer) {
            mOuter = new WeakReference<Outer>(outer);
        }

        @Override
        public void run() {
            // Do execution and update outer class instance fields.
            // Check for null as the outer instance may have been GC'd.
            if (mOuter.get() != null) {
                mOuter.get().mField = 1;
            }
        }
    }
}
```

In the code example, the Outer class is referenced through a *weak reference*, meaning that the static inner class holds a reference to the outer class and can access the outer instance fields. The weak reference is not a part of the garbage collector's reference counting, as all strong references, like normal references, are. So if the only remaining reference to the outer object is the weak reference from the inner class, the garbage collector sees this object as eligible for garbage collection and may deallocate the outer instance from the heap.

Stop Worker Thread Execution

Implementing Thread, Runnable, and Handler as static inner classes, nullifying explicit strong references, or using weak references will mitigate a memory leak but not totally prevent it. The executing thread may still hold some references that cannot be garbage collected. So to prevent the thread from delaying object deallocation, it should be terminated as soon as it is not required anymore.

Retain Worker Threads

Figure 6-7 shows how the lifecycle mismatch between component, activity, and thread can keep objects live longer than necessary. Typically, the long times are caused by changing the configurations of activities, where the old object is kept in memory for as long as the thread executes. By retaining the thread from the old to the new Activity and removing the thread reference from the old Activity, you can allow the Activity object to be garbage collected. The retention technique in practice differs according to the threading mechanisms available in the platform, and is explained for each mechanism in the chapters of Part II.

Clean Up the Message Queue

A message sent to a thread may be pending in the message queue either if it is sent with a long execution delay or if messages with a lower timestamp have not finished execution. If a message is pending when it is no longer needed, you should remove it from the message queue so that all its referenced objects can be deallocated.

Messages sent to a worker thread can be garbage collected once the worker thread finishes, but the UI thread cannot finish until the application process terminates. Therefore, cleaning up messages sent to the UI thread is a valuable way to avoid memory leaks. Both Message and Runnable can be removed from the queue:

```
removeCallbacks(Runnable r)
removeCallbacks(Runnable r, Object token)
removeCallbacksAndMessages(Object token)
removeMessages(int what)
removeMessages(int what, Object object)
```

The `Runnables` shall be removed with a reference to the instance, whereas the `Messag es` can be removed with the identifiers `what` and `token` (see "Message" on page 55).

Summary

This chapter has summarized the main reasons for memory leaks on Android, and shown both code design and execution lifecycle considerations you should take to avoid —or at least reduce—the memory leaks.

In Part II, more practical aspects of avoiding memory leaks for the asynchronous mechanisms in the platform are discussed.

PART II
Asynchronous Techniques

The simplest form of asynchronous execution on Android is the regular `java.lang.Thread` class, which is the basis for asynchronous behavior on Android. Other mechanisms build upon the `Thread` class to enable better resource control, message passing, or relief for the UI thread.

CHAPTER 7

Managing the Lifecycle of a Basic Thread

This chapter contains some of the basics of using threads, discusses threads in collaboration with Android components, and finishes with thread management. It covers the cancellation of tasks, how to retain threads across `Activity` and `Fragment` objects, and other essential techniques.

Basics

The `Thread` class in Android is no different from the `Thread` class in regular Java programming. It is the closest representation of the underlying Linux native thread an application gets. The `Thread` class creates the execution environment for tasks, represented by `Runnable`. The `Thread` implements `Runnable`, so the task to be executed is either defined by the thread itself or injected during thread creation.

Lifecycle

This section explains the observable states a thread can enter during its existence. These states are defined in the `Thread.State` class and are illustrated in Figure 7-1.

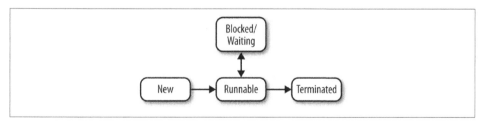

Figure 7-1. Lifecycle of a thread

New

Before the execution of a thread, a Thread object is created. The instantiation does not set up the execution environment, so it is no heavier than any other object instantiation. The default construction assigns the newly created thread to the same thread group as the thread that is doing the creation, with the same priority. Specifically, threads created from the UI thread belong to the same thread group, with the same priority, as the UI thread.

Runnable

When Thread.start() is called, the execution environment is set up and the thread is ready to be executed. It is now in the Runnable state. When the scheduler selects the thread for execution, the run method is called and the task is executed.

Blocked/Waiting

Execution can halt when the thread has to wait for a resource that is not directly accessible—for example, an I/O operation, synchronized resources used by other threads, blocking API calls, etc. But execution can also be given up explicitly:

1. Thread.sleep(): Let the thread sleep for certain amount of time and then make it available to be scheduled for execution again.

2. Thread.yield(): Give up execution, and let the scheduler make a new decision on which thread to execute. The scheduler freely selects which thread to execute, and there is no guarantee that the scheduler will choose a different thread.

Terminated

When the run method has finished execution, the thread is terminated and its resources can be freed up. This is the final state of the thread; no reuse of the Thread instance or its execution environment is possible. Setting up and tearing down the execution environment is a heavy operation; doing it over and over again is a sign that another solution, such as thread pools (see Chapter 9), is preferred.

Interruptions

Occasionally, an application wants to terminate the thread's execution before it has finished its task. For instance, if a thread is taking a long time to download a video and the user presses a button to cancel the download, the UI thread captures the button press and would like to terminate the downloading thread. There is, however, no way a thread can be directly terminated. Instead, threads can be *interrupted*, which is a request to the thread that is should terminate, but it is the thread itself that determines whether to oblige or not. Interruptions are invoked on the thread reference:

```
Thread t = new SimpleThread();
t.start(); // Start the thread
t.interrupt(); // Request interruption
```

Thread interruption is implemented collaboratively: the thread makes itself available to be interrupted, and other threads issue the call to interrupt it. Issuing an interruption has no direct impact on the execution of the thread; it merely sets an internal flag on the thread that marks it as interrupted. The interrupted thread has to check the flag itself to detect the interruption and terminate gracefully. A thread must implement *cancellation* points in order to allow other threads to interrupt it and get it to terminate:

```
public class SimpleThread extends Thread {

    @Override
    public void run() {
        while (isInterrupted() == false) {
            // Thread is alive
        }
        // Task finished and thread terminates
    }
}
```

Cancellation points are implemented by checking the interrupt flag with the `isInter rupted()` instance method, which returns a Boolean value of `true` if the thread has been interrupted, and `false` otherwise. If it returns `true`, the thread is informed that it is requested to terminate. Typically, cancellation points are implemented in loops, or before long-running tasks are executed, to enable the thread to skip the next part in the task execution.

The interrupt flag is also supported by most blocking methods and libraries; a thread that is currently blocked will throw an `InterruptedException` upon being interrupted. Hence, the thread can clean up the state of shared objects in the `catch` clause before the thread terminates. When an `InterruptedException` is thrown, the interrupted flag is reset—for example, `isInterrupted` will return `false` even though the thread has been interrupted. This may lead to problems further up in the thread callstack because no one will know that the thread has been interrupted. So if the thread doesn't have to perform any cleanup upon interruption, the thread should pass the `InterruptedExcep tion` further up in the callstack. If cleanup is required, it should be done in the catch-clause, after which the thread should interrupt itself again so that callers of the executed method are aware of the interruption, as shown in the following example:

```
void myMethod() {
    try {
        // Some blocking call
    } catch (InterruptedException e) {
        // 1. Clean up
        // 2. Interrupt again
        Thread.currentThread().interrupt();
    }
}
```

Interruption state can also be checked with the `Thread.interrup ted()` static method, which returns a Boolean value in the same way as `isInterrupted()`. However, `Thread.interrupted()` comes with a side effect: it clears the interruption flag.

 Do not use `Thread.stop()` to terminate an executing thread, because it can leave the shared objects in an inconsistent and unpredictable state. It has been deprecated since API Level 1.

Uncaught Exceptions

A running Java thread terminates normally when the code path reaches the end and there is no more code to execute—i.e., at the end of the `Runnable.run()` method. If, somewhere along the code path, an unexpected error occurs, the result may be that an unchecked exception is thrown. Unchecked exceptions are descendants of `RuntimeEx ception` and they do not require mandatory handling in a try/catch clause, so they can propagate along the callstack of the thread. When the starting point of the thread is reached, the thread terminates. To avoid unexpected errors from going unnoticed, a thread can be attached with an `UncaughtExceptionHandler` that is called before the thread is terminated. This handler offers a chance for the application to finish the thread gracefully, or at least make a note of the error to a network or file resource.

The `UncaughtExceptionHandler` interface is used by implementing the method un `caughtException` and attaching it to a thread. If thread is terminated due to an unexpected error, the implementation is invoked on the terminating thread before it terminates. The `UncaughtExceptionHandler` is attached to either all threads or a specific thread in the `Thread` class:

Thread global handler
```
static void setDefaultUncaughtExceptionHandler(
Thread.UncaughtExceptionHandler handler);
```

Thread local handler
```
void setUncaughtExceptionHandler(Thread.UncaughtExceptionHandler handler);
```

If a thread has both a global and a local handler set, the local handler has precedence over the global handler, which will not be called.

A local `UncaughtExceptionHandler` can be attached to the thread instance, either with `Thread.currentThread()` in the executing task or—as the code listing shows–by using the thread reference itself:

```
Thread t = new Thread(new Runnable() {
    @Override
```

```
    public void run() {
        throw new RuntimeException("Unexpected error occurred");
    }
});

t.setUncaughtExceptionHandler(new Thread.UncaughtExceptionHandler() {
    @Override
    public void uncaughtException(Thread thread, Throwable throwable) {
        // A basic logging of the message.
        // Could be replaced by log to file or a network post.
        Log.d(TAG, throwable.toString());
    }
});

t.start();
```

Unhandled Exceptions on the UI Thread

The Android runtime attaches a process global UncaughtExceptionHandler when an
application is started.[1] Thus, the exception handler is attached to all threads in the application, and it treats unhandled exceptions equally for all threads: the process is killed.

The default behavior can be overriden either globally for all threads—including the UI
thread—or locally for specific threads. Typically, the overriden behavior should only
add functionality to the default runtime behavior, which is achieved by redirecting the
exception to the runtime handler:

```
// Set new global handler
Thread.setDefaultUncaughtExceptionHandler(new ErrorReportExceptionHandler());

// Error handler that redirects exception to the system default handler.
public class ErrorReportExceptionHandler
    implements Thread.UncaughtExceptionHandler {

    private final Thread.UncaughtExceptionHandler defaultHandler;

    public ErrorReportExceptionHandler() {
        this.defaultHandler = Thread.getDefaultUncaughtExceptionHandler();
    }

    @Override
    public void uncaughtException(Thread thread, Throwable throwable) {
        reportErrorToFile(throwable);
        defaultHandler.uncaughtException(thread, throwable);
    }
}
```

1. *http://bit.ly/1iR1tU3*

Thread Management

Each application is responsible for the threads it uses and how they are managed. An application should decide on the number of threads to use, how to reuse them, when to interrupt them, and if they should be retained during a rotation change.

You can implement these qualities throughout the lifecycle of the thread, particularly at three phases: definition and start, retention, and cancellation.

Definition and Start

The lifecycles of threads, components, and their respective object do not match up (see "The lifecycle mismatch" on page 95). The thread can outlive several component lifecycles and keep old component objects in memory even if they are never reused. The way threads are defined and started has an impact on the both the risk and the size of a memory leak. We will now look into the most common ways of defining and starting worker threads on Android and observe the implications of each one.

The examples are based on generalized and simplified code, with an outer class (AnyObject) and threads that are started from a method (anyMethod) called in the UI thread.

Anonymous inner class

First, we will look at the properties of an inner class. The code example utilizes an anonymous inner class, because that is the syntactically shortest form, but the same principles apply to all nested and local classes as well:

```
public class AnyObject {
    @UiThread
    public void anyMethod() {
        new Thread() {
            public void run() {
                doLongRunningTask();
            }
        }.start();
    }
}
```

The anonymous inner class is simple to implement in the context of where it is used but it holds references to the outer class.

Public thread

A thread can be defined as a standalone class, not directly defined by the class that runs it:

```
class MyThread extends Thread {
    public void run() {
        doLongRunningTask();
```

```
        }
    }

    public class AnyObject {
        private MyThread mMyThread;

        @UiThread
        public void anyMethod() {
            mMyThread = new MyThread();
            mMyThread.start();
        }
    }
```

A standalone class holds no reference to the outer class, but the number of classes that needs to be defined can grow large.

Static inner class thread definition

Instead of defining the thread as an inner class, it can be defined as a static inner class, i.e., defined in the class object instead of the instance:

```
    public class AnyObject {
        static class MyThread extends Thread() {
            public void run() {
                doLongRunningTask();
            }
        };

        private MyThread mMyThread;

        @UiThread
        public void anyMethod() {
            mMyThread = new MyThread();
            mMyThread.start();
        }
    }
```

A static inner class only holds a reference to the class object of the outer class, and not the instance class. Hence, the memory allocated by instance object can't be leaked due to the thread reference.

Summary of options for thread definition

Inner classes have outer references that may leak larger memory chunks, a weakness avoided in both public classes and static inner classes. The anonymous inner class does not store any reference to the thread instance, which leaves the thread out of control. If there is no thread reference stored, the thread cannot be influenced by the application.

All the code examples have a problem with uncontrolled thread creation. If anyMe thod can be called often, for example following a button click, the number of threads cannot be controlled. New threads will be created over and over again, using up more memory with every creation. Also, the thread reference stored in the mMyThread member variable, for the public class and the static inner class, is overwritten on every execution and not usable anymore. The application can apply logic to store thread references in lists or make sure to start new threads only if the previously started thread is not alive anymore, but Thread may require some additional logic to constrain the number of concurrent tasks.

Thread pools (Chapter 9) or HandlerThread (Chapter 8) offer constraints on the number of executing threads.

Retention

A thread does not follow the lifecycle of an Android component that has started it or its underlying objects (see "The lifecycle mismatch" on page 95). Once a thread is started, it will execute until either its run method finishes or the whole application process terminates. Therefore, the thread lifetime can outlive the component lifetime.

When the thread finishes, it may have produced a result that was meant to be used by the component, but there is no receiver available. Typically, this situation occurs on configuration changes in Activity components. The default behavior is to restart the component when its configuration has changed, meaning that the original Activity object is replaced by a new one without any knowledge of the executing background thread.[2] Only the Activity object that started the thread knows that the thread was started, so the new Activity cannot utilize the thread's result; it has to restart the thread over again to collect the data.

This can lead to unnecessary work. For example, if a worker thread is set to download a large chunk of data, and a configuration change occurs during the download, it is a waste to throw the partial result away. Instead, a better approach is to retain the thread during the configuration change and let the new Activity object handle the thread started by the old Activity object.

Retaining threads is done differently depending on the platform version. Before API level 13 (Honeycomb), the retention is handled in the Activity but was simplified with the introduction of fragments. With the Support Library (*http://bit.ly/R7r7Jk*), Fragment is backported to older platform versions and the previous Activity retention methods are deprecated. We will now look into both methods, starting with the older Activity variant.

Retaining a thread in an Activity

The Activity class contains two methods for handling thread retention:

---

2. The default behavior can be overridden by android:configChanges in the *AndroidManifest.xml* file.

public Object onRetainNonConfigurationInstance()
> Called by the platform before a configuration change occurs, which causes the current `Activity` object to be destroyed and replaced by another instance. The implementation should return any object that you want to be retained across a configuration change (e.g., a thread) and passed to the new `Activity` object.

public Object getLastNonConfigurationInstance()
> Called in the new `Activity` object to retrieve the retained object returned in `onRetainNonConfigurationInstance()` after a configuration change has been made. It can be called in `onCreate` or `onStart` and returns `null` if the `Activity` is started for another reason than a configuration change.

As the `ThreadRetainActivity` listing shows, an alive thread can be passed across `Activity` objects during a configuration change. The example is simplified for brevity, so, for example, it doesn't show the preservation of UI state, network operation, etc.:

```java
public class ThreadRetainActivity extends Activity {

    private static class MyThread extends Thread { ❶
        private ThreadRetainActivity mActivity;

        public MyThread(ThreadRetainActivity activity) {
            mActivity = activity;
        }

        private void attach(ThreadRetainActivity activity) {
            mActivity = activity;
        }

        @Override
        public void run() {
            final String text = getTextFromNetwork();
            mActivity.setText(text);

        }

        // Long operation
        private String getTextFromNetwork() {
            // Simulate network operation
            SystemClock.sleep(5000);
            return "Text from network";
        }
    }

    private static MyThread t;
    private TextView textView;

    @Override
    public void onCreate(Bundle savedInstanceState) {
        super.onCreate(savedInstanceState);
```

```
        setContentView(R.layout.activity_retain_thread);
        textView = (TextView) findViewById(R.id.text_retain);

        Object retainedObject = getLastNonConfigurationInstance(); ❷
        if (retainedObject != null) {
            t = (MyThread) retainedObject;
            t.attach(this);
        }
    }

    @Override
    public Object onRetainNonConfigurationInstance() { ❸
        if (t != null && t.isAlive()) {
            return t;
        }
        return null;
    }

    public void onClickStartThread(View v) { ❹
        t = new MyThread(this);
        t.start();
    }

    private void setText(final String text) {
        runOnUiThread(new Runnable() {
            @Override
            public void run() {
                textView.setText(text);
            }
        });
    }
}
```

❶ Worker thread declared as a static inner class to avoid outer class references. The thread contains a reference to an Activity instance. The attach method is used to set the Activity reference to the currently executing object.

❷ If there is a retained thread object, it is restored. The new Activity instance is registered to the thread.

❸ Retains an executing thread before any configuration change occurs.

❹ Button click method.

 Retained objects—e.g., threads—bring their references over to the next Activity. Threads declared with references to the outer class —i.e., the Activity—will stop the garbage collector from reclaiming the old Activity and its view tree, although it will never be used anymore.

Retaining a thread in a Fragment

A `Fragment` normally implements part of the user interface in an `Activity`, but since instance retention is easier with a `Fragment`, the responsibility to retain `Thread` instances can be moved from an `Activity` to a `Fragment`. The `Fragment` can be added to an `Activity` just to handle thread retention, without containing any UI elements. In a `Fragment`, all that is required to retain a thread, or any other state, is to call `setRetai nInstance(true)` in `Fragment.onCreate()`. The `Fragment` is then retained during a configuration change. The actual `Fragment` lifecycle is changed so that it does not get destroyed during configuration changes. Worker threads remain in the same `Frag ment` instance while the platform handles the retention between the `Activity` and `Fragment`.

Let's take a look how a `Fragment` changes thread retainment compared to the `Threa dRetainActivity` listing. The `Activity` now refers to a `Fragment` instead of the worker thread:

```
public class ThreadRetainWithFragmentActivity extends Activity {
    private ThreadFragment mThreadFragment;
    private TextView mTextView;

    public void onCreate(Bundle savedInstanceState) {
        setContentView(R.layout.activity_retain_thread);
        mTextView = (TextView) findViewById(R.id.text_retain);

        FragmentManager manager = getFragmentManager(); ❶
        mThreadFragment =
            (ThreadFragment) manager.findFragmentByTag("threadfragment");
        if (mThreadFragment == null) {
            FragmentTransaction transaction = manager.beginTransaction();
            mThreadFragment = new ThreadFragment();
            transaction.add(mThreadFragment, "threadfragment");
            transaction.commit();
        }
    }

    // Method called to start a worker thread
    public void onStartThread(View v) {
        mThreadFragment.execute(); ❷
    }

    public void setText(final String text) { ❸
        runOnUiThread(new Runnable() {
            @Override
            public void run() {
                mTextView.setText(text);
            }
        });
    }
}
```

❶   Create the Fragment if this is the first time the Activity is started.

❷   Execution of the worker thread is delegated to the Fragment.

❸   Published method for the Fragment to set the produced worker thread result.

The Fragment defines the worker thread and starts it:

```java
public class ThreadFragment extends Fragment {
    private ThreadRetainWithFragmentActivity mActivity; ❶
    private MyThread t;

    private class MyThread extends Thread {
        @Override
        public void run() {
            final String text = getTextFromNetwork();
            mActivity.setText(text);
        }

        // Long operation
        private String getTextFromNetwork() {
            // Simulate network operation
            SystemClock.sleep(5000);
            return "Text from network";
        }
    }

    @Override
    public void onCreate(Bundle savedInstanceState) {
        super.onCreate(savedInstanceState);
        setRetainInstance(true); ❷
    }

    @Override
    public void onAttach(Activity activity) {
        super.onAttach(activity);
        mActivity = (ThreadRetainWithFragmentActivity) activity;
    }

    @Override
    public void onDetach() {
        super.onDetach();
        mActivity = null;
    }

    public void execute() { ❸
        t = new MyThread();
        t.start();
    }
}
```

❶   Reference to the parent Activity.

❷ Retain the platform handle on configuration changes.

❸ Interface for the `Activity` to start the worker thread.

 Worker threads that execute across the lifecycle of multiple activities are better handled with services (see Chapter 11 and Chapter 12).

Summary

A `java.lang.Thread` object represents the most fundamental abstraction in Android's underlying thread execution environment. Every started worker thread corresponds to a native Linux thread. A thread is started explicitly and terminates when the task has finished the execution. Interrupts are the only explicit way for an outsider to terminate a thread, but it is up to the thread itself to implement an interruption policy. An application should manage threads to reduce the risk and size of memory leaks and to control the starting and termination of threads. The Android platform contains many other asynchronous mechanisms built upon `Thread`, but application developers may still consider using simple worker threads for tasks that simply spawn worker threads to offload tasks, such as network communication.

CHAPTER 8

HandlerThread: A High-Level Queueing Mechanism

"Android Message Passing" on page 47 described background execution on a thread using a message queue and dispatch mechanism. The application explicitly coupled the message queue and the dispatch mechanism to a thread. Instead, you can use a Han dlerThread, a convenient wrapper that automatically sets up the internal message passing mechanisms.

This chapter covers:

- How to use the HandlerThread
- The advantages of HandlerThread compared to manually setting up the message passing mechanism
- Use cases for the HandlerThread

Fundamentals

HandlerThread is a thread with a message queue that incorporates a Thread, a Looper, and a MessageQueue. It is constructed and started in the same way as a Thread. Once it is started, HandlerThread sets up queuing through a Looper and MessageQueue and then waits for incoming messages to process:

```
HandlerThread handlerThread = new HandlerThread("HandlerThread");
handlerThread.start();

mHandler = new Handler(handlerThread.getLooper()) {
    @Override
    public void handleMessage(Message msg) {
        super.handleMessage(msg);
```

```
            // Process messages here
        }
    };
```

There is only one queue to store messages, so execution is guaranteed to be sequential —and therefore thread safe—but with potentially low throughput, because tasks can be delayed in the queue.

The `HandlerThread` sets up the `Looper` internally and prepares the thread for receiving messages. The internal setup gurantees that there is no race condition between creating the `Looper` and sending messages, which can occur in the manual setup (see "Example: Basic Message Passing" on page 49). The platform solves the race condition problem by making `handlerThread.getLooper()` a blocking call until the `HandlerThread` is ready to receive messages.

If additional setup is required on the `HandlerThread` before it starts to process messages, the application should override `HandlerThread.onLooperPrepared()`, which is invoked on the background thread when the `Looper` is prepared. The application can define any initialization code in `onLooperPrepared`, such as creating a `Handler` that will be associated with the `HandlerThread`.

Limit Access to HandlerThread

A `Handler` can be used to pass any data message or task to the `HandlerThread`, but the access to the `Handler` can be limited by keeping it private in a subclass implementation —MyHandlerThread, in the following example—and ensuring that the `Looper` is not accessible. The subclass defines public methods for clients to use so that the thread itself defines the communication contract for how it should be accessed:

```
public class MyHandlerThread extends HandlerThread {

    private Handler mHandler;

    public MyHandlerThread() {
        super("MyHandlerThread", Process.THREAD_PRIORITY_BACKGROUND);
    }

    @Override
    protected void onLooperPrepared() {
        super.onLooperPrepared();
        mHandler = new Handler(getLooper()) {
            @Override
            public void handleMessage(Message msg) {
                switch(msg.what) {
                    case 1:
                        // Handle message
                        break;
                    case 2:
```

```
                        // Handle message
                        break;
                }
            }
        };
    }

    public void publishedMethod1() {
        mHandler.sendEmptyMessage(1);
    }
    public void publishedMethod2() {
        mHandler.sendEmptyMessage(2);
    }
}
```

Lifecycle

A running HandlerThread instance processes messages that it receives until it is terminated. A terminated HandlerThread can not be reused. To process more messages after termination, create a new instance of HandlerThread. The lifecycle can be described in a set of states:

1. Creation: The constructor for HandlerThread takes a mandatory name argument and an optional priority for the thread:

    ```
    HandlerThread(String name)
    HandlerThread(String name, int priority)
    ```

    The name argument simplifies debugging, because the thread can be found more easily in both thread analysis and logging. The priority argument is optional and should be set with the same Linux thread priority values used in Process.set ThreadPriority (see "Priority" on page 34). The default priority is Pro cess.THREAD_PRIORITY_DEFAULT—the same priority as the UI thread—and can be lowered to Process.THREAD_PRIORITY_BACKGROUND to execute noncritical tasks.

2. Execution: The HandlerThread is active while it can process messages; i.e., as long as the Looper can dispatch messages to the thread. The dispatch mechanism is set up when the thread is started through HandlerThread.start and is ready when either HandlerThread.getLooper returns or on the onLooperPrepared callback. A HandlerThread is always ready to receive messages when the Handler can be created, as getLooper blocks until the Looper is prepared.

3. Reset: The message queue can be reset so that no more of the queued messages will be processed, but the thread remains alive and can process new messages. The reset will remove all pending messages in the queue, but not affect a message that has been dispatched and is executing on the thread:

```
public void resetHandlerThread() {
    mHandler.removeCallbacksAndMessages(null);
}
```

The argument to removeCallbacksAndMessages removes the message with that specific identifier. null, shown here, removes all the messages in the queue. Further details on message removal are described in "Removing Messages from the Queue" on page 68.

4. Termination: A HandlerThread is terminated either with quit or quitSafely, which corresponds to the termination of the Looper ("Looper termination" on page 59). With quit, no further messages will be dispatched to the HandlerThread, whereas quitSafely ensures that messages that have passed the dispatch barrier are processed before the thread is terminated. You can also send an interrupt to the HandlerThread to cancel the currently executing message, as explained in "Interruptions" on page 108:

```
public void stopHandlerThread(HandlerThread handlerThread) {
    handlerThread.quit();
    handlerThread.interrupt();
}
```

A terminated HandlerThread instance has reached its final state and cannot be restarted.

A HandlerThread can also be terminated by sending a finalization task to the Handler that quits the Looper, and consequently the HandlerThread:

```
handler.post(new Runnable() {
    @Override
    public void run() {
        Looper.myLooper().quit();
    }
});
```

The finalization task ensures that this will be the last executed task on this thread, once it has been dispatched by the Looper. There is, however, no guarantee that other tasks will not move ahead of the finalization task by being posted to the front of the queue through Handler.postAtFrontOfQueue (see "Message insertion" on page 62).

Use Cases

A HandlerThread is applicable to many background execution use cases, where sequential execution and control of the message queue is desired. This section shows a range of use cases where HandlerThread comes in handy.

Repeated Task Execution

Many Android components relieve the UI thread by executing tasks on background threads. If it is not necessary to have concurrent execution in several threads—for example, multiple independent network requests—the HandlerThread provides a simple and efficient way to define tasks to be executed sequentially in the background. Hence, the execution setup for this situation is the UI thread—available by default—and a HandlerThread with a lifecycle that follows that of the component. Thus, Handler Thread.start is called upon at the start of a component and HandlerThread.quit upon the termination of the component. In between, there is a background thread available for offloading the UI thread.

The tasks to execute can be either predefined Runnable or Message instances. Both types can be configured with input data as follows:

Runnable
> Provide input data through shared member variables. (Requires synchronization to ensure correct data.)

Message
> Pass data using the types shown Table 4-2.

 Don't mix long or blocking tasks with shorter tasks, because the shorter ones may be postponed unnecessarily. Instead, split execution among several HandlerThread or use an Executor (Chapter 9).

Related Tasks

Interdependent tasks—e.g., those that access shared resources, such as the file system —can be executed concurrently, but they normally require synchronization to render them thread safe and ensure uncorrupted data. The sequential execution of Handler Thread guarantees thread safety, task ordering, and lower resource consumption than the creation of multiple threads. Therefore, it is useful for executing nonindependent tasks.

Example: Data persistence with SharedPreferences

SharedPreferences is persistent storage for user preferences on the file system. Consequently, it should only be accessed from background threads. But file system access is not thread safe, so a HandlerThread—with sequential execution—makes the access thread safe without adding synchronization, which is normally a simpler approach. The following example shows how a HandlerThread can carry out the job:

```java
public class SharedPreferencesActivity extends Activity {

    TextView mTextValue;

    /**
     * Show read value in a TextView.
     */
    private Handler mUiHandler = new Handler() { ❶
        @Override
        public void handleMessage(Message msg) {
            super.handleMessage(msg);
            if (msg.what == 0) {
                Integer i = (Integer)msg.obj;
                mTextValue.setText(Integer.toString(i));
            }
        }
    };

    private class SharedPreferenceThread extends HandlerThread { ❷

        private static final String KEY = "key";
        private SharedPreferences mPrefs;
        private static final int READ = 1;
        private static final int WRITE = 2;

        private Handler mHandler;

        public SharedPreferenceThread() {
            super("SharedPreferenceThread", Process.THREAD_PRIORITY_BACKGROUND);
            mPrefs = getSharedPreferences("LocalPrefs", MODE_PRIVATE);
        }

        @Override
        protected void onLooperPrepared() {
            super.onLooperPrepared();
            mHandler = new Handler(getLooper()) {
                @Override
                public void handleMessage(Message msg) {
                    switch(msg.what) {
                        case READ:
                            mUiHandler.sendMessage(mUiHandler.obtainMessage(0,
                                                   mPrefs.getInt(KEY, 0)));
                            break;
                        case WRITE:
                            SharedPreferences.Editor editor = mPrefs.edit();
                            editor.putInt(KEY, (Integer)msg.obj);
                            editor.commit();
                            break;
                    }
                }
            };
        }
```

```java
        public void read() {
            mHandler.sendEmptyMessage(READ);
        }
        public void write(int i) {
            mHandler.sendMessage(Message.obtain(Message.obtain(mHandler,
                                 WRITE, i)));
        }
    }

    private int mCount;
    private SharedPreferenceThread mThread;


    @Override
    protected void onCreate(Bundle savedInstanceState) {
        super.onCreate(savedInstanceState);
        setContentView(R.layout.activity_shared_preferences);
        mTextValue = (TextView) findViewById(R.id.text_value);
        mThread = new SharedPreferenceThread();
        mThread.start(); ❸
    }

    /**
     * Write dummy value from the UI thread.
     */
    public void onButtonClickWrite(View v) {
        mThread.write(mCount++);
    }

    /**
     * Initiate a read from the UI thread.
     */
    public void onButtonClickRead(View v) {
        mThread.read();
    }

    /**
     * Ensure that the background thread is terminated with the Activity.
     */
    @Override
    protected void onDestroy() {
        super.onDestroy();
        mThread.quit();
    }
}
```

❶   Handler to the UI thread, used by the background thread to communicate with the UI thread.

❷   Background thread that reads and writes values to SharedPreferences.

❸   Start background thread when the Activity is created.

Task Chaining

A well-designed task executes a single contextual operation independently of other tasks. Contextual operations that should be executed on background threads in Android include retrieval of a network resource, data persistence, and image processing. Quite often, these types of operations are used in combination: download and persist, network data mashup, and so on. HandlerThread provides an infrastructure for task chaining with some favorable properties:

- Easy setup
- Independent, reusable tasks that may be chained
- Sequential execution
- Natural decision points, where you determine whether to continue with the next task in the chain or not
- Reporting the current state
- Easy passing of data from one task to another in the task chain

The task-chaining pattern is implemented in the Handler by defining tasks that are decoupled and reusable in handleMessage. The execution is controlled by the Message.what parameter; any of the tasks can be reached individually, for isolated execution, or executed consecutively through internal message passing within the Handler. Once a background task has finished, it can report the status to the UI thread, stop the task chain, or initiate a new task in the chain. Basically, every task has a natural decision point where the chain can stop or continue the execution.

Example: Chained network calls

Network-intensive applications commonly utilize the result from one network resource as input to a second network resource. When the first network operation finishes successfully, the call to the second network resource is made. Upon failure, the application stops the chain and terminates the background thread. During the execution, the user sees a progress dialog that can be controlled from every step in the chain: dismissed, updated, or just continuously shown until the chain has completed. This example has a HandlerThread with two chained tasks, where only the first task is exposed to the Activity. The second task can't be executed standalone; it only starts after a successful execution of the first task. The background thread communicates with the UI thread through a Handler that controls the dialog seen by the user:

```
public class ChainedNetworkActivity extends Activity {

    private static final int DIALOG_LOADING = 0;

    private static final int SHOW_LOADING = 1;
```

```java
    private static final int DISMISS_LOADING = 2;

    Handler dialogHandler = new Handler() { ❶
        @Override
        public void handleMessage(Message msg) {
            super.handleMessage(msg);
            switch (msg.what) {
                case SHOW_LOADING:
                    showDialog(DIALOG_LOADING);
                    break;
                case DISMISS_LOADING:
                    dismissDialog(DIALOG_LOADING);
            }
        }
    };

    private class NetworkHandlerThread extends HandlerThread {
        private static final int STATE_A = 1;
        private static final int STATE_B = 2;
        private Handler mHandler;

        public NetworkHandlerThread() {
            super("NetworkHandlerThread", Process.THREAD_PRIORITY_BACKGROUND);
        }

        @Override
        protected void onLooperPrepared() {
            super.onLooperPrepared();
            mHandler = new Handler(getLooper()) {
                @Override
                public void handleMessage(Message msg) {
                    super.handleMessage(msg);
                    switch (msg.what) {
                        case STATE_A: ❷
                            dialogHandler.sendEmptyMessage(SHOW_LOADING);
                            String result = networkOperation1();
                            if (result != null) {
                                sendMessage(obtainMessage(STATE_B, result));
                            } else {
                                dialogHandler.sendEmptyMessage(DISMISS_LOADING);
                            }
                            break;
                        case STATE_B: ❸
                            networkOperation2((String) msg.obj);
                            dialogHandler.sendEmptyMessage(DISMISS_LOADING);
                            break;
                    }
                }
            };
            fetchDataFromNetwork(); ❹
        }
```

```
            private String networkOperation1() {
                SystemClock.sleep(2000); // Dummy
                return "A string";
            }

            private void networkOperation2(String data) {
                // Pass data to network, e.g. with HttpPost.
                SystemClock.sleep(2000); // Dummy
            }

            /**
             * Publically exposed network operation
             */
            public void fetchDataFromNetwork() {
                mHandler.sendEmptyMessage(STATE_A);
            }
        }

        private NetworkHandlerThread mThread;


        public void onCreate(Bundle savedInstanceState) {
            super.onCreate(savedInstanceState);
            mThread = new NetworkHandlerThread();
            mThread.start();
        }

        @Override
        protected Dialog onCreateDialog(int id) {
            Dialog dialog = null;
            switch (id) {
                case DIALOG_LOADING:
                AlertDialog.Builder builder = new AlertDialog.Builder(this);
                builder.setMessage("Loading...");
                dialog = builder.create();
                break;
            }
            return dialog;
        }

        /**
         * Ensure that the background thread is terminated with the Activity.
         */
        @Override
        protected void onDestroy() {
            super.onDestroy();
            mThread.quit();
        }
    }
```

❶   DialogHandler that processes messages on the UI thread. It is used to control the dialogs shown to the user.

---

❷   The first network call, which is initiated in the `onCreate` method. It passes a message to the UI thread that initiates a progress dialog. When the network operation is done, the successful result is either passed on to the second task—STATE_B—or the progress dialog is dismissed.

❸   Execution of the second network operation.

❹   Initiate a network call when the background thread is started.

Conditional Task Insertion

`HandlerThread` offers great control over the `Message` instances in the queue and opportunites to observe their state. These features can be used to optionally insert new tasks in the queue, depending on the pending tasks in the queue when the message is sent. Message insertion control can be fine-grained, based on identifying messages in the queue by the `what` parameter and an optional tag:

```
handler.hasMessages(int what)
handler.hasMessages(int what, Object tag)
```

Conditional task insertion can be used in various ways, depending on the problem. A common use case is to ensure that your program does not send a message of a type that is already in the queue, because the queue should never contain more than one message of the same type at any time:

```
if (handler.hasMessages(MESSAGE_WHAT) == false) {
    handler.sendEmptyMessage(MESSAGE_WHAT);
}
```

Summary

`HandlerThread` provides a single-threaded, sequential task executor with fine-grained message control. It is the most fundamental form of message passing to a background thread, and it can be kept alive during a component lifecycle to provide low-resource background execution. The flexibility of message passing makes the `HandlerThread` a strong candidate for customizable sequential executors.

Message passing provides a powerful asynchronous mechanism, but is not always the most straightforward way to provide data to tasks. As we will see in the next chapters, the platform contains higher-level components that abstract message passing to make life easier for application developers and solve common asynchronous problems. However, when it comes to having full control of the background execution, `Handler Thread` and message passing are there to assist you!

CHAPTER 9

Control over Thread Execution Through the Executor Framework

Java's Executor framework opens up new dimensions of control over threads and the resources they use on the system. Sometimes you want to launch as many threads as the system can handle to resolve tasks quickly; other times you want to let the system manage the number of threads; and sometimes you want to cancel threads because they are no longer needed. The Executor framework, along with related classes, allows you to:

- Set up pools of worker threads and queues to control the number of tasks that can wait to be executed on these threads
- Check the errors that caused threads to terminate abnormally
- Wait for threads to finish and retrieve results from them
- Execute batches of threads and retrieve their results in a fixed order
- Launch background threads at convenient times so that results are available to the user faster

Executor

The fundamental component of the Executor framework is the simple `Executor` interface. Its main goal is to separate the creation of a task (such as a `Runnable`) from its execution, thus enabling the sorts of application behaviors listed at the beginning of the chapter. The interface includes just one method:

```
public interface Executor {
    void execute(Runnable command);
}
```

Despite its simplicity, the Executor is the foundation of a powerful execution environment, and is used more often than the basic Thread interface because it provides a better separation between submitting a task and its actual execution. The Executor does not execute any tasks by itself—it is merely an interface—so your implementations provide the actual execution and define how tasks will be executed. Normally, you only implement an Executor if there are special requirements. Instead—as we will soon see—there are provided Executor implementations in the platform, but first let's take a look at a custom implementation to grasp the concepts.

An Executor implementation in its simplest form creates a thread for every task (Example 9-1).

Example 9-1. One thread per task executor

```
public class SimpleExecutor implements Executor {
    @Override
    public void execute(Runnable runnable) {
        new Thread(runnable).start();
    }
}
```

The SimpleExecutor provides no more functionality than creating threads as anonymous inner classes directly, so it may look superfluous, but it provides advantages nevertheless: decoupling, scalability, and reduced memory references. You can alter the implementation in the Executor without affecting the code that submits the task through execute(Runnable), and scale the number of threads that handle the tasks. Furthermore, the SimpleExecutor holds no reference to the outer class, as an anonymous inner class does, and hence reduces the memory referenced by the thread.

In short, if you consider using the Thread class directly, but you don't know if the execution may change in the future, an Executor implementation can serve you well to simplify the change.

Other execution behaviors that can be controlled are:

- Task queueing
- Task execution order
- Task execution type (serial or concurrent)

An example of a more elaborate Executor is shown in Example 9-2. It implements a serial task executor, which is then used in the AsyncTask. (Chapter 10 explains the implications of this executor). The SerialExecutor implements a producer-consumer pattern, where producer threads create Runnable tasks and place them in a queue. Meanwhile, consumer threads remove and process the tasks off the queue.

Example 9-2. Serial executor

```
private static class SerialExecutor implements Executor {
    final ArrayDeque<Runnable> mTasks = new ArrayDeque<Runnable>();
    Runnable mActive;

    public synchronized void execute(final Runnable r) {
        mTasks.offer(new Runnable() {
            public void run() {
                try {
                    r.run();
                } finally {
                    scheduleNext();
                }
            }
        });
        if (mActive == null) {
            scheduleNext();
        }
    }

    protected synchronized void scheduleNext() {
        if ((mActive = mTasks.poll()) != null) {
            THREAD_POOL_EXECUTOR.execute(mActive);
        }
    }
}
```

The executor applies the following execution behavior:

Task queueing

An ArrayDeque—i.e., a double-ended queue—holds all submitted tasks until they are processed by a thread.

Task execution order

All tasks are put at the end of the double-ended queue through mTasks.offer(), so the result is a FIFO ordering of the submitted tasks.

Task execution type

Tasks are executed serially but not necessarily on the same thread. Whenever a task has finished executing—i.e., r.run() has finished—scheduleNext() is invoked. It takes the next task from the queue and submits it to another Executor in the thread pool, where any thread can execute the task.

In short, SerialExecutor constitutes an execution environment that guarantees serial execution with the the ability to process tasks on different threads.

Changing task execution type from serial to concurrent may give the application increased performance, but it raises thread safety concerns for the tasks that must be thread safe relative to each other.

As seen, the Executor is useful for asynchronous execution, but we seldom want to implement execution behavior from scratch. The most useful executor implementation is the thread pool, which we will look at next.

Thread Pools

A thread pool is the combination of a task queue and a set of worker threads that forms a producer-consumer setup (see "Pipes" on page 39). Producers add tasks to the queue and worker threads consume them whenever there is an idle thread ready to perform a new background execution. So, the worker thread pool can contain both active threads executing tasks, and idle threads waiting for tasks to execute.

There are several advantages with thread pools over executing every task on a new thread (thread-per-task pattern):

- The worker threads can be kept alive to wait for new tasks to execute. This means that threads don't have to be created and destroyed for every task, which compromises performance.

- The thread pool is defined with a maximum number of threads so that the platform isn't overloaded with background threads—that consume application memory—due to many background tasks.

- The lifecycle of all worker threads are controlled by the thread-pool lifecycle.

"ExecutorCompletionService" on page 152 contains a complete example showing a thread pool, along with other features discussed in this chapter.

Predefined Thread Pools

The Executor framework contains predefined types of thread pools, created from the factory class Executors:

Fixed size
> The fixed-size thread pool maintains a user defined number of worker threads. Terminated threads are replaced by new threads to keep the number of worker threads constant. This type of pool is created with Executors.newFixedThread Pool(n), where *n* is the number of threads.

This type of thread pool uses an unbounded task queue, meaning that the queue is allowed to grow freely as new tasks are added. Therefore, a producer will not fail at inserting a task.[1]

Dynamic size

The dynamic-size—-a.k.a. cached—thread pool creates a new thread if necessary when there is a task to process. Idle threads wait for 60 seconds for new tasks to execute and are then terminated if the task queue remains empty. Consequently, the thread pool grows and shrinks with the number of tasks to execute. This type of pool is created with `Executors.newCachedThreadPool()`.

Single-thread executor

This has only one worker thread to process the tasks from the queue. The tasks are executed serially and thread safety cannot be violated. This type of pool is created with `Executors.newSingleThreadExecutor()`.

 `Executors.newSingleExecutor()` and `Executors.newFixedThread Pool(1)` both have one worker thread to process tasks. The difference is that a single executor always has only one worker thread, whereas a fixed thread pool actually can reconfigure the number of worker threads after creation, for example, from one to four:

```
ExecutorService executor = Executors.newFixedThreadPool(1);
((ThreadPoolExecutor)executor).setCorePoolSize(4);
```

The reconfiguration API is accessible through the `ThreadPoolExecu tor` class, which can be used for customizing thread pools.

Custom Thread Pools

The predefined thread pool types from `Executors` cover the most common scenarios, but applications can create customized thread pools. The predefined `Executors` thread pools are based on the `ThreadPoolExecutor` class, which can be used directly to create thread pool behavior in detail. This section will go into more into the details of thread pools and their customization, including configuration and extension.

ThreadPoolExecutor configuration

A thread pool's behavior is based on a set of properties concerning the threads and the task queue, which you can set to control the pool. The properties are used by the `ThreadPoolExecutor` to define thread creation and termination as well as the queuing of tasks. The configuration is done in the constructor:

---

1. Actually, the upper limit is Integer.MAX, which, in practice, can be considered indefinite.

```
ThreadPoolExecutor executor = new ThreadPoolExecutor(
    int corePoolSize,
    int maximumPoolSize,
    long keepAliveTime,
    TimeUnit unit,
    BlockingQueue<Runnable> workQueue);
```

Core pool size

The lower limit of threads that are contained in the thread pool. Actually, the thread pool starts with zero threads, but once the core pool size is reached, the number of threads does not fall below this lower limit. If a task is added to the queue when the number of worker threads in the pool is lower than the core pool size, a new thread will be created even if there are idle threads waiting for tasks. Once the number of worker threads is equal to or higher than the core pool size, new worker threads are only created if the queue is full—i.e., queuing gets precedence over thread creation.

Maximum pool size

The maximum number of threads that can be executed concurrently. Tasks that are added to the queue when the maximum pool size is reached will wait in the queue until there is an idle thread available to process the task.

Maximum idle time (keep-alive time)

Idle threads are kept alive in the thread pool to be prepared for incoming tasks to process, but if the alive time is set, the system can reclaim noncore pool threads. The alive time is configured in `TimeUnits`, the unit the time is measured in.

Task queue type

An implementation of `BlockingQueue` ("BlockingQueue" on page 46) that holds tasks added by the consumer until they can be processed by a worker thread. Depending on the requirements, the queuing policy can vary.

Designing a Thread Pool

Thread pools help you manage the threads that should execute background tasks concurrently, but you should still configure it wisely to get high throughput with limited resource consumption. Basically, the goal is to create a thread pool that processes tasks at the highest speed allowed by the hardware, without consuming more memory than necessary.

Sizing

First, and most important, define the maximum size of the thread pool. If the maximum number of threads is too low, tasks may not be pulled from the queue at sufficient speed to not compromise performance. For example, if all threads are occupied by executing long I/O operations, there may be short-lived tasks waiting in the queue that don't get execution time until the IO operation has finished. On the other hand, too many threads can have a negative performance impact, as the scheduler has to switch threads more often, which leads to more time gaps where the CPU is occupied by thread management instead of execution.

It's good practice to base the thread pool size on the underlying hardware, more exactly the number of available CPUs. Android can retrieve the number of CPUs, referred to as N, from the `Runtime` class:

```
int N = Runtime.getRuntime().availableProcessors()
```

N is the maximum number of tasks that can be executed truly concurrently. Hence, a thread pool size of N can be sufficient for independent and nonblocking tasks, such as computation-intensive tasks. However, in reality, all threads can be stopped by the hardware for various reasons, so extra threads are needed to reach full CPU utilization.

It is not an exact science to find the optimal number of threads, and fortunately you don't have to be that exact. It's enough if you can roughly avoid too few and too many threads most of the time. There exist both theoretical and empirical suggestions of the thread pool size in the literature: for example, $N+1$ threads in *Java Concurrency in Practice* by Brian Goetz et al. (Addison-Wesley) for compute-intensive tasks, whereas Kirk Pepperdine suggests (*http://bit.ly/1g5mefe*) that a sizing of $2*N$ threads performs well. These values should serve Android applications well as a lower bound. However, the lower bound should not exceed the maximum number of concurrent tasks, as that may only lead to idle threads in the pool, without any tasks to execute.

When tasks that depend on each other execute in the same thread pool, it may not suffice to base the number of threads only on the underlying hardware. The executing threads can be occupied by tasks that—for some reason—aren't executing due to dependencies on other threads. Tasks can, for example, be dependent when they share a common state or rely upon a specific execution order. If so, some executing tasks may have dependencies on other tasks waiting in the queue, which in turn can't execute because the threads are occupied. Consequently, too few threads can lead to a deadlock situation for dependent tasks.

Likewise, tasks that block can delay other tasks in the queue if there are no idle threads available in the pool, which can lead to task starvation and low throughput. Consequently, a thread pool that you know is executing dependent or blocking tasks should be sized with a number of threads based not only on the number of CPUs, but also the number of dependent tasks.

Dynamics

Unless you define a fixed-sized thread pool, the number of threads changes during the thread pool lifetime. New threads may be created when needed and threads can be destroyed when unused. These dynamics are created with *core threads* and a *keep-alive time*.

The thread pool defines a set of core threads that the pool keeps alive, waiting for tasks to be submitted in the queue. The number of core threads ranges between 0 and the maximum number of threads. By default, the total number of threads in the pool changes dynamically between the number of core threads and the maximum number of threads. Therefore, if the core and maximum sizes are close, the pool becomes more static.

The keep-alive time of a thread pool defines how long idle threads should be kept in the pool before the system can start reclaiming memory by shutting down threads. Idle threads are available to execute new tasks that are added to the queue, which eliminates the overhead of destroying the old thread and creating a new one. Hence, a long idle time can give a slight performance improvement at the cost of using more memory.

For an Android application that normally has a limited number of worker threads, the performance gain from fine-tuning the idle time is small and rarely required. If the number of maximum threads are in the same order of magnitude as the number of CPUs, the memory held by the idle threads can be considered negligible and the idle time can be long—e.g., minutes. If you set the idle time to zero, the unused threads aren't terminated until the thread pool shuts down.

Bounded or unbounded task queue

A thread pool is normally used in combination with a bounded or unbounded task queue. An unbounded queue allows memory exhaustion because it can grow indefinitely, whereas the resource consumption of bounded queues is more manageable. On the other hand, bounded queues have to be tuned with both a size and a *saturation policy*, i.e., how the producer should handle rejected tasks. The rejection handling options are described in "Rejecting Tasks" on page 151.

The bounded and unbounded queue implementations are `LinkedBlockingQueue`, `PriorityBlockingQueue`, and `ArrayBlockingQueue`. The two latter queues are bounded, whereas the first one is unbounded by default but can be configured to be bounded. See the details of the blocking queue implementations in the official documentation (*https://developer.android.com/reference/java/util/concurrent/BlockingQueue.html*).

Thread configuration

The `ThreadPoolExecutor` defines not only the number of worker threads—and the pool's creation and termination—but also the properties of every thread. One common application behavior is to lower thread priorities so they don't compete with the UI thread.

Worker threads are configured through implementations of the `ThreadFactory` interface. Thread pools can define properties on the worker threads, such as priority, name, and exception handler. An example appears in Example 9-3.

Example 9-3. Fixed thread pool with customized thread properties

```
class LowPriorityThreadFactory implements ThreadFactory {
    private static int count = 1;

    public Thread newThread(Runnable r) {
        Thread t = new Thread(r);
        t.setName("LowPrio " + count++);
        t.setPriority(4);
        t.setUncaughtExceptionHandler(new Thread.UncaughtExceptionHandler()
        {
            @Override
            public void uncaughtException(Thread t, Throwable e)
            {
                Log.d(TAG, "Thread = " + t.getName() + ", error = " +
                    e.getMessage());
            }
        });
        return t;
    }
}
```

```
Executors.newFixedThreadPool(10, new LowPriorityThreadFactory());
```

Because thread pools often have many threads and they compete with the UI thread for execution time, it is normally a good idea to assign the worker threads a lower priority than the UI thread. (Priorities are described in "Priority" on page 34.) If the priority is not lowered by a custom `ThreadFactory`, the worker threads, by default, get the same priority as the UI thread.

Extending ThreadPoolExecutor

The `ThreadPoolExecutor` is commonly used standalone, but it can be extended to let the program track the executor or its tasks. An application can define the following methods to add actions taken each time a thread is executed:

`void beforeExecute(Thread t, Runnable r)`
Executed by the runtime library just before executing a thread

`void afterExecute(Runnable r, Throwable t)`
Executed by the runtime library after a thread terminates, whether normally or through an exception

`void terminated()`
Executed by the runtime library after the thread pool is shut down and there are no more tasks executing or waiting to be executed

The Thread and Runnable objects are passed to the first two methods; note that the order is reversed in the two methods. Example 9-4 illustrates a basic custom thread pool that tracks how many tasks are currently executing in the thread pool.

Example 9-4. Track the number of ongoing tasks in the thread pool

```
public class TaskTrackingThreadPool extends ThreadPoolExecutor{

    private AtomicInteger mTaskCount = new AtomicInteger(0);

    public TaskTrackingThreadPool() {
        super(3, 3, 0L, TimeUnit.SECONDS, new LinkedBlockingQueue<Runnable>());
    }

    @Override
    protected void beforeExecute(Thread t, Runnable r) {
        super.beforeExecute(t, r);
        mTaskCount.getAndIncrement();
    }

    @Override
    protected void afterExecute(Runnable r, Throwable t) {
        super.afterExecute(r, t);
        mTaskCount.getAndDecrement();
    }

    public int getNbrOfTasks() {
        return mTaskCount.get();
    }
}
```

beforeExecute increments the mTaskCounter before task execution, and afterExe
cute decrements the counter after execution. At any point, an external observer can request the number of tasks currently executing through getNbrOfTasks. The worker threads and external observer threads can access the shared member variable concurrently. Hence, it is defined as an AtomicInteger to ensure thread safety.

Lifecycle

The lifecycle of a thread pool ranges from its creation to the termination of all its worker threads. The lifecycle is managed and observed through the ExecutorService interface that extends Executor and is implemented by ThreadPoolExecutor. The internal thread pool states are shown in Figure 9-1.

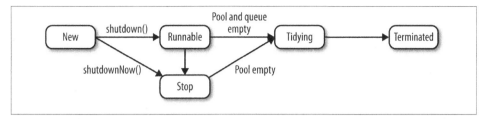

Figure 9-1. Thread pool lifecycle

Running

The initial state of the thread pool when it is created. It accepts incoming tasks and executes them on worker threads.

Shutdown

The state after `ExecutorService.shutdown` is called. The thread pool continues to process the currently executing tasks and the tasks in the queue, but new tasks are rejected.

Stop

The state after `ExecutorService.shutdownNow` is called. The worker threads are interrupted and tasks in the queue are removed.

Tidying

Internal cleaning.

Terminated

Final state. There are no remaining tasks or worker threads. `ExecutorSer vice.awaitTermination` stops blocking, and `ThreadPoolExecutor.terminated` is called. After the threads finish, all data structures related to the pool are freed.

The lifecycle states are irreversible; once a thread pool has left the `Running` state, it has initiated the path towards termination and it can not be reused again. The only controllable transitions at that point are to the Shutdown and Stop states. The subsequent transitions depend on the processing of the tasks and occur internally in the thread pool. Consequently, the actual termination of the threads and reclaiming of memory cannot be controlled without a cancellation policy—i.e., interrupt-handling—in the tasks.

Shutting Down the Thread Pool

Executors should not process tasks for longer than necessary; doing so can potentially leave a lot of active threads executing in the background for no good reason, holding on to memory that is not eligible for garbage collection. Typically, a fixed-size thread pool can keep a lot of threads alive in the background. Explicit termination is required to make the executor finish. Two methods—with somewhat different impacts—are available:

```
void shutdown()
List<Runnable> shutdownNow()
```

Table 9-1 explains the different impacts of the two calls on tasks in various states. Refer to Figure 9-2 for the numbers in the table.

Table 9-1. How tasks are affected by shutdown

Figure reference	shutdown()	shutdownNow()
1. Newly added tasks.	New tasks are rejected.	New tasks are rejected.
2. Tasks pending in the queue.	Pending tasks will be executed.	Pending tasks are not executed, but returned instead to a List<Runnable> so that they potentially can be executed on other threads.
3. Tasks being processed.	Processing continues.	Threads are interrupted.

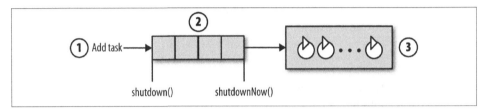

Figure 9-2. Executor shutdown

Consequently, shutdown() is considered to be a graceful termination of the executor, where both the executing and queued tasks are allowed to finish. shutdownNow() returns the queued tasks to the caller and tries to terminate currently executing tasks through interrupts. Hence, tasks should implement a cancellation policy to make them manageable. Without a cancellation policy, the tasks in the executor will terminate no earlier with shutdownNow() than with shutdown().

If the thread pool is not manually shut down, it will automatically do so when it has no remaining threads and is no longer referenced by the application. However, threads will remain in an idle state unless the keep-alive time is set. Consequently, the automatic shutdown applies only to thread pools where all threads have a keep-alive time set so that they terminate after a certain time. Automatic shutdown cannot occur earlier than the defined keep-alive time, as threads can still linger in the pool until the timeout occurs.

 Once the thread pool has initiated a shutdown, it cannot be reused for tasks. The application will have to create a new thread pool for subsequent tasks or to execute tasks returned by shutdownNow().

Thread Pool Uses Cases and Pitfalls

In this section, we'll take a look at a couple of unusual ways to treat thread pools, as well as pitfalls that can occur when defining a custom thread pool.

Favoring thread creation over queuing

By default, the alive time does not apply to core pool threads, but `allowCoreThreadTi meOut(true)` allows the system to also reclaim idle core pool threads. Hence, a thread pool can be defined to always favor thread creation over queueing:

```
int N = Runtime.getRuntime().availableProcessors();
ThreadPoolExecutor executor = new ThreadPoolExecutor(
            N*2,
            N*2,
            60L, TimeUnit.SECONDS,
            new LinkedBlockingQueue<Runnable>());
executor.allowCoreThreadTimeOut(true);
```

Handling preloaded task queues

A thread pool starts with zero worker threads and creates them when needed. Thread creation is triggered when tasks are submitted to the thread pool, but if no tasks are submitted, no worker threads are created even though there are tasks in the queue. Under those conditions, no tasks will be executed until a submission is done.

Preloaded task queues can be executed directly by prestarting the core threads with either `prestartAllCoreThreads()` or `prestartCoreThread()` on the `ThreadPoolExe cutor` instance. As the names suggest, the first method starts all the core threads you have configured in the pool, while the second starts a single thread to handle preloaded tasks. In either case, the preloaded tasks in the queue are processed:

```
BlockingQueue<Runnable> preloadedQueue = new LinkedBlockingQueue<Runnable>();
final String[] alphabet = {"Alpha","Beta", "Gamma","Delta","Epsilon","Zeta"};
for(int i = 0; i < alphabet.length; i++){
    final int j = i;
    preloadedQueue.add(new Runnable() {
        @Override
        public void run() {
            // Do long running operation
            // that uses "alphabet" variable.
        }
    });
}
ThreadPoolExecutor executor = new ThreadPoolExecutor(
    5, 10, 1, TimeUnit.SECONDS, preloadedQueue);
executor.prestartAllCoreThreads();
```

The danger of zero core threads

As described in "ThreadPoolExecutor configuration" on page 137, the core pool size determines how many threads will be started before queueing takes precedence over thread creation. As soon as the core pool size is reached, tasks are queued instead of being executed on a newly created thread:

```
int N = Runtime.getRuntime().availableProcessors();
ThreadPoolExecutor executor = new ThreadPoolExecutor(
            0,
            N*2,
            60L, TimeUnit.SECONDS,
            new ArrayBlockingQueue<Runnable>(10));
```

With zero-core threads and a bounded queue that can hold 10 tasks, no tasks actually run until the 11th task is inserted, triggering the creation of a thread.

Task Management

The execution environment running tasks can also be managed. In this section, we will look into the individual task and how we manage them.

Task Representation

A task is a unit of work that needs to be executed somewhere, at some point in time. It can be executed once or repeatedly, but the task itself should be independent of how it is executed; i.e., the task and the execution environment are separate entities. We have seen tasks represented by the Runnable interface; this section introduces the more powerful Callable interface, which can manage tasks and retrieve their results with the help of the Future interface.

The Runnable interface has been around since the first version of Java. It provides a simple interface that contains one method named run, which is called when the task is processed in an execution environment:

```
public interface Runnable {
    public void run();
}
```

Callable offers a much larger set of functionalities that you need to carry out the behaviors shown in this chapter. Among these functionalities are a way to cancel a thread (if it implements a cancellation policy) and to retrieve results from a thread, including the error from a thread that terminates abnormally.

Callable defines a call method that can return a value—defined as a generic type—and throw an exception:

```
public interface Callable<V> {
    public <V> call() throws Exception;
}
```

A `Callable` task cannot be directly executed by `Thread` instances because it was intro-duced first in Java 5. Instead, the execution environment should be based on `Executor Service` implementations—e.g., thread pools—to process the tasks. Once a `Callable` task is processed by the `ExecutorService`, it can be observed and controlled through the `Future` interface, which is available after task submission ("Submitting Tasks" on page 147).

Methods provided by `Future` are:

```
boolean cancel(boolean mayInterruptIfRunning)
V get()
V get(long timeout, TimeUnit unit)
boolean isCancelled()
boolean isDone()
```

The result from an asynchronous computation is retrieved with the blocking `get` meth-ods. It retrieves the result as a generic type, `V`, as declared in the task (e.g., `Calla ble<V>`). If the task does not end successfully by returning a result, it may have thrown a checked exception, `ExecutionException`, which can be caught by the caller of `get`.

`get` with no arguments blocks until the task exits, with no time limit. The two-argument version waits a limited amount of time, using the same timeout and unit shown in "Extending ThreadPoolExecutor" on page 141. If the task does not finish within the specified time, the calling thread stops waiting and continues to execute. The returned result is *null*.

A submitted task can be cancelled, in which case the executor tries to avoid executing it. If the task is still in the queue, it will be removed and is never executed. If it is currently executing, `cancel(false)` will not affect it, but `cancel(true)` interrupts the thread executing the task, and the task can terminate prematurely if it has implemented a cancellation policy.

`isCancelled` checks to see whether the task has been cancelled, but a return value `true` does not mean that the task will not execute—it just means someone wants this task to be cancelled. `isDone` returns `true` if the task is actually cancelled, has finished success-fully, or has thrown an exception.

Submitting Tasks

Before a task is submitted to a thread pool, it is by default an empty queue without threads. The state of the thread pool and queue of waiting threads determine how a thread pool can respond to a new task:

- If the core pool size has not been reached yet, a new thread can be created so the task can start immediately.
- If the core pool size has been reached but the queue has open slots, the task can be added to the queue.
- If the core pool size has been reached and the queue is full, the task must be rejected.

There are numerous ways of submitting tasks to a thread pool, both individually and batched. When there are multiple tasks to execute concurrently, they can be submitted one-by-one with the execute or submit methods. But the platform provides convenience methods that handle common use cases for batched submissions: invokeAll and invokeAny.

Individual submission

The most fundamental way to add a task to the thread pool is to build on its implementation of Executor and call the execute method:

```
ExecutorService executor = Executors.newSingleThreadExecutor();
executor.execute(new Runnable() {
    public void run() {
        doLongRunningOperation();
    }
});
```

The Executor interface can handle only Runnable tasks, but the ExecutorService extension contains more general methods allowing tasks to be submitted as instances of either Runnable or Callable. Every submitted task is represented by a Future to manage and observe the task, but only the Callable can be used for retrieving a result:

Callable
```
ExecutorService executor = Executors.newSingleThreadExecutor();
Future<Object> future = executor.submit(new Callable<Object>() {
    public Object call() throws Exception {
        Object object = doLongRunningOperation();
        return object;
    }
});

// Blocking call - Returns 'object' from the Callable
Object result = future.get();
```

Runnable without result
```
ExecutorService executor = Executors.newSingleThreadExecutor();
Future<?> future = executor.submit(new Runnable() {
    public void run() {
        doLongRunningOperation();
    }
});
```

```
// Blocking call - Always return null
Object result = future.get();
```

invokeAll

`ExecutorService.InvokeAll` executes mutiple independent tasks concurrently and lets the application wait for all tasks to finish by blocking the calling thread until all asynchronous computations are done or a timeout has expired:

```
List<Future<T>> invokeAll(Collection<? extends Callable<T>> tasks)
List<Future<T>> invokeAll(Collection<? extends Callable<T>> tasks,
                          long timeout, TimeUnit unit)
```

The call adds its collection of tasks to the thread pool in an ordered fashion. Depending on the thread pool definition, each added task may result in thread creation, task queuing or task rejection, similar to submit and execute. A timeout can be defined to expire when invokeAll should stop waiting for the background tasks to finish. If the timeout expires, the unfinished tasks are cancelled.

Once all tasks have finished, the results are stored in a list of futures, in the same order as the input tasks; i.e., the result is in the same position in the returned list as the task was in the input collection. After a task finishes, a call to Future.isDone returns true, and Future.get returns the task's result without blocking.

Example 9-5 utilizes invokeAll to execute two independent tasks concurrently on worker threads and combine the results when both have finished. It is typically used for retrieving network data from two different locations, where the results are mashed together before being used.

The data retrieval is initiated from a button click in an Activity—i.e., on the UI thread —but because invokeAll is a blocking call, it is executed from a SimpleExecutor (Example 9-1).

Example 9-5. Mashing data together from two network resources

```
public class InvokeActivity extends Activity {

    @UiThread
    public void onButtonClick(View v) {

        SimpleExecutor simpleExecutor = new SimpleExecutor();❶
        simpleExecutor.execute(new Runnable() {
            @Override
            public void run() {
                List<Callable<String>> tasks = new ArrayList<Callable<String>>();❷
                tasks.add(new Callable<String>() {
                    public String call() throws Exception {
                        return getFirstDataFromNetwork();
                    }
```

```
            });
            tasks.add(new Callable<String>() {
                public String call() throws Exception {
                    return getSecondDataFromNetwork();
                }
            });

            ExecutorService executor = Executors.newFixedThreadPool(2);❸
            try {
                List<Future<String>> futures = executor.invokeAll(tasks);❹
                String mashedData = mashupResult(futures);❺

            } catch (InterruptedException e) {
                e.printStackTrace();
            } catch (ExecutionException e) {
                e.printStackTrace();
            }

            executor.shutdown(); ❻
        }
    });
}

private String getFirstDataFromNetwork() { /* Network call omitted */ }

private String getSecondDataFromNetwork() { /* Network call omitted */ }

private String mashupResult(List<Future<String>> futures)
    throws ExecutionException, InterruptedException {
    for (Future<String> future : futures) {
        /* Get asynchronous computation result from future.get() */ ❼
        /* Mash data */
    }
    return /* Mashed data */
}
```

❶ Executor that offloads invokeAll from the UI thread.

❷ Collection that holds two long-running tasks, here simulated network calls.

❸ Execute the tasks on a fixed thread pool with two threads, because the example has only two tasks.

❹ Add the tasks in a batch to the thread pool. The call will block the simpleExe cutor thread, but not the UI thread.

❺ The result from the two asynchronous tasks are retrieved from the respective Future instances.

❻ Shut down the thread pool to terminate the worker threads.

❼ Presumably one would issue get calls with no arguments, so each would block until the thread it is tracking ends.

invokeAny

`ExecutorService.invokeAny` adds a collection of tasks to an executor, returns the result from the first finished task, and disregards the rest of the tasks. This can be useful in situations where you are doing a search through many different data sets and want to stop as soon as the item is found, or any similar situation where you need results from just one of the tasks you are running in parallel:

```
<T> invokeAny(Collection<? extends Callable<T>> tasks)
<T> invokeAny(Collection<? extends Callable<T>> tasks, long timeout,
    TimeUnit unit)
```

`invokeAny` blocks until one of the tasks has returned a result, and then cancels the remaining tasks in the executor by issuing `future.cancel(true)` on each. If, however, the remaining tasks do not respond to interruption, the tasks will continue to execute on worker threads in the background without reporting a result. Hence, lingering tasks may have side effects—e.g., changing a shared variable—even after `invokeAll` has returned. If the execution times out, `invokeAll` stops blocking, but no result is returned.

 Tasks added with `invokeAll` should normally utilize a thread pool with a number of threads that can allow for concurrent execution of all tasks, without queuing. Delaying any of the tasks defeats the value of running them all to get the fastest possible result. So the minimum core pool size should not be lower than the number of tasks.

Rejecting Tasks

Task addition can fail for two reasons: because both the number of worker threads and the queue are saturated, or because the executor has initiated a shutdown. The application can customize rejection handling by providing an implementation of `RejectedExecutionHandler` to the thread pool. `RejectedExecutionHandler` is an interface with a single method that is called upon task rejection:

```
void rejectedExecution(Runnable r, ThreadPoolExecutor executor)
```

The platform provides four predefined handlers for rejected tasks, implemented as inner classes of the `ThreadPoolExecutor`:

`AbortPolicy`
> Rejects the task by throwing a `RejectedExecutionException`. Unless another rejection policy is defined for the thread pool, this is the default behavior.

`CallerRunsPolicy`
> Executes the task in the caller's thread—i.e., synchronously. This is not an alternative when long tasks are added from the UI thread.

`DiscardOldestPolicy`
> Removes the oldest task in the queue and inserts the rejected task again. Hence, the task first in the queue is removed, and the added task is placed last in the queue.

`DiscardPolicy`
> Silently ignores the rejection of the task.

ExecutorCompletionService

A thread pool manages a task queue and the worker threads, but does not manage the results of the finished task. That is done by the `ExecutorCompletionService`. It holds a completion queue (based on a `BlockingQueue`) of finished tasks, as shown in Figure 9-3. When a task finishes, a `Future` object is placed in the queue, which is available to consumer threads so they can process the results in the order that the tasks have finished.

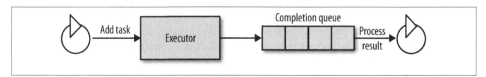

Figure 9-3. ExecutorCompletionService

Displaying multiple downloaded images in an `Activity` is a common use case. The UI is populated asynchronously, and a downloaded image should be displayed as soon as it is available, independently of the other image downloads. This is a job that fits well with an `ExecutorCompletionService`, because downladed images can be put in the completion queue and processed as soon as they are available.

The following example illustrates the use of an `ExecutorCompletionService` to display downloaded images in an `Activity`. The image download is done with a dynamic sized thread pool of worker threads, when the `Activity` is created. The downloaded images are held in the completion queue and processed by a consumer thread:

```
public class ECSImageDownloaderActivity extends Activity {
    private LinearLayout layoutImages;

    private class ImageDownloadTask implements Callable<Bitmap> { ❶

        @Override
        public Bitmap call() throws Exception {
            return downloadRemoteImage();
        }

        private Bitmap downloadRemoteImage() {
            /* Do image download */
```

```
        }
    }

    private class DownloadCompletionService extends ExecutorCompletionService { ❷

        private ExecutorService mExecutor;

        public DownloadCompletionService(ExecutorService executor) {
            super(executor);
            mExecutor = executor;
        }

        public void shutdown() {
            mExecutor.shutdown();
        }

        public boolean isTerminated() {
            return mExecutor.isTerminated();
        }
    }

    private class ConsumerThread extends Thread { ❸

        private DownloadCompletionService mEcs;

        private ConsumerThread(DownloadCompletionService ecs) {
            this.mEcs = ecs;
        }

        @Override
        public void run() {
            super.run();
            try {
                while(!mEcs.isTerminated()) { ❹
                    Future<Bitmap> future = mEcs.poll(1, TimeUnit.SECONDS); ❺
                    if (future != null) {
                        addImage(future.get());
                    }
                }
            } catch (InterruptedException e) {
                e.printStackTrace();
            } catch (ExecutionException e) {
                e.printStackTrace();
            }
        }
    }

    public void onCreate(Bundle savedInstanceState) { ❻
        DownloadCompletionService ecs =
        new DownloadCompletionService(Executors.newCachedThreadPool());
        new ConsumerThread(ecs).start();
```

```
                 for (int i = 0; i < 5; i++) {
                     ecs.submit(new ImageDownloadTask());
                 }

                 ecs.shutdown();
             }


         private void addImage(final Bitmap image) { ❼
             runOnUiThread(new Runnable() {
                 @Override
                 public void run() {
                     ImageView iv = new ImageView(ECSImageDownloaderActivity.this);
                     iv.setImageBitmap(image);
                     layoutImages.addView(iv);
                 }
             });
         }
     }
```

❶ A `Callable` instance that represents a task producing a result. It returns a bitmap image when downloaded over a network connection.

❷ A `ExecutorCompletionService` that holds the `Executor` and exposes lifecycle methods—`shutdown` and `isTerminated`—to control the executor.

❸ A consumer thread that polls the completion queue for results from finished tasks.

❹ If the executor is terminated, all tasks have finished and it is safe to stop polling the completion queue for more tasks. The consumer thread will finish once the executor is terminated.

❺ Polling mechanism: the consumer thread waits for one second, in every iteration, for finished tasks. After that it continues execution to check again if the executor has terminated, as described in the previous item.

❻ Create the `Activity` that initiates `DownloadCompletionService` with a cached thread pool and a `ConsumerThread`. Five download tasks are submitted.

❼ Shut down the executor gently; let the submitted tasks finish before the worker threads terminate.

Summary

The Executor framework provides a cornerstone in the Android-specific asynchronous techniques. It is often used with message passing ("Android Message Passing" on page 47) to create application-specific asynchronous execution behaviors. If the Android-specific techniques seem limiting, the Executor framework provides the developer with full control of the asynchronous execution. It separates tasks from their execution environment, providing greater flexibility and simplifying future change to execution. Tasks designed with independence in mind can be executed in any execution environment, and if the Executor interface abstracts the actual execution, it can be easily altered without concerning the tasks. The platform's concrete implementations of Executor—thread pools—provide applications with better thread management and ways to manage concurrency in sophisticated ways. Queues and rejection policies help maintain a balance between CPU resources and tasks that need to be executed.

CHAPTER 10

Tying a Background Task to the UI Thread with AsyncTask

The most important role for asynchronous tasks on Android, as we've discussed, is to relieve the UI thread from long-running operations. This calls for defining an execution environment, creating the task to do the long operation, and finally determining how the UI thread and the background threads communicate. All of these properties are encapsulated in an AsyncTask to make asynchronous execution as easy as it gets.

This chapter gets into the details of AsyncTask class and shows how smoothly it can handle background task execution, but also raises concerns about the pitfalls you need to watch for.

Fundamentals

As the name indicates, an AsyncTask is an asynchronous task that is executed on a background thread. The only method you need to override in the class is doInBackground(). Hence, a minimal implementation of an AsyncTask looks like this:

```java
public class MinimalTask extends AsyncTask {
    @Override
    protected Object doInBackground(Object... objects) {
        // Implement task to execute on background thread.
    }
}
```

The task is executed by calling the execute method, which triggers a callback to doInBackground on a background thread:

```java
new MinimalTask().execute(Object... objects);
```

When an `AsyncTask` finishes executing, it cannot be executed again—i.e., `execute` is a one-shot operation and can be called only once per `AsyncTask` instance, the same behavior as a `Thread`.

In addition to background execution, `AsyncTask` offers a data passing mechanism from `execute` to `doInBackground`. Objects of any type can be passed from the initiating thread to the background thread. This is like `HandlerThread` (Chapter 8), but with `AsyncTask` you do not have to be concerned about sending and processing `Message` instances with a `Handler`.

 The data passed in `execute` to `doInBackground` is shared by both threads and needs to be accessed in a mutually exclusive way. In other words, synchronization is required to protect the data from corruption.

In the common case we discussed at the beginning of the chapter, where you want to execute a task in the background and deliver a result back to the UI thread, `AsyncTask` shines; it is all about handling the flow of preparing the UI before executing a long task, executing the task, reporting progress of the task, and finally returning the result. All of this is available as optional callbacks to subclasses of the `AsyncTask`, which look like this:

```java
public class FullTask extends AsyncTask<Params, Progress, Result> {
    @Override
    protected void onPreExecute() { ... }

    @Override
    protected Result doInBackground(Params... params) { ... }

    @Override
    protected void onProgressUpdate(Progress... progress) { ... }

    @Override
    protected void onPostExecute(Result result) { ... }

    @Override
    protected void onCancelled(Result result) { ... }
}
```

This implementation extends the `AsyncTask` and defines the arguments of the objects that are passed between threads:

Params
    Input data to the task executed in the background.

Progress

> Progress data reported from the background thread—i.e., from `doInBackground`—to the UI thread in `onProgressUpdate`.

Result

> The result produced from the background thread and sent to the UI thread.

All callback methods are executed sequentially, except `onProgressUpdate`, which is initiated by and runs concurrently with `doInBackground`. Figure 10-1 shows the lifecycle of an `AsyncTask` and its callback sequence.

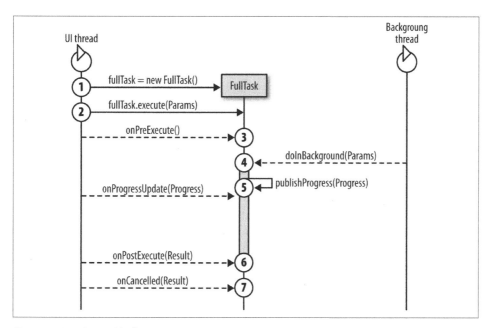

Figure 10-1. AsyncTask overview

The steps in the figure are:

1. Create the `AsyncTask` instance.
2. Start execution of the task.
3. First callback on the UI thread: `onPreExecute`. This usually prepares the UI for the long operation—e.g., by displaying a progress indicator on the screen.
4. Callback on a background thread: `doInBackground`. This executes the long-running task.
5. Report progress updates from the `publishProgress` method on the background thread. These trigger the `onProgressUpdate` callback on the UI thread, which typ-

ically handles the update by changing a progress indicator on the screen. The progress is defined by the `Progress` parameter.

6. The background execution is done and is followed by running a callback on the UI thread to report the result. There are two possible callbacks: `onPostExecute` is called by default, but if the `AsyncTask` has been cancelled, the callback `onCancelled` gets the result instead. It is guaranteed that only one of the callbacks can occur.

The progress update mechanism solves two use cases:

- Displaying to the user how the long-running operation is progressing, by continuously reporting how many of the total tasks are executed.

- Delivering the result in portions, instead of delivering everything at the end in `onPostExecute`. For example, if the task downloads multiple images over the network, the `AsyncTask` does not have to wait and deliver all images to the UI thread when they are all downloaded; it can utilize `publishProgress` to send one image at the time to the UI thread. In that way, the user gets a continuous update of the UI.

Creation and Start

`AsyncTask` implementations are created with the default constructor, which should be called from the UI thread. If another thread creates the `AsyncTask`—on platforms prior to the Jelly Bean release—the callbacks may not occur on the correct thread. The thread where the `AsyncTask` is created decides what thread runs the callbacks to `onProgressUpdate`, `onPostExecute`, and `onCancelled`.

Actually, the first created `AsyncTask` in the application process controls the callback threads for all consecutive `AsyncTask` implementations in the application. The callback thread is set only once per application lifetime. Starting with Jelly Bean, an `AsyncTask` is class-loaded at application start on the UI thread, so that the callbacks are guaranteed to occur on the UI thread.

No configuration parameters are offered by the constructor. Instead, arguments are passed to the start of the task:

```
execute(Object... objects);
```

The input consists of a variable-sized object list that can receive any number of objects of arbitrary type. The input arguments are retrieved in the `doInBackground` callback. In this way, data is shared between the UI thread and the background thread, and is always available to both.

The execute method should be called from the UI thread; otherwise, the onPreExe cute callback will not occur on the UI thread. Execution is a one-shot task; calling it more than once generates an IllegalStateException error.

Cancellation

If the UI thread decides not to use the results of an AsyncTask (perhaps because the user indicated that she changed her mind or put the app in the background), it can send a termination request through a call to cancel(boolean):

```
// Start the task
AsyncTask task = new MyAsyncTask().execute(/* Omitted */);
// Cancel the task
task.cancel(true);
```

If the argument to the call is false, the call merely sets a flag that the background thread can check through isCancelled(). If the argument is true, an interrupt is also sent ("Interruptions" on page 108). Sending the interrupt is a stronger message because blocking methods calls are released, and the background thread can catch the Inter ruptedException or check the Thread.isInterrupted() flag.

As usual with background tasks, it is best to terminate as early as possible if the result of the background execution cannot be used anymore. Termination releases allocated resources and reduces the risk of memory leaks. Just like a Thread, an AsyncTask cannot be forced to terminate, but requires a cancellation strategy ("Interruptions" on page 108) to end the execution gracefully.

When it receives a cancellation request, the task skips the call to onPostExecute and calls one of the cancel callbacks—onCancelled() or onCancelled(Result)—instead. You can use the cancel callbacks to update the UI with a different result or a different message to the user from the ones that take place when the asynchronous task finishes successfully. A cancelled task does not necessarily finish earlier than it would without cancellation, because cancellation only ensures that the onCancelled callback is called after the background task execution.

A cancellation policy involves two parts: Finish doInBackground when a blocking method throws InterruptedException, and use checkpoints in the code to see whether the task has been cancelled before starting any long operation. Checkpoints can be inserted anywhere in the code, but it becomes impractical to add them everywhere, so they are best used as a condition in a loop or between two long operations. The check-point condition can be determined either by checking AsyncTask.isCancelled or catching an interrupt. But the two checkpoint conditions responds differently to the cancel method, as shown in Table 10-1.

Table 10-1. Difference between cancellation and interruption check

cancel(boolean)	isCancelled() returns	Thread.currentThread().isInterrupted() returns
false	true	false
true	true	true

The strongest checkpoint condition is `isCancelled`, because it observes the actual call to `cancel` and not the interruption. Hence, the strongest cancellation policy is to combine checkpoints and interrupt-handling as follows:

```
public class InterruptionTask extends AsyncTask<String, Void, Void> {
    @Override
    protected Void doInBackground(String... s) {
        try {
            while (!isCancelled()) {
                doLongInterruptibleOperation(s[0]);
            }
        } catch (InterruptedException iex) {
            // Do nothing. Let's just finish.
        }
        return null;
    }
}
```

States

An `AsyncTask` has the following possible states: `PENDING`, `RUNNING` and `FINISHED`, in that order:

PENDING
> The `AsyncTask` instance is created, but `execute` has not been called on it.

RUNNING
> Execution has started; i.e., `execute` is called. The task remains in this state when it finishes, as long as its final method (such as `onPostExecute`) is still running.

FINISHED
> Both the background execution and the optional final operation—`onPostExe cute` or `onCancelled`—is done.

Backward transitions are not possible, and once the task is in `RUNNING` state, it is not possible to start any new executions. `FINISH` is a terminal state; a new `AsyncTask` instance must be created for every execution.

The state of the `AsyncTask` can be observed with `AsyncTask.getStatus()`, and it is useful for determining whether a task is currently executing, as shown in the following example.

Example: Limiting an AsyncTask execution to one at the time

If an AsyncTask should not be allowed to execute while another task is executing, you can store a reference to the task and check the task's status before a new execution is allowed. In the AsyncTaskStatusActivity, the AsyncTask is started from the onExe cute method, which could be called from anywhere on the UI thread—e.g., from the onClick() method triggered by a button click:

```
public class AsyncTaskStatusActivity extends Activity {

    private AsyncTask mMyAsyncTask;

    // Activity lifecycle code omitted.

    public void onExecute(View v) {
        if (mMyAsyncTask != null && mMyAsyncTask.getStatus() !=
            AsyncTask.Status.RUNNING) {
            mMyAsyncTask = new MyAsyncTask().execute();
        }
    }

    private static class MyAsyncTask extends AsyncTask<String, Void, Void> {
        @Override
        protected Void doInBackground(String... s) {
            // Details omitted.
            return null;
        }
    }
}
```

Implementing the AsyncTask

Implementing an AsyncTask is straightforward: create a subclass, override doInBack ground for background execution, and add helper methods for any desired UI updates before, during, and after the background execution. Despite its simplicity, there are a few more things to consider:

Avoid memory leaks

As long as the worker thread is alive, all of its referenced objects are held in memory, as explained in "Thread-Related Memory Leaks" on page 91. The AsyncTask should therefore be declared as a standalone or static inner class so that the worker thread avoids implicit references to outer classes.

Coupling with a Context *and its lifecycle*

An AsyncTask usually issues updates to the UI thread that may reference the Con text, typically an Activity with a view hierarchy. But you should avoid referencing the view hierarchy so that the views won't be kept in memory when they are not needed. Hence, the AsyncTask should be declared as a static inner class that holds a reference to the associated Context. The reference is removed by setting it to null when it is not needed anymore.

Cancellation policy

Allow tasks to be interrupted and cancelled, as explained in "Cancellation" on page 161 and "Interruptions" on page 108.

Example: Downloading Images

This example shows the implementation of an Activity that displays four images that are downloaded from the network with an AsyncTask. The UI consists of a determinate progress bar—an mProgressBar—that shows the number of downloaded images) and a layout—using mLayoutImages—whose children constitute the downloaded images. The download starts upon Activity creation and is cancelled on destruction:

```java
public class FileDownloadActivity extends Activity {

    private static final String[] DOWNLOAD_URLS = {  ❶
        "http://developer.android.com/design/media/
        devices_displays_density@2x.png",
        "http://developer.android.com/design/media/
        iconography_launcher_example2.png",
        "http://developer.android.com/design/media/
        iconography_actionbar_focal.png",
        "http://developer.android.com/design/media/
        iconography_actionbar_colors.png"
    };

    DownloadTask mFileDownloaderTask;

    // Views from layout file
    ProgressBar mProgressBar;
    LinearLayout mLayoutImages;

    @Override
    public void onCreate(Bundle savedInstanceState) {
        super.onCreate(savedInstanceState);

        setContentView(R.layout.activity_file_download);
        mProgressBar = (ProgressBar) findViewById(R.id.progress_bar);
        mProgressBar.setMax(DOWNLOAD_URLS.length);
        mLayoutImages = (LinearLayout) findViewById(R.id.layout_images);

        mFileDownloaderTask = new DownloadTask(this);
        mFileDownloaderTask.execute(DOWNLOAD_URLS);  ❷
    }

    @Override
    protected void onDestroy() {  ❸
        super.onDestroy();
```

```
        mFileDownloaderTask.setActivity(null);
        mFileDownloaderTask.cancel(true);
    }

    private static class DownloadTask extends AsyncTask<String, Bitmap, Void> { ❹

        private FileDownloadActivity mActivity; ❺
        private int mCount = 0;

        public DownloadTask(FileDownloadActivity activity) {
            mActivity = activity;
        }

        public void setActivity(FileDownloadActivity activity) { ❻
            mActivity = activity;
        }

        @Override
        protected void onPreExecute() {
            super.onPreExecute();
            mActivity.mProgressBar.setVisibility(View.VISIBLE); ❼
            mActivity.mProgressBar.setProgress(0);
        }

        @Override
        protected Void doInBackground(String... urls) {
            for (String url : urls) {
                if (!isCancelled()) { ❽
                    Bitmap bitmap = downloadFile(url); ❾
                    publishProgress(bitmap); ❿
                }
            }
            return null;
        }

        @Override
        protected void onProgressUpdate(Bitmap... bitmaps) { ⓫
            super.onProgressUpdate(bitmaps);
            if (mActivity != null)  {
                mActivity.mProgressBar.setProgress(++mCount);
                ImageView iv = new ImageView(mActivity);
                iv.setImageBitmap(bitmaps[0]);
                mActivity.mLayoutImages.addView(iv);
            }
        }

        @Override
        protected void onPostExecute(Void aVoid) {
            super.onPostExecute(aVoid);
            if (mActivity != null) {
                mActivity.mProgressBar.setVisibility(View.GONE); ⓬
            }
```

```
        }

        @Override
        protected void onCancelled() {
            super.onCancelled();
            if (mActivity != null) {
                mActivity.mProgressBar.setVisibility(View.GONE); ⓭
            }
        }


        private Bitmap downloadFile(String url) {
            Bitmap bitmap = null;
            try {
                bitmap = BitmapFactory
                        .decodeStream((InputStream) new URL(url)
                                .getContent());
            } catch (MalformedURLException e) {
                e.printStackTrace();
            } catch (IOException e) {
                e.printStackTrace();
            }
            return bitmap;
        }

    }
}
```

❶   URLs of the images.

❷   Pass the URLs to `doInBackground`.

❸   When the `Activity` is destroyed, the `AsyncTask` is cancelled and its reference to the destroyed `Activity` is nullified so that it can be garbage collected, although the worker thread is alive.

❹   Definition of `AsyncTask`: An array of `String` objects is passed to `doInBackground`, and `Bitmap` objects are returned during background execution. The background thread does not pass a result to the UI thread, so the last parameter is declared `Void`.

❺   The `Activity` is referenced for updates on the UI thread.

❻   Setter for changing or nullifying the `Activity` reference. The `Activity` is changed upon task retention during a configuration change.

❼   Show the progress bar before the background task executes.

❽   Check whether the task is cancelled before starting the download of the next image, so that the task can terminate as early as possible.

❾   Download the image over the network and assign it to the `Bitmap` argument passed to the `AsyncTask`.

⑩　Send the image to the UI thread.

⑪　Respond to the progress update sent by the background thread by updating the progress bar and displaying the new image.

⑫ ⑬　Remove the progress bar.

Background Task Execution

Because `AsyncTask` executes its tasks asynchronously, multiple tasks can be executed either sequentially or concurrently. The execution environment can be defined explicitly in the application; otherwise, it is set implicitly by the platform. The method that starts the execution determines how the task is executed. Table 10-2 shows the possibilities.

Table 10-2. Overview of task execution

Execution method	Lowest API level	Return value	Executor	Background task	Execution type
`execute(Params…)`	3	The started AsyncTask	Defined in AsyncTask	`doInBackground`	Sequential or concurrent
`(static) execute(Runnable)`	11	None	Defined in AsyncTask	`Runnable`	Sequential only
`executeOnExecutor(Executor, Params…)`	11	The started AsyncTask	Customizable	`doInBackground`	Customizable

Before API level 11, only the first option in the table is available. From API level 11 onward, the `AsyncTask` offers three methods for task execution, with different properties:

`execute(Params…)`
> The version described above and the only method available on all platform versions. It utilizes the `AsyncTask` internal execution environment, but this has changed during platform evolution. See "Execution Across Platform Versions" on page 170.

`execute(Runnable)`
> Added in API level 11 for executing `Runnable` tasks instead of overriding `doInBackground`. The `Runnable` is processed in the `AsyncTask` internal execution environment but does not use message passing to communicate between threads. `onPreExecute`, `onPostExecute`, and `onCancelled` are not called and progress can not be published. This use case should probably be replaced with a different solution (see "Using execute(Runnable)" on page 174).

```
executeOnExecutor(Executor, Params…)
```
Added in API level 11 for configuring the actual execution environment on which the task is processed. It can utilize internal execution environments or use a custom `Executor`.

The `Executor` argument `executeOnExecutor` can be one of the following execution environments:

```
AsyncTask.THREAD_POOL_EXECUTOR
```
Tasks are processed concurrently in a pool of threads. In KitKat, the thread pool sizing is based on the number of available CPU cores: $N+1$ core threads and a maximum of $2*N+1$ threads, and the work queue can hold 128 tasks. Hence, a device with four available cores can hold a maximum of 137 tasks.

```
AsyncTask.SERIAL_EXECUTOR
```
A sequential task scheduler that ensures thread-safe task execution. It contains no threads of its own, relying instead on `THREAD_POOL_EXECUTOR` for execution. It stores the tasks in an unbounded queue and passes each one to the `THREAD_POOL_EX ECUTOR` to be executed in sequence. The tasks can be executed in different threads of the thread pool, but the `SERIAL_EXECUTOR` guarantees that consecutive tasks are not added to the thread pool until the previous task has finished, so thread safety is preserved.

Figure 10-2 summarizes how these two execution environments operate and use the thread pool.

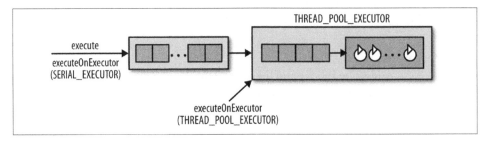

Figure 10-2. AsyncTask execution

Both execution environments use the `AsyncTask` worker threads for the `doInBack ground` callbacks. The threads have no `Looper` attached, so the `AsyncTask` cannot receive messages from other threads. Furthermore, the threads' priority is lowered to `Pro cess.THREAD_PRIORITY_BACKGROUND` so that it will interfere less with the UI thread (priorities are described in "Priority" on page 34).

Application Global Execution

`AsyncTask` implementations can be defined and executed from any component in the application, and several instances in the `RUNNING` state can coexist. However, all `AsyncTask` instances shared an application-wide, global execution property (Figure 10-3). That means that even if two different threads launch two different tasks (as in the following example) at the same time, they will be executed sequentially. Whichever happens to be executed first by the runtime environment will keep the other from executing until it terminates:

```
new FirstLongTask().execute();
...
new SecondLongTask().execute();
```

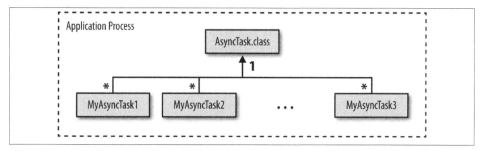

Figure 10-3. AsyncTask application global behavior

It does not matter whether the `AsyncTask` implementations are executed from an `Activity`, a `Service`, or any other part of the application—they still use the same application global execution environment and run sequentially

 The application global execution of `AsyncTask` instances poses a risk that the execution environment gets saturated and that background tasks get delayed, or worse still, not executed at all.

Because all `AsyncTask` instances share this global execution, they all can have an impact on each other, which depends on the execution environment:

Sequential execution (`SERIAL_EXECUTOR`)
Tasks that are executed sequentially will not be processed on a worker thread until all the preceding tasks in the application have been processed. This applies to any tasks launched through `executeOnExecutor(AsyncTask.SERIAL_EXECUTOR)` or through `execute()` on API level 13 or higher.

Concurrent execution (`THREAD_POOL_EXECUTOR`*)*

> A quad-core device with all cores available can handle five `AsyncTask`s concurrently. When a sixth task is started, it will be placed in the waiting queue until one of the first five tasks has finished and left a worker thread idle. This may seem odd, because I previously stated that the `THREAD_POOL_EXECUTOR` can hold 137 tasks, but the reason lies in the implementation of the `ThreadPoolExecutor` with five core pool threads. When the core pool threads are all occupied, the implementation chooses queuing over the creation of new threads (see "ThreadPoolExecutor configuration" on page 137).

Execution Across Platform Versions

It may be important to know whether tasks are being executed sequentially or concurrently if they depend on the guaranteeed ordering or thread safety of sequential execution. Tasks launched through `execute` run sequentially, whereas `executeOnExecutor` can be run with a concurrent `Executor`. However, `executeOnExecutor` was added first in API level 11 (Honeycomb). This section explains what you need to know to handle the `AsyncTask` across platform versions. The differences in execution are summarized in Table 10-3.

Table 10-3. Execution differences depending on platform version

API level	execute	executeOnExecutor
1 - 3	Sequential	Not available
4 - 10	Concurrent	Not available
11 - 12	Concurrent	Sequential/concurrent (customizable)
13+	Sequential	Sequential/concurrent (customizable)

At first, execution was always sequential, but to gain performance, the `execute` method was changed in API level 4 to process tasks concurrently. Unfortunately, tasks that depended on ordered or thread-safe execution could fail when they were exposed to a nonordered and non-thread–safe enviroment. So in API level 11, the API was extended with the `executeOnExecutor` method; and in API level 13, the `execute` method was reverted to sequential execution to restore the previous safe behavior. The `executeOnExecutor` method supports custom `Executor` implementations, which can be used for concurrent execution.

Also in API level 13, the platform added a check to the `targetSdkVersion` in the applications' *AndroidManifest.xml* file to avoid unexpected behavior for existing applications:

targetSdkVersion<13

> `execute` keeps concurrent execution, even on platforms with API level 13 or higher.

targetSdkVersion>=13

> execute causes sequential execution on platforms with API level 13 or higher.

 The execution behavior of execute is dependent both on the API level of the platform and the targetSdkVersion in the application's Manifest.

An application that needs consistent execution behavior on all platform versions has to handle this itself by setting targetSdkVersion.

Until API level 13, it is not possible to achieve sequential execution across all platform versions with an AsyncTask.[1] Concurrent execution across platform versions is achieved either by setting targetSdkVersion < 13+ or by changing the actual executor, depending on the platform version:

Consistent sequential execution

> Sequential execution of AsyncTask instances cannot be guaranteed on API levels 4-10 because execute is concurrent and executeOnExecutor is not available until API level 11. Instead, background tasks that require consistent sequential execution should utilize either Executors.newSingleThreadExecutor (Chapter 9) or Han dlerThread (Chapter 8).

Consistent concurrent execution

> The targetSdkVersion setting determines how concurrent execution can be consistently achieved across platform versions. For API levels lower than 13, the exe cute method suffices, but for higher API levels, the application has to vary the execution call depending on the build:

```
if (Build.VERSION.SDK_INT <= Build.VERSION_CODES.HONEYCOMB_MR1) {
    new MyAsyncTask().execute();
} else {
    new MyAsyncTask().executeOnExecutor(AsyncTask.THREAD_POOL_EXECUTOR);
}
```

Because checking the API for every execution is tedious, you can define a wrapper class that can be implemented to handle the platform check:

```
public class ConcurrentAsyncTask {
    public static void execute(AsyncTask as) {
        if (Build.VERSION.SDK_INT < Build.VERSION_CODES.HONEYCOMB_MR2) {
            as.execute(...);
        } else {
            as.executeOnExecutor(AsyncTask.THREAD_POOL_EXECUTOR, ...);
```

---

1. API levels 1-3 are considered to be obsolete, and are therefore omitted.

```
            }
        }
    }
```

The caller passes `AsyncTask` it wants executed to the wrapper class:

```
ConcurrentAsyncTask.execute(new MyAsyncTask());
```

Custom Execution

The predefined executors—`SERIAL_EXECUTOR` and `THREAD_POOL_EXECUTOR`—in the `AsyncTask` are application global, which risks a performance penalty when the application executes a lot of tasks. To circumvent global execution, tasks should be processed in a custom `Executor`:

```
new AsyncTask().executeOnExecutor(Params, MyCustomExecutor);
```

The custom executor replaces the execution environment in the `AsyncTask` but preserves the communication between threads for progress updating: the overridden methods are called in the same way as they would have been with a predefined executor.

Sequential execution can be handled better by using a customized—nonglobal—executor in combination with the `AsyncTask`; e.g., the single threaded executor described in Chapter 9.

Example: Nonglobal sequential execution

Sequential execution that is shared globally in an application may cause unexpected execution delays if a task from one component has to wait for a task from another component to finish. Hence, to utilize sequential execution—but avoid the application global behavior—a custom executor should be shared between the tasks.

The following, very bare-bones example shows the use of a sequential executor, `Executors.newSingleThreadExecutor`, in both an `Activity` and a `Service`. Because the tasks are executed in different components–but still require the same executor—the executor instance is held in the `Application` instance:

```
public class EatApplication extends Application {
    private Executor customSequentialExecutor;

    public Executor getCustomSequentialExecutor() {
        if (customSequentialExecutor == null) {
            customSequentialExecutor = Executors.newSingleThreadExecutor();
        }
        return customSequentialExecutor;
    }
}

public class MyActivity extends Activity {
    private void executeTaskSequentially() {
```

```
        new MyActivityAsyncTask().executeOnExecutor(
            ((EatApplication)getApplication).getCustomSequentialExecutor());
    }
    public class MyService extends Service {
        private void executeTaskSequentially() {
            new MyServiceAsyncTask().executeOnExecutor(
                ((EatApplication)getApplication).getCustomSequentialExecutor());
    }
```

AsyncTask Alternatives

Due to its simplicity, the AsyncTask is a popular asynchronous technique. It allows background task execution in combination with thread communication, offering a generic and adaptable asynchronous technique that can be applied on many use cases —the AsyncTask itself does not impose any constraints. However, as we have seen in this chapter, it has a couple of concerns you need to consider:

- Because AsyncTask has a global execution environment, the more tasks you execute with an AsyncTask, the higher the risk that tasks will not be processed as expected because there are other tasks in the application that hold the execution environment.

- Inconsistency in execution environments over different platform versions makes it more difficult to either optimize execution for performance (concurrent execution) or thread safety (sequential execution).

The AsyncTask is often overused in applications, due to its simplicity. It is not a silver-bullet solution for asynchronous execution on Android. For many use cases, you should look into alternative techniques, for reasons of architecture, program design, or just because they are less error prone.

When an AsyncTask Is Trivially Implemented

Two trivial use cases where the AsyncTask can cause more complexity than the alternatives are:

*Running the task without parameters (*AsyncTask<Void, Void, Void>*)*
An AsyncTask that does not define any parameters cannot pass data between the UI thread and the background thread. Data cannot be entered into the background thread, no progress can be reported, and no result is passed from the background thread to the UI thread.

Implementing only the doInBackground *method*
Without the callbacks that give progress updates or report results, the AsyncTask is merely a background task.

In either of these cases, use a Thread (Chapter 7) or HandlerThread (Chapter 8) instead.

Background Tasks That Need a Looper

The worker thread that executes the background task under `AsyncTask` has no associated `Looper` or `MessageQueue`, so message passing is unfeasible. In theory, it is possible to associate a `Looper` with the worker thread in either `doInBackground` or an executed `Runnable`, but this will block the used worker thread until the `Looper` finishes. When sequential execution is in effect, it will block all other `AsyncTask` executions in the application.

Even if the `Looper` is just prepared—but does not loop through the message queue—it will not be removed from the worker thread so that the thread can be used by other task executions. If a second task tries to prepare another `Looper` on that thread, a `RuntimeException` will be thrown.

If your application wants a `Looper`, use a `HandlerThread` (Chapter 8) instead of an `AsyncTask`.

Local Service

A local `Service` executes in parallel with other components in an application, typically to handle execution of long operations. The `Service` executes in the UI thread of the hosting application and requires additional background threads to execute the long operations. The `AsyncTask` is a candidate, but the application of global execution of tasks allows other components to utilize the execution environment simultaneously, and interfere with each other.

Services, therefore, should use one of these alternative solutions:

- `Thread` (Chapter 7)
- The Executor framework (Chapter 9)
- `HandlerThread` (Chapter 8)
- An `AsyncTask` with a custom executor

Using execute(Runnable)

Executing tasks as `Runnable` instances eliminates the major advantages of the `AsyncTask`; it merely puts the `Runnable` in the working queue and runs it when an idle thread is available in the thread pool. Because message passing is not enabled, the UI thread will receive no callbacks. Hence, this use case is like execution with a regular `Thread`, but with two main differences:

- Advantage: The task is executed in the `AsyncTask` internal thread pool that may already exist, which makes it resource-efficient.

- Disadvantage: The task always executes in the application global execution environment and can interfere with other tasks.

Alternative solutions include `Thread` (Chapter 7) and the Executor framework (Chapter 9).

Summary

This chapter looked into the—probably—most popular asynchronous technique in Android. It is easily understood, because it abstracts away many of the underlying complexities of background execution and thread communication. For clean use cases— e.g., executing a background task in an `Activity` in which the UI should be updated before, during, and after the execution—it is a great option. It is less desirable if execution is done in a `Service` or if it is necessary to tweak the `AsyncTask` to something it is not—e.g., a background thread with a `Looper`.

CHAPTER 11

Services

Android provides the `Service` component to run operations that are invisible to the user or that should be exposed to other applications. This chapter focuses on asynchronous execution with `Service`, although it is not an asynchronous execution environment by itself. The `Service` runs in the UI thread, so it can degrade responsiveness and cause ANRs, even though it does not interact directly with the UI. Still, the `Service` in combination with an asynchronous executor is a powerful tool for background task execution.

Why Use a Service for Asynchronous Execution?

Two risks are inherent in using regular threads instead of services for background operation:

Decouple lifecycles of components and threads
> The thread lifecycle is independent of the Android components and their underlying Java object lifecycles. A thread continues to run until the task either finishes or the process is killed, even after the component that started the thread finishes itself. Threads may keep references to Java objects so that they cannot be garbage collected until the thread terminates, as described in Chapter 6.

Lifecycles of the hosting processes
> If the runtime terminates the process, all of its threads are terminated. Thus, background tasks are terminated and not restarted by default when the process is restored. The runtime terminates processes depending on their process rank—as described in "Application termination" on page 7—and a process with no active components has a low ranking and is likely to be eligible for termination. This may cause unexpected termination of background tasks that should be allowed to finish. For example, an `Activity` that stores user data to a database in a background thread while the user navigates back leaves an empty process if there are no other com-

ponents running. This increases the risk of process termination, aborting the background thread before it can persist the data.

A `Service` can mitigate both the risk for memory leaks and the risk of having tasks terminated prematurely. The `Service` has a lifecycle that can be controlled from background threads: it couples the component lifecycle with the thread's lifetime. Hence, the `Service` component can be active while the background thread runs and be destroyed when it finishes, which enables better lifecycle control. As Figure 11-1 illustrates, the `BroadcastReceiver` and `Activity` lifecycles are decoupled from the background thread's execution, whereas the `Service` lifecycle can end when the background task is done. Consequently, the process contains a `Service` component throughout the background thread's execution. The details of starting and stopping `Services` are explained later in this chapter.

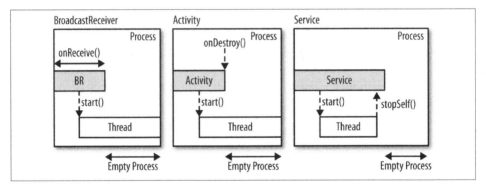

Figure 11-1. Background thread execution in BroadcastReceiver and Activity compared to Service; both can execute in the same process as other components or in separate processes

To offload background execution, a `BroadcastReceiver` or `Activity` should start a `Service` that then starts a thread, as shown in Figure 11-2.

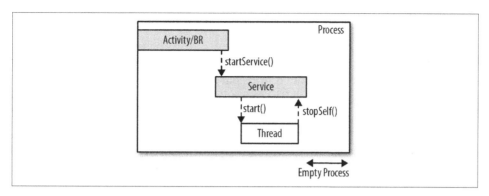

Figure 11-2. Offloading background tasks to Service

Local, Remote, and Global Services

A Service is started through intents that are sent from other components, referred to as *client components*. The invocation can occur either local to the process or across process boundaries, depending on where the Service runs with respect to the client component. If the Service is used within the same process as the client, it is local, whereas a Service used from external processes is remote. Figure 11-3 shows the possibilities.

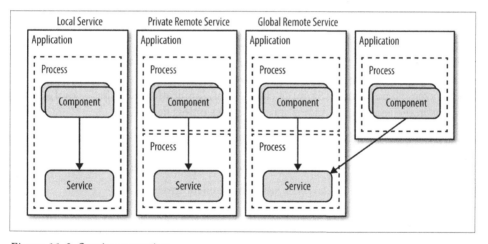

Figure 11-3. Service execution

Local service

> The Service runs in the same process as the invoking component; i.e., the components run on the same UI thread and share the same heap memory area. Hence,

the `Service` can share Java objects with clients so that the shared objects run on the calling thread in the client.

Private remote service

The `Service` runs in a remote process but is accessible only to client components that belong to the application. The remote process has its own UI thread. Thus, the `Service` UI thread does not delay the execution of the UI threads of the client components. The remote `Service` cannot expose objects directly to the clients, as they do not share the the same heap memory area. Instead, clients call the `Service` through the binder mechanism in Android—see Chapter 5—which contains a pool of binder threads used to invoke the remote methods. Thus, method invocations can be invoked concurrently on different threads from the binder thread pool, although the clients call the methods sequentially. The `Service` has to ensure thread safety during remote access from binder threads.

Global remote service

The `Service` is exposed to other applications. It has the same properties as the private remote service with its own UI thread, heap memory, and execution on binder threads, but it cannot be referred to by the `Service` class name because that is not known to external applications. Instead, external access is provided through intent filters.

By far the most common use case is to run the `Service` in the local process, where it executes background tasks deployed by client components—e.g., a music player service. The advantage of the local service are simplicity and saving memory. The possibility of sharing Java objects within the process avoids the complexities of IPC and AIDL. Furthermore, the `Service` is part of an already running process—i.e., you don't need to run another process that consumes memory. Each process consumes several megabytes of RAM, even if it only hosts a `Service` component. Applications should be good Android citizens in the ecosystem and not start processes unless needed.

In short, the advantages with running in the local process are:

- Easier and faster communication through shared Java objects instead of IPC
- Control over `Service` task execution from client threads
- Less memory consumption

Although local services are normally preferred and sufficient, there may be requirements that call for remote execution. Typically, that's when multiple applications require the same functionality that is independent enough to be shared across the applications —e.g., a GPS or music service. Another advantage of remote execution is that errors that stop the `Service` are contained in the remote process and do not affect the processes run by the client components.

Creation and Execution

Services are defined as extensions of the `Service` class and must be defined in the Android Manifest. The `<name>` attribute contains a fully qualified classname, which points to an implementation class that extends `Service` in the application:[1]

```
<service
    android:name="com.wifill.eat.EatService"/>
```

By default, the `Service` component runs locally in the application process where it is defined and shares the same UI thread with all other components in that process. But just as with all Android components, the `Service` can be assigned to run in a remote process, in which case it is not executing on the same UI thread as the other application components. The assigned process is defined by the `android:process` attribute, which declares the name of the process and the access rights. A private remote process has an attribute value that starts with a colon (":"):

```
<service
    android:name="com.wifill.eat.EatService"
    android:process=":com.wifill.eat.PrivateProcess"/>
```

Execution in a global remote process—accessible from other applications with the right permissions (*http://bit.ly/R7NNJn*)—is defined by leading off the process name with a capital letter:

```
<service
    android:name="com.wifill.eat.EatService"
    android:process="Com.wifill.eat.PrivateProcess">
    <intent-filter>
        <action android:name="..." />
        <category android:name="..." />
    </intent-filter>
</service>
```

As the `Service` class name is not visible to other applications, it defines an `IntentFilter` (*http://bit.ly/1iH6oYC*) that external applications have to match against.

Lifecycle

A `Service` component is active between the callbacks to `onCreate` and `onDestroy`—both are called once per lifecycle—where the implementation can initialize and clean up data, respectively:

```
public class EatService extends Service {
```

---

1. See the documentation for the `<service>` element (*http://bit.ly/1i68xHa*) for the full list of attributes and elements.

```java
    @Override
    public void onCreate() { /* Initialize component */ }

    @Override
    public void onDestroy() { /* Clean up used resources */ }

    @Override
    public IBinder onBind(Intent intent) { /* Return communication interface */ }
}
```

The only mandatory method is onBind, which returns a communication interface to clients that bind to the Service. Through this interface, clients can invoke methods defined in the Service either in the local process or remotely.

There are two types of services:

Started Service

> Created by the first start request and destroyed by the first stop request. In between, start requests only pass data to the Service.

Bound Service

> Created when the first component binds to the Service and destroyed when all components have unbound from it. In other words, a bounded Service lifecycle is based on the number of binding components. As long at least one component is bound to the Service, it stays active.

The Service component is created by client components that either start it through Context.startService or bind to it through Context.bindService. These are two fundamentally different approaches with different access methods and communication mechanisms, summarized in Table 11-1.

Table 11-1. Started versus bound Service

	Started	Bound
Create	Context.startService(Intent)	Context.bindService
Destroy	Context.stopService(Intent) from a client component or Service.stopSelf() from itself.	Occurs when all bound components have unbound from the Service with Context.unbind Service().
Communication	Data is passed in the Intent of the start request.	Binding component receives a communication interface.

If some process starts a Service component, the component lasts until it stops itself or is stopped externally. If processes bind to a Service component, it starts when the first remote process binds to it, and lasts until all processes that have bound to it unbind from it. If one process starts the component and others bind to it, it lasts as long as both conditions hold: it will not be terminated until it is explicitly stopped and all processes have unbound from it. The various cases are shown in Figure 11-4.

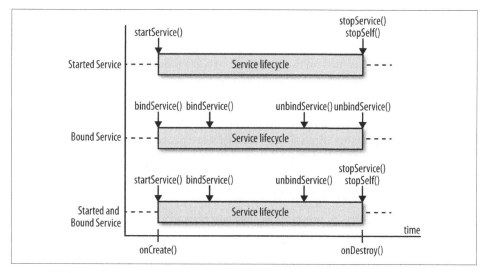

Figure 11-4. Service lifecycle

Started Service

Components invoke `Context.startService(Intent)` to send start requests to a `Service`, which can be invoked by multiple components and multiple times from every component during a lifecycle. The first start request creates and starts the `Service`, whereas consecutive start requests just pass on the `Intent` to the started `Service` so that the data conveyed in the `Intent` can be processed.

Services always have to implement `onBind`, but started services—which do not support binding—should provide a trivial implementation that just return `null`:

```
public class StartedEatService extends Service {

    @Override
    public int onStartCommand(Intent intent, int flags, int startId) { ... }

    @Override
    public IBinder onBind(Intent intent) { return null; }

}
```

Started services must implement an `onStartCommand` method that handles start requests. The method is invoked each time a start request (`Context.startService`) from a client component is ready to be processed. Start requests are delivered sequentially to `onStartCommand` and remain pending in the runtime until preceding start requests are processed or offloaded from the UI thread. In spite of the sequential processing of start requests, calls to `startService` do not block even if they have to wait to be processed in the `Service`. A start request supplies an `Intent` that conveys data that can be processed in the `Service`.

`onStartCommand` is executed on the UI thread, so you should spawn background threads within the method to execute long-running operations, not only to preserve responsiveness but also to enable concurrent execution of multiple start requests.

The sequential processing of `onStartCommand` on the UI thread guarantees thread safety. No synchronization is required unless the tasks are processed concurrently on background threads spawned from the UI thread.

Implementing onStartCommand

`onStartCommand` is the key method for implementing started `Services` and initiating asynchronous task execution. Tasks should be offloaded to an asynchronous executor that can be either sequential or concurrent. Because the `Service` process, along with all its background threads, can be terminated by the runtime, `onStartCommand` includes a flag that defines how start requests—both pending and processed—should be handled after process termination.

The arguments are:

Intent
> Data to be used for the asynchronous execution; e.g., a URL to a network resource that shall be retrieved.

Delivery method
> A flag reflecting the history of the start request. This argument may contain other flags in future versions of Android. Possible values are currently 0, `START_FLAG_RE DELIVERY` (value of 1), or `START_FLAG_RETRY` (value of 2). The following section will explain this argument.

Start ID
> A unique identifier provided by the runtime for this start request. If the process is terminated and restarted, `onStartCommand` is called with the same start ID.

The return value tells the runtime whether to restart the `Service` and resubmit the `Intent` argument, in case the runtime has to terminate the process for lack of resources and then restart it. This will be explained in the following section.

Options for Restarting

Like any Android application, your `Service` may be terminated by the runtime if there are too many processes running on the device. In fact, as a background process, your `Service` has a greater chance of being killed than many other processes ("Application termination" on page 7). A client can also terminate your `Service` through a `Context.stopService` call. Finally, a `Service` can terminate itself through `Service.stopSelf`. This section covers termination by either the runtime or a client, not a clean termination through `Service.stopSelf`.

The return value of `onStartCommand` and the second argument (the delivery method flag) let you control what happens after your `Service` is terminated. You may want to restart the same request, which you can do by asking the runtime to resubmit the `Intent` that you received in this `onStartCommand` call. Or you may abandon that `Intent`. If you abandon the current `Intent`, you have another choice:

- You can ask the runtime to restart your `Service` only if other requests are pending, and if there are none, to restart the `Service` when a new request comes from a client.

- You can ask the runtime to restart your `Service` as soon as it can, even if there are no requests.

 If a `Service` is terminated while the `onStartCommand` method is running, the `Intent` that was submitted never gets a chance to start. Therefore, it is still considered a pending request, not a started request.

All of these options are enabled by the return value from the call, which is called the *operational mode*:

START_STICKY

The `Service` will be restarted in a new process whether or not there are any requests pending. The `Intent` of the request that was terminated will not be resubmitted. However, the `Service` will receive any pending start requests that remained undelivered when the previous `Service` process was terminated. The pending start requests are delivered with the `START_FLAG_RETRY` flag set in the call's second argument. If there are no pending start requests, `onStartCommand` is invoked with a `null` value for the `Intent` argument.

START_NOT_STICKY

Like `START_STICKY`, except that the `Service` will be restarted only if there were pending start requests when the process was terminated. An `Intent` will always be passed.

START_REDELIVER_INTENT

The `Service` will be restarted and receives both pending requests and requests that were previously started and had no chance to finish. The pending requests are delivered with the START_FLAG_RETRY flag set in the second argument, whereas the previously started requests are redelivered with the START_FLAG_REDELIVERY set.

Value 0
> Default value, used when a new request is submitted. A new process is started to run the Service.

START_FLAG_REDELIVERY *(value 1)*
> Indicates that the Intent is one that was previously submitted to the Service.

START_FLAG_RETRY *(value 2)*
> Indicates that the Intent was not previously submitted or never had a chance to start, but was pending when the Service was terminated and restarted.

Here are sample use cases for the return value:

Restart a single background task
> In this scenario, you want the Service to execute a background task that should be controlled from the client components. The Service should not finish until one component has invoked stopService. Return START_STICKY so that the Service is always restarted and the background task can be restarted.

Ignore background tasks
> In this scenario, the Service executes a task that should not be resumed after process termination. An example might be a periodic task that can wait until its next scheduled execution. Return START_NOT_STICKY so that the Service will not be automatically restarted.

Restart unfinished background tasks
> In this scenario, the Service executes background tasks that you want to be resumed. Return START_REDELIVER_INTENT so that all the Intents are redelivered, and the tasks can be restarted on new threads. Furthermore, the tasks can be configured with the same data from the Intent as the original task.

User-Controlled Service

User-controlled services may be used for operations that should be running until instructed by other Android components that they should terminate. The termination is typically triggered by a user action. Applications that should continue to execute operations and handle events without a visible UI are candidates for extracting functionality to a Service: for instance, playing music, managing location, tracking updates from a network resource, or setting up a Bluetooth connection, as "Example: Bluetooth connection" on page 187 illustrates.

Long-running or blocking operations need to be executed asynchronously on background threads created by the Service. But the Service lifecycle does not control the lifetime of background threads: they continue to run after the component has been destroyed. In other words, the threads are asynchronous tasks that run after a client has called stopService. As Chapter 6 showed, the lingering threads pose a risk for leaking the memory of the objects they reference. A Service that is started and stopped repeatedly can leave more threads lingering for every lifecycle, each one referencing a different Service instance and forcing it to be retained in memory.[2] To reduce the risk for memory leaks and performance issues caused by many lingering threads, the Service should not be restarted repeatedly, if possible. It is better to let the Service stay alive as long as needed in order to limit the number of lingering threads and the memory leakage.

Example: Bluetooth connection

A Bluetooth connection is generally initialized by the user when pairing with another device. The pairing can take a long time, and while waiting, the user may navigate away from the application. Therefore, to ensure that the pairing process can continue independently of the user navigation, the pairing should be done in a Service. The Bluetooth pairing API is synchronous and cannot be called from the UI thread methods, so the Service requires additional asynchronous pairing in a background thread.

The following example contains a user-controlled BluetoothService to set up and cancel the pairing, and a basic BluetoothActivity with two buttons that control the Service lifecycle. When the BluetoothService is started—i.e., onStartCommand is called—it initiates a Thread to handle the pairing and keeps a state variable—mListening—to ensure that only one pairing operation is active. Consequently, only one thread at the time will be alive. The pairing task defined in a Runnable executes until a connection is set up or cancelled, after which the background thread terminates.

The BluetoothService shares an entry point–COMMAND_START_LISTENING–to start the pairing process, but no method for stopping it. Instead, the pairing process is terminated when the BluetoothService stops itself, and its onDestroy method cancels the pairing so that the background thread can terminate. Hence, there are no lingering background threads after the Service is destroyed:

```
public class BluetoothService extends Service {

    public static final String COMMAND_KEY = "command_key";
    public static final String COMMAND_START_LISTENING =
        "command_start_discovery";

    private static final UUID MY_UUID = ...;
    private static final String SDP_NAME = ...;
```

---

2. Like activities, a new Service object is created for every lifecycle of the Service component.

```java
private BluetoothAdapter mAdapter;
private BluetoothServerSocket mServerSocket;
private boolean mListening = false;
private Thread listeningThread;

public IBinder onBind(Intent intent) {
    return null;
}

@Override
public void onCreate() {
    super.onCreate();
    mAdapter = BluetoothAdapter.getDefaultAdapter();
}

@Override
public int onStartCommand(Intent intent, int flags, int startId) {
    if (mAdapter != null) {
        if (intent.getStringExtra(COMMAND_KEY).equals
            (COMMAND_START_LISTENING)
            && mListening == false) { ❶
            startListening();
        }
    }
    return START_REDELIVER_INTENT; ❷
}

private void startListening() {
    mListening = true;
    listeningThread = new Thread(new Runnable() {

        @Override
        public void run() {
            BluetoothSocket socket = null;
            try {
                mServerSocket =
                    mAdapter.listenUsingInsecureRfcommWithServiceRecord(
                    SDP_NAME, MY_UUID);
                socket = mServerSocket.accept(); ❸

                if (socket != null) {
                    // Handle BT connection
                }

            } catch (IOException e) {
                Log.d(TAG, "Server socket closed");
            }
        }
    });
    listeningThread.start();
}
```

```
        private void stopListening() {
            mListening = false;
            try {
                if (mServerSocket != null) {
                    mServerSocket.close(); ❹
                }
            } catch (IOException e) {
                // Handle error
            }
        }

        @Override
        public void onDestroy() {
            super.onDestroy();
            stopListening(); ❺
        }
    }
```

❶   Control the number of threads so that only one pairing at the time can be done.

❷   If the process is shut down, the Intent will be redelivered so that we can resume the pairing.

❸   Blocking call.

❹   Release the blocking call.

❺   The Service is destroyed and stops the pairing so that the background thread can finish.

The BluetoothActivity controls the Service lifecycle with a start command that initiates the pairing and then stops the pairing by destroying the BluetoothService that manages the background thread:

```
public class BluetoothActivity extends Activity {

    public void onCreate(Bundle savedInstanceState) {
        ...
    }

    public void onClickStartListening(View v) {
        Intent intent = new Intent(this, BluetoothService.class);
        intent.putExtra(BluetoothService.COMMAND_KEY,
        BluetoothService.COMMAND_START_LISTENING);
        startService(intent);
    }


    public void onClickStopListening(View v) {
        Intent intent = new Intent(this, BluetoothService.class);
        stopService(intent);
    }
}
```

Task-Controlled Service

Task-controlled services are typically used to ensure that background threads can be allowed to finish execution with reduced risk of being stopped due to process termination. When the Service stops itself with stopSelf, control over the Service component's lifecycle lies with the processed task. In other words, the task determines when the component will be destroyed.

The lifetime of the background thread determines the lifetime of the Service, as shown earlier in Figure 11-2. Therefore, the component is always active while the task is running on the background thread, which raises its chances of being kept alive. (As "Application termination" on page 7 explained, an empty process is among the first to be terminated by the runtime.) So task-controlled services allow applications to utilize a Service for long-running operations on background threads.

Example: Concurrent download

This example illustrates the use of a concurrent file download executor running in a Service. The time it takes to download a file over the network is nondeterministic—and often very long—because it depends on both the file size and the network connection quality. Therefore, we want to avoid downloading the files from an Activity because the user can navigate away from the application during download, leaving an empty process that can be terminated by the runtime before the download has finished. Instead, we let the download be handled by a task-controlled Service that is independent of user navigation and reduces the probability that the runtime terminates the process during the download.

The implementation fulfills some requirements:

- Concurrent downloads improve performance.

- The Service can resume downloading of unfinished files if the process is terminated by the runtime.

- The Service stops when there are no more download requests to handle so that its process can be terminated, freeing up resources once it is no longer needed. In this example, the Service runs in the application process, but it can easily be configured to run in a separate process ("Creation and Execution" on page 181).

The DownloadService is registered in the Android Manifest with an action and a scheme:

```
<service android:name=".DownloadService">
    <intent-filter>
        <action android:name="com.wifill.eat.ACTION_DOWNLOAD"/>
        <data android:scheme="http" />
```

```
        </intent-filter>
    </service>
```

The file download can be triggered from any application component by issuing an Intent with an ACTION_DOWNLOAD action, as shown in the following code from the DownloadActivity. Typically, the intent would be started by a button click that triggers the onStartDownload callback:

```
public class DownloadActivity extends Activity {

    String mUrl = ...; // url details omitted

    public void onStartDownload(View v) {
        Intent intent = new Intent("com.wifill.eat.ACTION_DOWNLOAD");
        intent.setData(Uri.parse(mUrl));
        startService(intent);
    }
}
```

The DownloadService is defined to be started and not bound to, and it stops once all the start requests have been processed. Concurrent execution is done in a thread pool with a fixed size of four worker threads. The long-operating requests are submitted to the thread pool to offload them from the UI thread and to make the Service available to receive new start requests:

```
public class DownloadService extends Service {

    private ExecutorService mDownloadExecutor;
    private int mCommandCount; ❶

    public IBinder onBind(Intent intent) { ❷
        return null;
    }

    @Override
    public void onCreate() {
        super.onCreate();
        mDownloadExecutor = Executors.newFixedThreadPool(4);
    }

    @Override
    public void onDestroy() {
        super.onDestroy();
        mDownloadExecutor.shutdownNow();
    }

    @Override
    public int onStartCommand(Intent intent, int flags, int startId) {
        synchronized (this) {
            mCommandCount++;
        }
        if (intent != null) {
```

```
            downloadFile(intent.getData(), startId);
        }
        return START_REDELIVER_INTENT; ❸
    }

    private void downloadFile(final Uri uri) {
        mDownloadExecutor.submit(new Runnable() {
            @Override
            public void run() {

                // The file download code is omitted

                synchronized (this) { ❹
                    if (--mCommandCount <= 0) {
                        stopSelf();
                    }
                }
            }
        });
```

❶ Track the number of ongoing file downloads. The variable is incremented when a start request is received and decremented when the background task is finished.

❷ The interface requires an onBind method to be implemented, but because this is a started—and not a bound—Service, we do not have to return an IBinder implementation; instead return null.

❸ If the process is terminated by the runtime, we want the Service to be restarted with the intents from the start requests that hold the URLs to download so that the downloads can be resumed. Hence, we return START_REDELIVER_INTENT.

❹ When a download has finished, the task checks whether it is time to stop the Service. If it is the last start request, indicated when mCommandCount <= 0, we stop the Service.

Bound Service

A bound Service defines a communication interface that the binding components—referred to as *client components*—can utilize to invoke methods in the Service. The communication interface is defined as a set of methods that the Service implements and executes in the Service process. The client components can bind to a Service through Context.bindService. Multiple client components can bind to a Service—and invoke methods in it—simultaneously.

The Service is created when the first binding is set up, and is destroyed when there are no more client components keeping the binding alive. Internally, the Service keeps a reference counter on the number of bound components, and when the reference counter is decremented to zero, the Service is destroyed. A client component can terminate a binding explicitly with `Context.unbindService`, but the binding is also terminated by the runtime if the client component lifecycle ends.

The outline for a bound `Service` is:

```
public class EatService extends Service {

    @Override
    public IBinder onBind(Intent intent) { /* Return communication interface */ }

    @Override
    public boolean onUnbind(Intent intent) { /* Last component has unbound */ }
}
```

onBind
: Called when a client binds to a `Service` the first time through `Context.bindSer vice`. The invocation supplies an `Intent` and the method returns an `IBinder` implementation that the client can use to interact with the `Service`.

onUnbind
: Called when all bindings are unbound.

Components bind to services and retrieve a communication interface for sending requests and receiving responses, either within the process or across processes, as in IPC through a `Binder`. The communication interface consists of methods to be invoked by the client component, but the execution is implemented in the `Service` component.

A bound `Service` returns an `IBinder` implementation from `onBind` that the client can use as a communication channel. The `IBinder` is returned to the client through the `ServiceConnection` interface that the binding client supplies when invoking `bindSer vice`:

```
boolean bindService (Intent service, ServiceConnection conn, int flags)
```

The `Intent` identifies the `Service` to bind to, but it cannot pass on any `Extra` parameters to the `Service`. The binding is observed by the `ServiceConnection`, and the binding client component provides an implementation to get notified when the binding is established:

```
private class EatServiceConnection implements ServiceConnection {

    @Override
    public void onServiceConnected(ComponentName componentName,
                                   IBinder iBinder) {
        /* Connection established.
           Retrieve communication interface from the IBinder */
    }

    @Override
    public void onServiceDisconnected(ComponentName componentName) {
        /*  Service not available.
```

```
                          Remote service process is probably terminated. */
        }
```

The `flags` argument can be either 0 or a collection of allowed arguments (*http://bit.ly/ 1i6d1O2*). Options for this argument can adjust the rank of the `Service`'s process or determine the strategy for restarting the `Service`. The most commonly used flag is `BIND_AUTO_CREATE`, which recreates the `Service` if it is destroyed, as long as a client component is bound to it.

From a client perspective, the fundamental binding to the `Service` is the same regardless of which process the `Service` runs in. However, if the `Service` runs in the local process, communication is easier than with remote processes. Also, the behavior and management of asynchronous execution differ between the three communication types:

- Local binding, covered in the following section
- Remote binding with `Messenger`, covered in "Message Passing Using the Binder" on page 83
- Remote binding with AIDL, covered in "AIDL" on page 77

Local Binding

Local binding to a `Service` is the most common type. A client component that binds to a `Service` in the same application and process can benefit because both components run in the same VM and share the same heap memory. There is no need to be concerned with the complexities of IPC. Instead, the `Service` can define the communication interface as a Java class and send it to the client wrapped in a `Binder` object. The following example provides itself as a communication interface (through `return BoundLocal Service.this`), but it could just as well define the interface as an internal class:

```
public class BoundLocalService extends Service {
    private final ServiceBinder mBinder = new ServiceBinder();

    public IBinder onBind(Intent intent) {
        return mBinder;
    }

    public class ServiceBinder extends Binder {
        public BoundLocalService getService() {
            return BoundLocalService.this;
        }
    }

    // Methods published to clients.
    public void publishedMethod1() { ... }
    public void publishedMethod2() { ... }
```

```
    }
```

The BoundLocalService creates a Binder subclass called ServiceBinder, which wraps the Java object of the Service and returns it to the binding client components. The Service implements methods that can be invoked by bound clients.

The clients retrieve the Binder implementation in the ServiceConnection.onService Connected() callback, which contains the communication interface.

The client BoundLocalActivity retrieves the communication interface—i.e., the Bound LocalService object itself—from the ServiceBinder and stores it as a member variable for later reference:

```
public class BoundLocalActivity extends Activity {
    private LocalServiceConnection mLocalServiceConnection =
        new LocalServiceConnection();
    private BoundLocalService mBoundLocalService;
    private boolean mIsBound;

    public void onCreate(Bundle savedInstanceState) {
        super.onCreate(savedInstanceState);
        bindService(new Intent(BoundLocalActivity.this, BoundLocalService.class),
            mLocalServiceConnection, Service.BIND_AUTO_CREATE);
        mIsBound = true;
    }

    @Override
    protected void onDestroy() {
        super.onDestroy();
        if (mIsBound) {
            try {
                unbindService(mLocalServiceConnection);
                mIsBound = false;
            } catch (IllegalArgumentException e) {
                // No bound service
            }
        }
    }

    private class LocalServiceConnection implements ServiceConnection {

        @Override
        public void onServiceConnected(ComponentName componentName,
                                IBinder iBinder) {
            mBoundLocalService = ((BoundLocalService.ServiceBinder)iBinder)
                            .getService();

            // At this point clients can invoke methods in the Service,
            // i.e. publishedMethod1 and publishedMethod2.

        }
```

```
        @Override
        public void onServiceDisconnected(ComponentName componentName) {
            mBoundLocalService = null;
        }
    }
}
```

When the client has bound to the local Service, it can invoke the methods that were published in its communication interface. The invocations are done directly to the Java object created in the Service, and they are executed on the thread of the calling client. Thus, long operations that require execution off the UI thread can utilize asynchronous behavior implemented either in the client or in the Service.

Our BoundLocalService executes tasks on a new background thread for every invocation of the published method in the communication interface:

```
public class BoundLocalService extends Service {

    public interface OperationListener {❶
        public void onOperationDone(int i);
    }

    public void doLongAsyncOperation(final int i,
            final OperationListener listener) { ❷
        new Thread(new Runnable() {
            @Override
            public void run() {
                int result = longOperation(i);
                listener.onOperationDone(result); ❸
            }
        }).start();
    }

    private int longOperation(int i) {
        // Return a result from the long operation.
    }
}
```

❶   Callback listener to report the result to the client.

❷   Communication interface published to the client.

❸   The thread holds a reference to the listener that is defined in the binding client component. This poses a risk for a memory leak of the object tree that the listener references in the client.

A BoundLocalActivity, which invokes BoundLocalService and its executor, defines an implementation of the OperationListener to retrieve the result from the background execution and use it on the UI thread, which is a common use case. In the BoundLocalService, the background thread references the listener; anything referenced in the listener cannot be garbage collected while the thread is running (see Chapter 6). Hence, our `BoundLocalActivity` defines a static inner class `ServiceListener` with weak references to the `Activity`:

```java
public class BoundLocalActivity extends Activity {

    // Activity creation and Service binding omitted.
    // See previous BoundLocalService listing.

    private static class ServiceListener implements
        BoundLocalService.OperationListener {

        private WeakReference<BoundLocalActivity> mWeakActivity;

        public ServiceListener(BoundLocalActivity activity) {
            this.mWeakActivity =
            new WeakReference<BoundLocalActivity1>(activity);
        }

        @Override
        public void onOperationDone(final int someResult) {
            final BoundLocalActivity localReferenceActivity =
            mWeakActivity.get();
            if (localReferenceActivity != null) {
                localReferenceActivity.runOnUiThread(new Runnable(){
                    @Override
                    public void run() {

                        // Update on the UI thread

                    }
                });
            }
        }
    }

    public void onClickExecuteOnClientUIThread(View v) {
        if (mBoundLocalService != null) {
            mBoundLocalService.doLongAsyncOperation(new ServiceListener(this));
        }
    }
}
```

Choosing an Asynchronous Technique

Asynchronous task execution in `Services` can be sequential or concurrent, and can utilize any of the techniques described in this book. However, for two use cases, alternatives may be considered:

Sequential execution for a task-controlled service

A task controlled `Service` can execute tasks concurrently or sequentially, depending on used asynchrounous technique. When the tasks are executed sequentially—e.g., with a `HandlerThread`, `Executors.newSingleThreadExecutor`, or any customized `Executor`—it is better to use an `IntentService` (Chapter 12) because it has built-in support for sequential task execution that terminates the `Service` when there are no more tasks to execute.

`AsyncTask` *with global executor in local process*

The `Service` component runs independently of—and often simultaneously with—other components in the same process. Hence, background tasks are likely to execute at the same time as background tasks of other components in the process. The `AsyncTask` risks delaying tasks because it has a process global executor, as described in Chapter 10, and the same executor is shared for all tasks. Hence, `AsyncTasks` that execute in the same process as other components should use a custom executor—i.e., a nonglobal executor—or an alternative technique, such as a thread pool.

Summary

A `Service` runs in the background on the UI thread and it is of great use to offload tasks to background threads. The lifecycle of the `Service` component can be better controlled to fit background threads without letting user interaction interfere with the destruction of the component, as with an `Activity`. The `Service` can be active until all background tasks have finished.

CHAPTER 12

IntentService

In Chapter 11 we discussed how the Service lifecycle can handle asynchronous execution while increasing the process rank and avoiding termination of the background threads by the runtime. The Service, however, is not an asynchronous technique by itself, because it executes on the UI thread. This shortcoming is addressed in the In tentService, which extends the Service class. The IntentService has the properties of the Service lifecycle but also adds built-in task processing on a background thread.

Fundamentals

The IntentService executes tasks on a single background thread—i.e., all tasks are executed sequentially. Users of the IntentService trigger the asynchronous execution by passing an Intent with Context.startService. If the IntentService is running, the Intent is queued until the background thread is ready to process it. If the Intent Service is not running, a new component lifecycle is initiated and finishes when there are no more Intents to process. Hence, the IntentService runs only while there are tasks to execute.

Like a task-controlled Service ("Task-Controlled Service" on page 190), an IntentSer vice always has an active component, reducing the risk of terminating the task prematurely.

 The background task executor in the IntentService is a Handler Thread. Unlike the default executor in AsyncTask, the IntentSer vice executor is per instance and not per application. So an application can have multiple IntentService instances, where every instance executes tasks sequentially but independent of other Intent Service instances.

To use the `IntentService`, override it with an application-specific implementation, declaring it in the `AndroidManifest.xml` as a `Service` component:

```
<service android:name=".SimpleIntentService"/>
```

`IntentService` subclasses only have to implement the `onHandleIntent` method, as the following `SimpleIntentService` shows:

```
public class SimpleIntentService extends IntentService {
    public SimpleIntentService() {
        super(SimpleIntentService.class.getName());
        setIntentRedelivery(true);
    }

    @Override
    protected void onHandleIntent(Intent intent) {
        // Called on a background thread
    }
}
```

The constructor has to call the superclass with a string that names the background thread —for debugging purposes. Here is also where to specify whether the `IntentService` shall be restored if the process is killed. By default, the `IntentService` is restored only if there are pending start requests, but an invocation of `setIntentRedelivery(true)` will redeliver the last delivered intent.

 The `IntentService` internally handles the two start types `START_NOT_STICKY` and `START_REDELIVER_INTENT` described in "Options for Restarting" on page 184. The first is default, so the latter needs to be set with `setIntentRedelivery(true)`.

Clients that want to use the `IntentService` create a start request with `Context.start` `Service` and pass an `Intent` with data that the service should handle:

```
public class SimpleActivity extends Activity {

    public void onButtonClick(View v) {
        Intent intent = new Intent(this, SimpleIntentService.class);
        intent.putExtra("data", data);
        startService(intent);
    }
}
```

 There is no need to stop the `IntentService` with `stopSelf`, because that is done internally.

Good Ways to Use an IntentService

The `IntentService` is suitable for when you want to offload tasks easily from the UI thread to a background thread with sequential task processing, giving the task a component that is always active in order to raise the process rank.

Sequentially Ordered Tasks

Tasks that should be executed sequentially and independently of the originating component can use an `IntentService` to ensure that all submitted tasks are queued in the active `IntentService` component.

Example: Web service communication

Communication with network resources, such as web services, are often done in a sequential manner—i.e., one resource is retrieved that contains future instructions on how to interact with other resources.[1] The HTTP protocol interacts with the network resources using the GET, POST, PUT and DELETE request types. The request can originate in a user interaction or a scheduled system operation, but can be processed by an `IntentService`.

In this example, the request originates from an `Activity`, typically initialized by a user action. For simplicity's sake, only the most common types of requests are handled: GET for retrieving data and POST for sending it. Both are offloaded to an `IntentService`. The responses from the requests are returned in a `ResultReceiver`:

```java
public class WebServiceActivity extends Activity {

    private final static String getUrl = "...";
    private final static String postUrl = "...";

    private ResultReceiver mReceiver;

    public WebServiceActivity() {
        mReceiver = new ResultReceiver(new Handler()) { ❶
            @Override
            protected void onReceiveResult(int resultCode, Bundle resultData) {
                int httpStatus = resultCode;
                String jsonResult = null;
                if (httpStatus == 200) { // OK
                    if (resultData != null) {
                        jsonResult= resultData.getString(
                        WebService.BUNDLE_KEY_REQUEST_RESULT);
                        // Omitted: Handle response
                    }
```

---

1. This is the basis of a REST interface.

```
                }
                else {
                    // Omitted: Handle error
                }
            }

        };
    }

    private void doPost() { ❷
        Intent intent = new Intent(this, WebService.class);
        intent.setData(Uri.parse(postUrl));
        intent.putExtra(WebService.INTENT_KEY_JSON, "{\"foo\":\"bar\"}");
        intent.putExtra(WebService.INTENT_KEY_RECEIVER, mReceiver);
        startService(intent);
    }

    private void doGet() { ❸
        Intent intent = new Intent(this, WebService.class);
        intent.setData(Uri.parse(getUrl));
        intent.putExtra(WebService.INTENT_KEY_RECEIVER, mReceiver);
        startService(intent);
    }

}
```

❶   Create the ResultReceiver that is passed to the IntentService so that the result of the operation can be returned.

❷   Issue a POST request with JSON-formatted content.

❸   Issue a GET request.

The IntentService receives the requests in onHandleIntent and processes them sequentially. The data from the WebServiceActivity determines the request type, URL, ResultReceiver, and possibly the data to be sent:

```
public class WebService extends IntentService {
    private static final String TAG = WebService.class.getName();
    public static final int GET = 1;
    public static final int POST = 2;

    public static final String INTENT_KEY_REQUEST_TYPE =
    "com.eat.INTENT_KEY_REQUEST_TYPE";
    public static final String INTENT_KEY_JSON =
    "com.eat.INTENT_KEY_JSON";
    public static final String INTENT_KEY_RECEIVER =
    "com.eat.INTENT_KEY_RECEIVER";
    public static final String BUNDLE_KEY_REQUEST_RESULT =
    "com.eat.BUNDLE_KEY_REQUEST_RESULT";

    public WebService() {
```

```
        super(TAG);
}

@Override
protected void onHandleIntent(Intent intent) {

    Uri uri = intent.getData(); ❶
    int requestType = intent.getIntExtra(INTENT_KEY_REQUEST_TYPE, 0);
    String json = (String)intent.getSerializableExtra(INTENT_KEY_JSON);
    ResultReceiver receiver = intent.getParcelableExtra(INTENT_KEY_RECEIVER);

    try {
        HttpRequestBase request = null;
        switch (requestType) { ❷
            case GET: {
                request = new HttpGet();
                // Request setup omitted
                break;
            }
            case POST: {
                request = new HttpPost();
                if (json != null) {
                    ((HttpPost)request).setEntity(new StringEntity(json));
                }
                // Request setup omitted
                break;
            }
        }

        if (request != null) {
            request.setURI(new URI(uri.toString()));
            HttpResponse response = doRequest(request); ❸
            HttpEntity httpEntity = response.getEntity();
            StatusLine responseStatus = response.getStatusLine();
            int statusCode = responseStatus != null ?
            responseStatus.getStatusCode() : 0;

            if (httpEntity != null) {
                Bundle resultBundle = new Bundle();
                resultBundle.putString(BUNDLE_KEY_REQUEST_RESULT,
                EntityUtils.toString(httpEntity));
                receiver.send(statusCode, resultBundle); ❹
            }
            else {
                receiver.send(statusCode, null);
            }
        }
        else {
            receiver.send(0, null);

        }
    }
```

```
            catch (IOException e) {
                receiver.send(0, null);
            } catch (URISyntaxException e) {
                e.printStackTrace();
            }
        }

        private HttpResponse doRequest(HttpRequestBase request) throws IOException {
            HttpClient client = new DefaultHttpClient();

            // HttpClient configuration omitted

            return client.execute(request);
        }
    }
```

❶ Retrieve the necessary data from the `Intent`.

❷ Create request type depending on `Intent` data.

❸ Do the network request.

❹ Return the successful result to the `WebServiceActivity`.

Asynchronous Execution in BroadcastReceiver

A `BroadcastReceiver` is an application entry point—i.e., it can be the first Android component to be started in the process. The start can be triggered from other applications or system services. Either way, the `BroadcastReceiver` receives an `Intent` in the `onReceive` callback, which is invoked on the UI thread. Hence, asynchronous execution is required if any long-running operations shall be executed.

However, the `BroadcastReceiver` component is active only during the execution of `onReceive`. Thus, an asynchronous task may be left executing after the component is destroyed—leaving the process empty if the `BroadcastReceiver` was the entry point—which potentially makes the runtime kill the process before the task is finished. The result of the task is then lost.

To circumvent the problem of an empty process, the `IntentService` is an ideal candidate for asynchronous execution from a `BroadcastReceiver`. Once a start request is sent from the `BroadcastReceiver`, it is not a problem that `onReceive` finishes because a new component is active during the background execution.

Prolonged Lifetime with goAsync

As of API level 11, the `BroadcastReceiver.goAsync()` method is available to simplify asynchronous execution. It keeps the state of the asynchronous result in a `BroadcastReceiver.PendingResult` and extends the lifetime of the broadcast until the Broad

---

`castReceiver.PendingResult` is explicitly terminated with `finish`, which can be called after the asynchronous execution is done.

A minimalistic asynchronous receiver is shown in `AsyncReceiver`, where the `BroadcastReceiver` is kept alive until the `PendingResult` is finished:

```
public class AsyncReceiver extends BroadcastReceiver {
    public void onReceive(Context context, Intent intent) {
        final PendingResult result = goAsync();

        new Thread() {
            public void run() {

                // Do background work

                result.finish();
            }
        }.start();
    }
}
```

Example: Periodical long operations

Applications that should trigger periodical tasks even when the applications themselves are not executing can utilize the `AlarmManager` system service in the platform. This can be configured with a periodic interval when it will send an `Intent` to a `BroadcastReceiver` in the application. Thus, if the application is not running, the `BroadcastReceiver` is the entry point of the application, and long-running operations should be executed in another component, typically an `IntentService`.

This example checks a network resource to see whether any updates have been made since the last time the `IntentService` ran.[2] If so, a notification is added to the status bar.

The `BroadcastReceiver` and `AlarmManager` are set up in an `Activity`:

```
public class AlarmBroadcastActivity extends Activity {
    private static final long ONE_HOUR = 60 * 60 * 1000;

    AlarmManager am;
    AlarmReceiver alarmReceiver;

    public void onCreate(Bundle savedInstanceState) {
        super.onCreate(savedInstanceState);

        alarmReceiver = new AlarmReceiver();
```

2. Use Google Cloud Messaging (*http://bit.ly/1iRxMSA*), if applicable, before implementing your own mechanism.

```
        registerReceiver(alarmReceiver, new IntentFilter(
        "com.eat.alarmreceiver")); ❶

        PendingIntent pendingIntent = PendingIntent.getBroadcast(this, 0,
            new Intent("com.eat.alarmreceiver"),
            PendingIntent.FLAG_UPDATE_CURRENT);

        am = (AlarmManager)(this.getSystemService( Context.ALARM_SERVICE ));
        am.setRepeating(AlarmManager.ELAPSED_REALTIME,
            SystemClock.elapsedRealtime() + ONE_HOUR, ONE_HOUR, pendingIntent); ❷
    }
}
```

❶   Register the `BroadcastReceiver` that will receive `Intent` from the `AlarmManag`
    `er`.

❷   Configure the `AlarmManager` so that it starts the application every hour.

The `AlarmReceiver` is started every hour and redirects the invocation to an `IntentSer`
`vice` that can handle the network operation:

```
public class AlarmReceiver extends BroadcastReceiver {
    public void onReceive(Context context, Intent intent) {
        context.startService(new Intent(context,
        NetworkCheckerIntentService.class));
    }
}
```

The `NetworkCheckerIntentService` receives the start request in `onHandleIntent`,
makes a network call, and possibly updates the status bar:

```
public class NetworkCheckerIntentService extends IntentService {

    public NetworkCheckerIntentService() {
        super("NetworkCheckerThread");
    }

    @Override
    protected void onHandleIntent(Intent intent) {
        if (isNewNetworkDataAvailable()) { ❶
            addStatusBarNotification();
        }
    }

    private boolean isNewNetworkDataAvailable() {
        // Network request code omitted. Return dummy result.
        return true;
    }

    private void addStatusBarNotification() {
        Notification.Builder mBuilder =
                new Notification.Builder(this)
```

```
                    .setSmallIcon(R.drawable.new_data_available)
                    .setContentTitle("New network data")
                    .setContentText("New data can be downloaded.");

        NotificationManager mNotificationManager =
                (NotificationManager) getSystemService(
                Context.NOTIFICATION_SERVICE);
        mNotificationManager.notify(1, mBuilder.build());
    }
}
```

❶   Contains the network call.

IntentService Versus Service

The `IntentService` inherits its character from the `Service`: same declaration, same impact on process rank, and same start request procedure for clients. It implements the start request handling semantics of the `Service` so that an application that uses `Intent Service` just has to implement `onHandleIntent`. Thus, the use of `IntentService` matches the commonly used task-controlled `Service` ("Task-Controlled Service" on page 190), but with built-in support for asynchronous execution and component life-cycle management.

The `IntentService` is appealingly simple to use and is often the perfect solution for the right use case, such as the one just described. However, the simplicity comes with limitations, and a `Service` may be preferred:

Control by clients
   When you want the lifecycle of the component to be controlled by other components, choose a user-controlled `Service` ("User-Controlled Service" on page 186). This goes for both started and bound services.

Concurrent task execution
   To execute tasks concurrently, starting multiple threads in `Service`.

Sequential and rearrangeable tasks
   Tasks can be prioritized so that the task queue can be bypassed. For example, a music service that is controlled by buttons—play, pause, rewind, fast forward, stop, etc.—would typically prioritize a stop request so that it is executed prior to any other tasks in the queue. This requires a `Service`.

Summary

The `IntentService` is an easy-to-use, sequential task processor that is very useful for offloading operations not only from the UI thread, but also from other originating components. Other sequential task processors discussed in this book, such as `Handler`

Thread, Executors.newSingleThreadExecutor, and to some extent AsyncTask, can be compared to the IntentService, but IntentService has the advantage of running as an independent component, which the others do not.

CHAPTER 13

Access ContentProviders with AsyncQueryHandler

AsyncQueryHandler is a utility class that specializes in handling CRUD (Create, Read, Update, and Delete) operations on a ContentProvider asynchronously. The operations are executed on a separate thread, and when the result is available, callbacks are invoked on the initiating thread. Most commonly, the class is used to offload the ContentProvider operations from the UI thread, which receives the result once the background task has finished.

This chapter covers:

- ContentProvider basics and concurrent access
- How to implement and use the AsyncQueryHandler
- Understanding the background execution

Brief Introduction to ContentProvider

This section contains some basic information on content providers. For more details, see the official documentation (*https://developer.android.com/guide/topics/providers/ content-providers.html*). A ContentProvider is an abstraction of a data source that can be accessed uniformly within the application or from other applications running in separate processes. The ContentProvider exposes an interface where data can be read, added, changed, or deleted through a database-centric CRUD approach with four access methods, as the skeleton code for EatContentProvider—a custom provider—shows:

```
public class EatContentProvider extends ContentProvider {

    private final static String STRING_URI=
```

```
"content://com.eat.provider/resource";
public final static Uri CONTENT_URI= Uri.parse(STRING_URI);

@Override
public Cursor query(Uri uri, String[] projection, String selection,
    String[] selectionArgs, String sortOrder) {
    // Read data source
    return null;
}

@Override
public Uri insert(Uri uri, ContentValues values) {
    // Add data
    return null;
}

@Override
public int delete(Uri uri, String selection, String[] selectionArgs) {
    // Remove data
    return 0;
}

@Override
public int update(Uri uri, ContentValues values, String selection,
    String[] selectionArgs) {
    // Change data
    return 0;
}
}
```

The access methods originate from the most common use case for providers: to expose data stored in a SQLite database (*http://bit.ly/1n5NpJ0*) across application boundaries. SQLite databases are private to applications but can be exposed to other applications through the ContentProvider class, providing application entry points that are registered at application installation. The definition is done in the AndroidManifest, with an authority that identifies the provider and an exported attribute that determines whether it is accessible to other applications:

```
<provider
    android:name="EatContentProvider"
    android:authorities="com.eat.provider"
    android:exported="true"/>
```

The access methods are defined by the implementation and can be invoked through the ContentResolver class, which identifies the ContentProvider through a unique Uri that it defines in a syntax like *content://com.eat.provider/resource*. The ContentResolver contains the same range of data access methods as the provider: query, insert, delete, and update:

```
final Cursor query (Uri uri, String[] projection, String selection,
    String[] selectionArgs, String sortOrder)
```

```
final Uri insert (Uri url, ContentValues values)
final int delete (Uri url, String where, String[] selectionArgs)
final int update (Uri uri, ContentValues values, String where,
    String[] selectionArgs)
```

When called, these methods invoke the corresponding provider methods. For example, EatContentProvider.query(…) is invoked when the query method of a resolver with the correct Uri is called:

```
public final static Uri CONTENT_URI= Uri.parse(
"content://com.eat.provider/resource");

ContentResolver cr = getContentResolver();
Cursor c = cr.query(CONTENT_URI, null, null, null, null);
```

The platform defines a range of providers (*http://bit.ly/1oaakQE*) of its own that are accessible to all applications, so that common content —e.g., contacts, calender appointments, bookmarks, etc.—can be stored in one place.

Justification for Background Processing of a ContentProvider

A ContentProvider cannot control how many clients will access the data or if it can happen simultaneously. The encapsulated data of a provider can be accessed concurrently from multiple threads, which can both read and write to the data set. Consequently, concurrent access to a provider can lead to data inconsistencies (see "Data inconsistency" on page 18) unless the provider is thread safe. Thread safety can be achieved by applying synchronization to the query, insert, update, and delete data access methods, but it is required only if the data source needs it. SQLite database access, for example, is thread safe in itself because the transaction model of the database is sequential, so that the data can not be corrupted by concurrent accesses.

Faster Database Access with Write-Ahead Logging

SQLite databases are sequential by default, which can lead to low throughput when reading and writing data intensively from multiple threads. To improve concurrent throughput, the database offers a technique called Write-Ahead Logging (*http://sqlite.org/wal.html*) (WAL) that can be enabled explicitly:

```
SQLiteDatabase db = SQLiteDatabase.openDatabase( ... );
db.enableWriteAheadLogging();
```

Once enabled, the database can handle multiple transactions in parallel and allows simultaneous read transactions to access the database concurrently because multiple readers cannot cause data inconsistency. WAL still ensures that read and write transactions cannot occur concurrently on the same data set: a write is done on a copy of the database and is not written to the original database until there are no active read transactions.

Access to a ContentProvider commonly involves interaction with persistant storage—database or file—so it should not be executed on the UI thread because it may become a long task that can delay UI rendering. Instead, background threads should handle the provider execution. The background threads should be created by the user of the provider, such as the application that invokes the ContentResolver. The provider implementation is invoked on the same thread as the caller of the ContentResolver if the call originates from a component in the same application process. If, however, the Content Provider is called from another process, the provider implementation is invoked on binder threads instead.

Spawning new threads in the ContentProvider implementation is a viable asynchronous solution only if the callers of the provider do not care about the result of the calls. This may be the case for in sert, delete, or update, but not for query, where the purpose of the call is to retrieve a data set. If data needs to be returned, the background thread would have to block in the provider until the result is ready. Consequently, the call is not asynchronous and will not relieve the thread that uses the provider.

The data stored in a ContentProvider is most often handled from the UI thread—e.g., data reads are shown in view components and data writes are initiated on button clicks. But because providers should not be accessed directly from the UI thread, asynchronous mechanisms are required. Execution must be processed on a background thread and the result must be communicated back to the UI thread. This is the most common use case and can be carried out with any of the general concurrent constructs previously discussed in this book, in combination with message passing between the threads. However, the platform contains two special purpose mechanisms for providers: Asyn cQueryHandler and CursorLoader. This chapter discusses the first, and Chapter 14 describes the second.

Using the AsyncQueryHandler

AsyncQueryHandler is an abstract class that simplifies asynchronous access to Content Providers by handling the ContentResolver, background execution, and the message passing between threads. Applications subclass the AsyncQueryHandler and implement a set of callback methods that contain the result of a provider operation. The Asyn

---

cQueryHandler contains four methods that wrap the provider operations of a Conten tResolver:

```
final void startDelete(int token, Object cookie, Uri uri, String selection,
    String[] selectionArgs)
final void startInsert(int token, Object cookie, Uri uri,
    ContentValues initialValues)
final void startQuery(int token, Object cookie, Uri uri, String[] projection,
    String selection, String[] selectionArgs, String orderBy)
final void startUpdate(int token, Object cookie, Uri uri, ContentValues values,
    String selection, String[] selectionArgs)
```

Each method wraps the equivalent ContentResolver method and executes the request on a background thread. When the provider operation finishes, it reports the result back to the AsyncQueryHandler, which invokes the following callbacks that the implementation should override. The token and cookie objects permit communication between the caller, the background thread, and the callback, which we'll look at momentarily:

```
public class EatAsyncQueryHandler extends AsyncQueryHandler{

    public EatAsyncQueryHandler(ContentResolver cr) {
        super(cr);
    }

    @Override
    protected void onDeleteComplete(int token, Object cookie, int result) { ... }

    @Override
    protected void onUpdateComplete(int token, Object cookie, int result) { ... }

    @Override
    protected void onInsertComplete(int token, Object cookie, Uri result) { ... }

    @Override
    protected void onQueryComplete(int token, Object cookie, Cursor result) { }
}
```

The type of the provider result depends on the request; it corresponds to the result type of the underlying ContentResolver method. Thus, the result arguments of the onDe leteComplete and onUpdateComplete methods contain the number of records affected; whereas the onInsertComplete result contains a URI pointing to the added record, and the onQueryComplete result contains a cursor with the results of the query.

The first two arguments of the calls and callbacks are used as follows:

Cookie

Request identifier and data container of any object type. It is passed with the provider request and returned in the callback so that data can be passed from the request to the response and individual requests can be identified if necessary.

Token

> Request type, which defines the kind if requests that can be made (see "Example: Expanding Contact List" on page 214). It also identifies the requests so that unprocessed requests can be cancelled. Thus, if the caller issues `cancelOperation(to ken)`, unprocessed requests that were submitted with that token will not start processing. However, the cancellation will not affect requests that already started.

The `AsyncQueryHandler` can be created and invoke provider operations on any thread, but it is most commonly used in the UI thread. The callbacks are, however, always called on the thread that created the `AsyncQueryHandler`.

> AsyncQueryHandler cannot be used for asynchronous interaction with the SQLite database directly. Instead, the database should be wrapped in a `ContentProvider` that can be accessed through a `Con tentResolver`

Example: Expanding Contact List

The contacts stored on a device are exposed through a system provider so that all applications on a device can share the same contacts. The contact provider is exposed through the nontrivial `ContactsContract` interface (*http://bit.ly/1mldz6S*). This example shows how to list all the available contacts in the contact book with the help of an `AsyncQueryHandler`. The list items display the contact name, and the list is expandable so that the phone numbers of the contact are shown when the list item is clicked. The example originates from the Android SDK sample applications,[1] with some minor modifications.

The contacts list is backed by a `SimpleCursorTreeAdapter` that can expose data from multiple cursors. The contact list is populated asynchronously with the custom `Query Handler` when the `Activity` is created. The `QueryHandler` queries the contact database both for display names as well as phone numbers, but as they belong to different database tables, two queries are made: first, one for the display names, followed by a query for the phone numbers.

```
public class ExpandableContactListActivity extends ExpandableListActivity {

    private static final String[] CONTACTS_PROJECTION = new String[] {
            Contacts._ID,
            Contacts.DISPLAY_NAME
    };
```

---

1. *android_sdk_install_dir*/samples/*platform_version*/ApiDemos/src/com/example/android/
apis/view/ExpandableList2

```java
private static final int GROUP_ID_COLUMN_INDEX = 0;

private static final String[] PHONE_NUMBER_PROJECTION = new String[] {
        Phone._ID,
        Phone.NUMBER
};

private static final int TOKEN_GROUP = 0; ❶
private static final int TOKEN_CHILD = 1;

private QueryHandler mQueryHandler;
private CursorTreeAdapter mAdapter;

@Override
public void onCreate(Bundle savedInstanceState) {
    super.onCreate(savedInstanceState);

    // Set up our adapter
    mAdapter = new MyExpandableListAdapter(
            this,
            android.R.layout.simple_expandable_list_item_1,
            android.R.layout.simple_expandable_list_item_1,
            new String[] { Contacts.DISPLAY_NAME }, // Name for group layouts
            new int[] { android.R.id.text1 },
            new String[] { Phone.NUMBER }, // Number for child layouts
            new int[] { android.R.id.text1 });

    setListAdapter(mAdapter);

    mQueryHandler = new QueryHandler(this, mAdapter);

    // Query for people
    mQueryHandler.startQuery(TOKEN_GROUP, ❷
            null,
            Contacts.CONTENT_URI,
            CONTACTS_PROJECTION,
            Contacts.HAS_PHONE_NUMBER,
            null,
            Contacts.DISPLAY_NAME + " ASC");
}

@Override
protected void onDestroy() {
    super.onDestroy();
    mQueryHandler.cancelOperation(TOKEN_GROUP); ❸
    mQueryHandler.cancelOperation(TOKEN_CHILD);
    mAdapter.changeCursor(null);
    mAdapter = null;
}

private static final class QueryHandler extends AsyncQueryHandler {
    private CursorTreeAdapter mAdapter;
```

```
    public QueryHandler(Context context, CursorTreeAdapter adapter) {
        super(context.getContentResolver());
        this.mAdapter = adapter;
    }

    @Override
    protected void onQueryComplete(int token, Object cookie, Cursor cursor) {
        switch (token) {
            case TOKEN_GROUP:
                mAdapter.setGroupCursor(cursor); ❹
                break;

            case TOKEN_CHILD:
                int groupPosition = (Integer) cookie;
                mAdapter.setChildrenCursor(groupPosition, cursor); ❺
                break;
        }
    }
}

public class MyExpandableListAdapter extends SimpleCursorTreeAdapter {

    // Note that the constructor does not take a Cursor.
    // This is done to avoid querying the database on the main thread.
    public MyExpandableListAdapter(Context context, int groupLayout,
                                   int childLayout, String[] groupFrom,
                                   int[] groupTo, String[] childrenFrom,
                                   int[] childrenTo) {

        super(context, null, groupLayout, groupFrom, groupTo, childLayout,
            childrenFrom, childrenTo);
    }

    @Override
    protected Cursor getChildrenCursor(Cursor groupCursor) {
        // Given the group, we return a cursor for all the children
        // within that group

        // Return a cursor that points to this contact's phone numbers
        Uri.Builder builder = Contacts.CONTENT_URI.buildUpon();
        ContentUris.appendId(builder, groupCursor.getLong(
        GROUP_ID_COLUMN_INDEX));
        builder.appendEncodedPath(Contacts.Data.CONTENT_DIRECTORY);
        Uri phoneNumbersUri = builder.build();

        mQueryHandler.startQuery(TOKEN_CHILD, ❻
                groupCursor.getPosition(),
                phoneNumbersUri,
                PHONE_NUMBER_PROJECTION,
                Phone.MIMETYPE + "=?",
                new String[] { Phone.CONTENT_ITEM_TYPE },
```

```
                null);

            return null;
        }
    }
}
```

❶ Define tokens that represent request types that the QueryHandler handles: one for contact name requests and one for phone number requests.

❷ Start an asynchronous query for contact names.

❸ Cancel pending provider operations if the Activity is destroyed.

❹ Receive the result for the contact name requested in mQueryHandler.start Query. The adapter initiates a consecutive query on the child cursor—i.e., the phone numbers.

❺ Receive result for the phone number query, with a cookie that identifies the contact it belongs to.

❻ Start asynchronous query for phone numbers that belong to the contacts.

Understanding the AsyncQueryHandler

The AsyncQueryHandler holds a ContentResolver, an execution environment for background processing, and handles the thread communication to and from the background thread. When one of the provider requests (startQuery, startInsert, start Delete or startUpdate) is invoked, a Message with the request is added to a Message Queue processed by one background thread. Figure 13-1 shows the elements of the exchange.

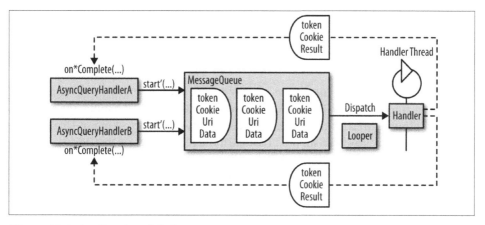

Figure 13-1. Application global execution

The message is populated with `ContentResolver` arguments, the `cookie` object, and the `token` argument, which becomes a `what` parameter in the `Message`. Hence, the token can be used to remove requests from the queue ("Removing Messages from the Queue" on page 68) with `cancelOperation(token)`.

The background thread processes the provider requests sequentially and passes the result back in a `Message` to the calling `AsyncQueryHandler` instance. The processing on the background thread is application global—i.e., all `AsyncQueryHandler` instances within an application add provider requests to the same queue. The application-global behavior is similar to the execution environment in an `AsyncTask` (described in "Application Global Execution" on page 169), but is not as inherently problematic because the `AsyncQueryHandler` is used only to access providers and not longer tasks, as network connections do.

Limitations

The simplicity of an `AsyncQueryHandler` is an advantage, but it has been around since API level 1, without being updated for later additions to the Android platform. Hence, there are some newer functions that require a more general asynchronous handling, using one of the previously discussed techniques in this book:

Batch operations
> API level 5 added `ContentProviderOperation` (*http://bit.ly/1udXULU*) to support batch operations on providers—a set of insertions that can be executed atomically in one transaction to avoid multiple transactions for a larger data set.

`CancellationSignal`
> API level 16 added the possibility of cancelling `ContentResolver` queries with the help of `CancellationSignal` (*http://bit.ly/R7Wrrj*), but it's not supported by the `AsyncQueryHandler`, so it should still use `cancelOperation(token)`.

Summary

The `AsyncQueryHandler` constitutes an easy-to-use asynchronous mechanism for accessing the full set of CRUD operations on a `ContentProvider`. It handles the execution on a background thread and the message passing between the invoking and background thread. It does not, however, support a couple more recent features that have been added in later versions of the platform. As we will see in the next chapter, it can—advantageously—be used in conjunction with a `CursorLoader`, where the data query is handled by the `CursorLoader` and insertions, updates, and deletions are handled by the `AsyncQueryHandler` ("Example: Use CursorLoader with AsyncQueryHandler" on page 229).

CHAPTER 14

Automatic Background Execution with Loaders

The Loader framework offers a robust way to run asynchronous operations with content providers or other data sources. The framework can load data asynchronously and deliver it to your application when content changes or is added to the data source. The Loader framework was added to the Android platform in Honeycomb (API level 11), along with the compatibility package.

You can connect to the Loader framework from an `Activity` or a `Fragment`. When you create the `Loader` object, you request a loader that manages your connection with the data source. (Note that I'm using uppercase for the framework and lowercase for the object you connect.)

When you connect with a content provider, the framework contains a loader named `CursorLoader` that you can hook into. For other data sources, you can code up a custom loader. For any loader type, you have to define three callbacks: one that creates a new loader, one that runs whenever the loader delivers new data, and one that runs when the loader is reset—i.e., the loader stops delivering data.

Some of the features offered by the Loader framework are:

Asynchronous data management
> The loader reacts in the background to the data source and triggers a callback in your app when the data source has new data.

Lifecycle management
> When your `Activity` or `Fragment` stops, its loader stops as well. Furthermore, loaders that are running in the background continue to do their work after configuration changes, such as an orientation change.

Cached data

> If the result of an asynchronous data load can't be delivered, it is cached so that it can be delivered when there is a recipient ready—e.g., when an `Activity` is recreated due to a configuration change.

Leak protection

> If an `Activity` undergoes a configuration change, the Loader framework ensures that the `Context` object is not lost to a leak. The framework operates only on the `Application` context so that major thread-related leaks don't occur (see "The lifecycle mismatch" on page 95).

 As we have seen, loaders that are running when the `Activity` undergoes a configuration change are kept alive so they can run again with a new `Activity`. Because the loaders are preserved, they could cause a memory leak.

All callbacks—most importantly, the delivery of data—are reported on the UI thread.

Because a loader can work with either an `Activity` or a `Fragment`, I'll use the term *client* in this chapter to refer to the `Activity` or `Fragment`.

This chapter breaks down into two major sections: using a loader offered by a content provider and creating a custom loader for another data source.

Loader Framework

The Loader framework is an API in the `android.app`-package that contains the `LoaderManager`, `Loader`, `AsyncTaskLoader`, and `CursorLoader` classes. Figure 14-1 shows how the relate to one another. The API is rather comprehensive, but most of it is required only for custom loaders and not when using loaders from a client. Hence, I'll focus on how to use loaders from a client in this section, and postpone other parts of the framework to "Implementing Custom Loaders" on page 233.

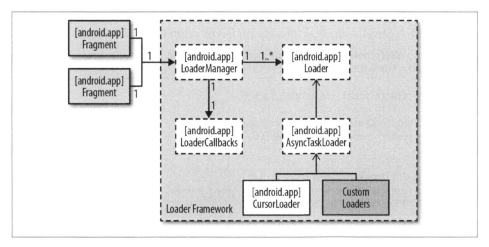

Figure 14-1. Framework core classes

The LoaderManager is responsible for handling the loaders in a client. A loader is a concrete implementation based on the Loader and AsyncTaskLoader classes. The only concrete loader in the platform is the CursorLoader, whereas customized loaders can be implemented by extending the AsyncTaskLoader and adhere to the Loader lifecycle.

LoaderManager

The LoaderManager is an abstract class that manages all loaders used by an Activity or a Fragment. The LoaderManager acts as an intermediary between a client and its loaders. A client holds one LoaderManager instance, which is accessible through the Activity or Fragment class:

```
LoaderManager getLoaderManager();
```

The LoaderManager API primarily consists of four methods:

```
Loader<D> initLoader(int id, Bundle args, LoaderCallbacks<D> callback)
Loader<D> restartLoader(int id, Bundle args, LoaderCallbacks<D> callback)
Loader<D> getLoader(int id)
void destroyLoader(int id)
```

All methods contain an identifier that represents the loader that the LoaderManager should interact with. Every loader should have a unique identifier. Typically, an application only has to call initLoader or restartLoader to start the loader.

Clients interact with the LoaderManager via the LoaderManager.LoaderCallbacks interface, which must be implemented by the client.

A skeleton example follows of a typical loader setup with callbacks in an Activity (Example 14-1).

Example 14-1. Skeleton example of a typical loader setup with callbacks

```
public class SkeletonActivity extends Activity implements
LoaderManager.LoaderCallbacks<D> {

    private static final int LOADER_ID = 0;

    public void onCreate(Bundle savedInstanceState) {
        getLoaderManager().initLoader(LOADER_ID, null, this);
    }

    // LoaderCallback methods
    public Loader<D> onCreateLoader(int id, Bundle args) {
        /* TODO: Create the loader. */
    }

    public void onLoadFinished(Loader<D> loader, D data) {
        /* TODO: Use the delivered data. */
    }
    public void onLoaderReset(Loader<D> loader) {
        /* TODO: The loader data is invalid, stop using it. */
    }
}
```

SkeletonActivity initializes the loader in onCreate, which tells the framework to invoke the first callback in the code, onCreateLoader(). In that callback, the client should return a loader implementation that will be managed by the platform. Once the loader is created, it initiates data loading. The result is returned in onLoadFinished() on the UI thread so that the client can use the result to update the UI components with the latest data. When a previously created loader is no longer available, onLoadReset() is invoked, after which the data set being handled by the loader is invalidated and shouldn't be used anymore.

When a client changes state—through Activity.onStart(), Activity.onStop(), etc. —the LoaderManager is triggered internally so that the application doesn't have to manage any loaders' lifecycles itself. For example, an Activity that starts will initiate a data load and listen for content changes. When the Activity stops, all the loaders are stopped as well, so that no more data loading or delivery is done.

The client can explicitly destroy a loader through destroyLoader(id) if it wants to stay active but doesn't need the data set any more.

initLoader vs restartLoader

The LoaderManager initializes a loader with either initLoader() or restartLoad er(), which have the same argument list:

id

A loader identifier, which must be unique for all loaders within the same client. Loaders for two different clients—each a separate `Activity` or `Fragment`—can use the same numbers to identify their loaders without interference.

args

A set of input data to the loader, packaged in a Bundle (*https://develop er.android.com/reference/android/os/Bundle.html*). This parameter can be `null` if the client has no input data. The arguments are passed to `LoaderCallbacks.on CreateLoader()`. Typically, the arguments contain a set of query parameters.

callback

A mandatory implementation of the `LoaderCallback` interface, which contains callback methods to be invoked by the framework.

Even though they look similar, there are important differences between the two method calls:

- `initLoader()` reuses an available loader if the identifier matches. If no loader exists with the specified identifier, `onCreateLoader` first requests a new loader, after which a data load is initiated and the result is delivered in `onLoadFinished`. If the loader identifier already exists, the latest data load result is delivered directly in `onLoad Finished`. `initLoader()` is typically called when the client is created so that you can either create a new loader or retrieve the result of an already existing loader. This means that a loader is reused after a configuration change and no new data load has to be made: the cached result in the loader can be delivered immediately.

- `restartLoader()` does not reuse loaders. If there is an existing loader with the specified identifier, `restartLoader()` destroys it—and its data—and then creates a new `Loader` by calling `onCreateLoader`. This then launches a new data load. Because previous loader instances are destroyed, their cached data is removed.

`initLoader` should be chosen when the underlying data source is the same throughout a client lifecycle; e.g., an `Activity` that observes the same `Cursor` data from a content provider. The advantage is that `initLoader` can deliver a cached result if data from a previous load is available, which is useful after configuration changes. The fundamental setup is shown in Example 14-1.

If, however, the underlying data source can vary during a client lifecycle, `restartLoad er` should be used. A typical variation would be to change the query to a database, in which case previously loaded `Cursor` instances are obsolete, and a new data load that can return a new `Cursor` should be initiatied.

LoaderCallbacks

These are mandatory interfaces that set up or tear down communication between the LoaderManager and the client. The interface consists of three methods:

```
public Loader<D> onCreateLoader(int id, Bundle args)
public void onLoadFinished(Loader<D> loader, D data)
public void onLoaderReset(Loader<D> loader)
```

The implementation of the interface is adapted to the content to be loaded. The loader is defined as Loader<D>, where <D> is a generic parameter corresponding to the data type that the loader returns; for example, <D> is a Cursor if the loader is a content provider.

The callbacks are triggered depending on the loader events that occur, as Figure 14-2 shows.

The normal sequence of events is:

Loader initialization

Typically, the client initializes the loader when creating it so that it can start the background data loading as soon as possible. Loader initialization is triggered through LoaderManager.initLoader(), passing a unique identifier for the loader to be initialized. If there is no loader available with the requested identifier, the onCreateLoader—callback is invoked so that the client can create a new loader and return it to the LoaderManager. The LoaderManager now starts to manage the lifecycle and data loading from the loader.

If the client requests initialization on an existing loader identifier, there is no need to create a new loader. Instead, the existing loader will deliver the last loaded result by invoking the client's onLoadFinished callback.

Data loading

The framework can initiate new data loading when the data source has updated its content or when the client becomes ready for it. The client itself can also force a new data load by calling Loader.forceLoad(). In any case, the result is delivered to the LoaderManager, which passes on the result by calling the client's onLoadFinished callback.

Clients can also cancel initiated loads with Loader.cancelLoad(). If this is issued before the load starts, the load request is simply canceled. If the load has started, the results are discarded and not delivered to the client.

Loader reset

A loader is destroyed when the client is destroyed or when it calls LoaderManager.destroyLoader(id). The client is notified of the destruction through the on

`LoaderReset(Loader)` callback. At this point, the client may want to free up the data that was previously loaded if it should't be used anymore.

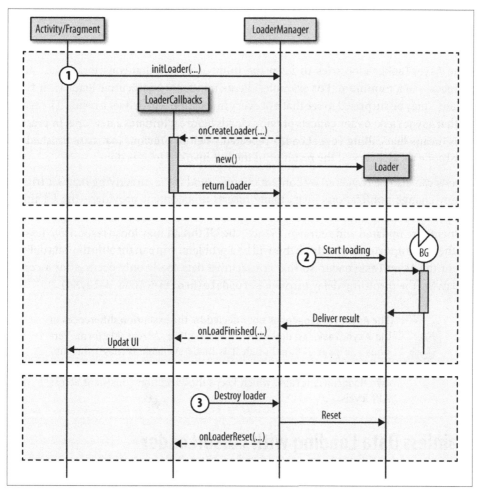

Figure 14-2. Sequence diagram of the loader callbacks

AsyncTaskLoader

The loader asynchronous execution environment is provided by the `AsyncTaskLoad er`, which extends the `Loader` class. The class contains an `AsyncTask` to process the background loading, and relies on the `AsyncTask.executeOnExecutor()` method for background execution. Hence, it does not suffer from the variations between behavior on different versions of Android (described in "Background Task Execution" on page 167).

The `AsyncTaskLoader` in the compatibility package does not rely on the public `AsyncTask` in the platform, because that may execute sequentially. Instead, the compatibility package is bundled with an internal `ModernAsyncTask` implementation that processes the data loads concurrently.

The `AsyncTaskLoader` tries to keep the number of simultaneous tasks—i.e., active threads—to a minimum. For example, clients that force consecutive loads with `force Load()` may be surprised to see that not every invocation will deliver a result. The reason is that `AsyncTaskLoader` cancels previous loads before it initiates a new one. In practice, this means that calling `forceLoad()` repeatedly before previous loads are finished will postpone the delivery of the result until the last invoked load is done.

Loads can also be triggered by content changes, and if the underlying data set triggers many change notifications—e.g., many inserts in a content provider—the UI thread may receive many `onLoadFinished` invocations on the UI thread, where the UI components are updated and redrawn. Hence, the UI thread may loose responsiveness due to the many updates. If you think this will be a problem, you can throttle the data delivery from the `AsyncTaskLoader` so that consecutive data loads only occur after a certain delay. Set the throttling delay through `setUpdateThrottle(long delayMs)`.

The `AsyncTaskLoader` is not affected by the execution differences of the `AsyncTask`, as described in "Execution Across Platform Versions" on page 170, although it is made available through the support package from API level 4. The support package implements its own `ModernAsyncTask`, which keeps the execution consistent across API levels.

Painless Data Loading with CursorLoader

Data loading from loaders is handled by the abstract `Loader` class, which should be subclassed and connected to a data source. Out of the box, the framework currently supports only `ContentProvider` data sources, using the `CursorLoader`. The greatness of the `CursorLoader` arises from the design choice that has been made: it does not try to provide a general asynchronous technique that can be adapted to many different situations. Instead, it is a special-purpose functionality that focuses on data loading from content providers, and simplifies that use case only.

The `CursorLoader` can be used only with `Cursor` objects delivered from content providers, not those that come from SQLite databases.

Using the CursorLoader

The `CursorLoader` is an extension of the abstract `AsyncTaskLoader` class that implements the asynchronous execution ("AsyncTaskLoader" on page 225). `CursorLoader` monitors `Cursor` objects that can be queried from a content provider. In other words, it is a loader with a `Cursor` data type and is passed to the `LoaderManager` through calls such as `Loader<Cursor>`. The `CursorLoader` registers a ContentObserver (*http://bit.ly/1pWSPbo*) on the `Cursor` to detect changes in the data set.

The content provider is identified through a URI that identifies the data set to query. The `Cursor` to monitor is defined with the query parameters that are normally used for providers and that can all be defined in the constructor:

```
CursorLoader(Context context, Uri uri, String[] projection, String selection,
        String[] selectionArgs, String sortOrder)
```

The `Cursor` lifecycle is managed by the `CursorLoader`: it replaces the `managedQuery` and `startManagingCursor` methods that were deprecated in the `Activity` class after the `CursorLoader` was introduced. Consequently, clients should not interfere with this internal lifecycle management and try to close the `Cursor` themselves.

Example: Contact list

Before we get into the details of the framework, let us peek at an example that illustrates the power and simplicity a `Loader` can provide.

The following example lists the contacts in the contact provider by using the concrete `CursorLoader` loader implementation class that is available in the platform. The concept is to set up the `CursorLoader` with an `Activity` or `Fragment` and implement the methods in `LoaderCallback`:

```
public class ContactActivity extends ListActivity implements
LoaderManager.LoaderCallbacks<Cursor>{

    private static final int CONTACT_NAME_LOADER_ID = 0;

    // Projection that defines just the contact display name
    static final String[] CONTACTS_SUMMARY_PROJECTION = new String[] { ❶
            ContactsContract.Contacts._ID,
            ContactsContract.Contacts.DISPLAY_NAME
    };
```

```
    SimpleCursorAdapter mAdapter;

    public void onCreate(Bundle savedInstanceState) {
        super.onCreate(savedInstanceState);
        initAdapter();
        getLoaderManager().initLoader(CONTACT_NAME_LOADER_ID, null, this); ❷
    }

    private void initAdapter() {
        mAdapter = new SimpleCursorAdapter(this,
                android.R.layout.simple_list_item_1, null,
                new String[] { ContactsContract.Contacts.DISPLAY_NAME },
                new int[] { android.R.id.text1}, 0);
        setListAdapter(mAdapter);
    }

    @Override
    public Loader<Cursor> onCreateLoader(int id, Bundle args) { ❸
        return new CursorLoader(this, ContactsContract.Contacts.CONTENT_URI,
                CONTACTS_SUMMARY_PROJECTION, null, null,
                ContactsContract.Contacts.DISPLAY_NAME + " ASC");
    }

    @Override
    public void onLoadFinished(Loader<Cursor> loader, Cursor c) { ❹
      ou  mAdapter.swapCursor(c);
    }

    @Override
    public void onLoaderReset(Loader<Cursor> loader) { ❺
        mAdapter.swapCursor(null);
    }
}
```

❶ The loader only queries the display name of the contacts.

❷ Initiate a loader with the LoaderManager, which is followed by a callback to onCreateLoader.

❸ The first callback. The Activity creates a loader and hands it over to the platform.

❹ Whenever data has finished loading on a background thread, the data is served on the UI thread.

❺ When the loader is reset, the last callback is invoked and the Activity releases the references to the loader data.

CursorLoader closes the old Cursor after a new data set is loaded. Hence, use swapCursor in onLoadFinished and not the changeCursor alternative, as that also closes the old Cursor.

Adding CRUD Support

Loaders are intended to read data, but for content providers, it is often a requirement to also create, update, and delete data, which isn't what the CursorLoader supports. Still, the content observation and automatic background loading also brings simplicity to a full CRUD solution. You do, however, need a supplemantary mechanism for handling the writing to the provider, such as an AsyncQueryHandler, as the following example shows.

Example: Use CursorLoader with AsyncQueryHandler

In this example, we create a basic manager for the Chrome browser bookmarks stored in the content provider. The example consists of an Activity that shows the list of stored bookmarks and a button that opens a Fragment where new bookmarks can be added. If the user long-clicks on an item, it is directly deleted from the list.

Consequently, the bookmark manager invokes three provider operations that should be handled asynchronously:

List bookmarks

> Use CursorLoader to query the provider, so that we can utilize the feature of content observation and automatic data loading.

Add or delete a bookmark

> Use AsyncQueryHandler to insert new bookmarks from the fragment and delete bookmarks when list items are long clicked.

Much of the example carries out display and cursor handling activities common to many Android applications. The comments will focus on what's special about using a CursorLoader. In the example, the bookmark list is shown in the ChromeBookmarkActivity:

```
public class ChromeBookmarkActivity extends Activity implements
    LoaderManager.LoaderCallbacks<Cursor> {

    // Definition of bookmark access information.
    public interface ChromeBookmark {
        final static int ID = 1;
        final static Uri URI= Uri.parse(
        "content://com.android.chrome.browser/bookmarks"); ❶
        final static String[] PROJECTION = {
                Browser.BookmarkColumns._ID,
                Browser.BookmarkColumns.TITLE,
```

```
                    Browser.BookmarkColumns.URL
        };
    }

    // AsyncQueryHandler with convenience methods for
    // insertion and deletion of bookmarks.
    public static class ChromeBookmarkAsyncHandler extends AsyncQueryHandler {

        public ChromeBookmarkAsyncHandler(ContentResolver cr) {
            super(cr);
        }

        public void insert(String name, String url) {
            ContentValues cv = new ContentValues();
            cv.put(Browser.BookmarkColumns.BOOKMARK, 1);
            cv.put(Browser.BookmarkColumns.TITLE, name);
            cv.put(Browser.BookmarkColumns.URL, url);
            startInsert(0, null, ChromeBookmark.URI, cv);
        }

        public void delete(String name) {
            String where = Browser.BookmarkColumns.TITLE + "=?";
            String[] args = new String[] { name };
            startDelete(0, null, ChromeBookmark.URI, where, args);
        }
    }

    ListView mListBookmarks;
    SimpleCursorAdapter mAdapter;
    ChromeBookmarkAsyncHandler mChromeBookmarkAsyncHandler;

    public void onCreate(Bundle savedInstanceState) {
        super.onCreate(savedInstanceState);
        setContentView(R.layout.activity_bookmarks);
        mListBookmarks = (ListView) findViewById(R.id.list_bookmarks);

        mChromeBookmarkAsyncHandler =
        new ChromeBookmarkAsyncHandler(getContentResolver());

        initAdapter();

        getLoaderManager().initLoader(ChromeBookmark.ID, null, this);
    }

    private void initAdapter() {
        mAdapter = new SimpleCursorAdapter(this,
                android.R.layout.simple_list_item_1, null,
                new String[] { Browser.BookmarkColumns.TITLE },
                new int[] { android.R.id.text1}, 0);
        mListBookmarks.setAdapter(mAdapter);
        mListBookmarks.setOnItemLongClickListener(
        new AdapterView.OnItemLongClickListener() {
```

```
        @Override
        public boolean onItemLongClick(AdapterView<?> adapterView, View view,
            int pos, long id) {

            Cursor c =
            ((SimpleCursorAdapter) adapterView.getAdapter()).getCursor();
            c.moveToPosition(pos);
            int i = c.getColumnIndex(Browser.BookmarkColumns.TITLE);

            mChromeBookmarkAsyncHandler.delete(c.getString(i)); ❷

            return true;
        }
    });
}

@Override
public Loader<Cursor> onCreateLoader(int i, Bundle bundle) {
    return new CursorLoader(this, ChromeBookmark.URI,
            ChromeBookmark.PROJECTION, null, null,
            Browser.BookmarkColumns.TITLE + " ASC"); ❸
}

@Override
public void onLoadFinished(Loader<Cursor> loader, Cursor newCursor) {
    mAdapter.swapCursor(newCursor);
}

@Override
public void onLoaderReset(Loader loader) {
    mAdapter.swapCursor(null);
}


public void onAddBookmark(View v) {
    FragmentTransaction ft = getFragmentManager().beginTransaction();
    Fragment prev = getFragmentManager().findFragmentByTag("dialog");
    if (prev != null) {
        ft.remove(prev);
    }
    ft.addToBackStack(null);
    // Create and show the dialog.
    DialogFragment newFragment = EditBookmarkDialog.
        newInstance(mChromeBookmarkAsyncHandler);
    newFragment.show(ft, "dialog");
}
}
```

❶   Provider Uri for the Chrome browser bookmarks.

❷   Asynchronous deletion of bookmarks.

❸   Use a CursorLoader for asynchronous data retrieval.

New bookmarks are added via an `EditBookmarkDialog` that contains a button and two input fields: one for the bookmark name and one for the bookmark URL. When the button is pressed, the bookmark name and URL are inserted in the provider and the dialog is dismissed:

```
public class EditBookmarkDialog extends DialogFragment {

    static EditBookmarkDialog newInstance(
        ChromeBookmarkActivity.ChromeBookmarkAsyncHandler asyncQueryHandler) {

        EditBookmarkDialog dialog = new EditBookmarkDialog(asyncQueryHandler);
        return dialog;
    }

    ChromeBookmarkActivity.ChromeBookmarkAsyncHandler mAsyncQueryHandler;

    public EditBookmarkDialog(
        mChromeBookmarkActivity.ChromeBookmarkAsyncHandler asyncQueryHandler) {
        mAsyncQueryHandler = asyncQueryHandler;
    }

    @Override
    public View onCreateView(LayoutInflater inflater, ViewGroup container,
                             Bundle savedInstanceState) {
        View v = inflater.inflate(R.layout.dialog_edit_bookmark, container,
                                  false);
        final EditText editName = (EditText) v.findViewById(R.id.edit_name);
        final EditText editUrl = (EditText) v.findViewById(R.id.edit_url);
        Button buttonSave = (Button) v.findViewById(R.id.button_save);

        buttonSave.setOnClickListener(new View.OnClickListener() {
            public void onClick(View v) {
                String name = editName.getText().toString();
                String url = editUrl.getText().toString();
                mAsyncQueryHandler.insert(name, url); ❶
                dismiss();
            }
        });

        return v;
    }
}
```

❶ Insert the bookmark asynchronously in the provider.

Once a bookmark has been inserted or deleted via the `ChromeBookmarkAsyncHandler`, the content changes and the `CursorLoader` automatically requeries the `Cursor`. Hence, insertions and deletions are automatically updated in the list.

Implementing Custom Loaders

Loaders are most commonly used with content providers because they are already supported by the platform, but other data sources can be handled with custom loaders. Of course, this requires both more work and a deeper insight into the framework. Custom loaders should be implemented so that they behave as expected from a client's point of view. A fully fledged loader should support a range of features:

- Loader lifecycle
- Background loading
- Content management
- Deliver cached result

 To avoid leaking outer class objects referenced from inner classes—typically `Activity` and `Fragment`—a custom loader has to be declared as a static or external class. If you don't do this, a `RuntimeEx ception` is thrown when the loader is returned from `onCreateLoader`.

Loader Lifecycle

The base class for a loader is the `Loader`. It holds the state of the loader, which defines whether data should be delivered to the client or not. The loader contains a set of state transition methods that invoke methods that a custom loader may implement:

```
void startLoading()  -> void onStartLoading()
void stopLoading()   -> void onStopLoading()
void reset()         -> void onReset()
void abandon()       -> void onAbandon()
```

The loader delivers data only in the *started* state—i.e., after `Loader.startLoading()` has been invoked, which changes the state and initiates a data load.

The transitions between states, and the role of these methods, are shown in Figure 14-3. States are:

Reset
> The initial and final state of a loader, where it has released any cached data.

Started
> Starts an asynchronous data load and delivers the result through a callback invocation of `LoaderCallback.onLoadFinished`.

Stopped

The loader stops delivering data to the client. It may still load data in the background on content change, but the data is cached in the loader so that the latest data can be retrieved easily without initiating a new data load.

Abandoned

Intermediate state before reset, where data is stored until a new loader is connected to the data source. This is rarely used; the LoaderManager abandons loaders on restart so that the data is available while the restart is underway.

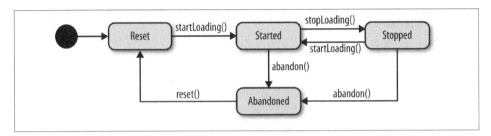

Figure 14-3. Loader states

The lifecycle of a loader is controlled by the LoaderManager, and clients normally shouldn't modify the state directly with the Loader methods. Instead, the client should issue initLoader and restartLoader to ensure that there is a started loader and leave it up to the LoaderManager to interact with the loader.

Data loading can be explicitly initiated by forcing an update:

```
void forceLoad ()
```

forceLoad() differs from startLoading() in that it only forces a new data load, but it does not change the state of the loader. Forceload should be called only in the started state; otherwise, the result will not delivered to the client.

Background Loading

Data should be loaded asynchronously on a background thread, and it's up to the loader to choose execution environment. Normally, the choice is not difficult; the platform provides the AsyncTaskLoader, which can be extended by custom loaders to facilitate the offloading from the UI thread. An implementation of AsyncTaskLoader must only override one method:

```
public D loadInBackground() {
    ...
}
```

loadInBackground is called on a background thread and should execute the long task of the loader and return content from the load. The return type is generic, so the D must be replaced by the data type of the underlying content and the callback should return data in that data type.

Example: Simple custom loader

The following is a basic loader that extends AsyncTaskLoader to load an integer value from a dummy data source. It simulates a long loading time to reflect the environment for real loaders:

```
public class BasicLoader extends AsyncTaskLoader<Integer>{

    public BasicLoader(Context context) {
        super(context);
    }

    @Override
    protected void onStartLoading() {
        super.onStartLoading();
        forceLoad(); ❶
    }

    @Override
    public Integer loadInBackground() {
        return loadDummyData(); ❷
    }

    private int loadDummyData() {
        SystemClock.sleep(1000);
        Random rand = new Random();
        return rand.nextInt(50);
    }
}
```

❶ When the client calls startLoading(), the loader changes state to started and invokes the onStartLoading(), where the custom loader should trigger a new load—i.e., calling forceLoad().

❷ Load a long-running task on the background thread and return the result.

BasicActivity is a client that uses BasicLoader to load integer values and display them:

```
public class BasicActivity extends Activity implements
LoaderManager.LoaderCallbacks<Integer>{

    private static final int BASIC_LOADER_ID = 0;

    TextView tvResult;

    public void onCreate(Bundle savedInstanceState) {
```

```
    super.onCreate(savedInstanceState);
    setContentView(R.layout.activity_basic);
    tvResult = (TextView) findViewById(R.id.text_result);
    getLoaderManager().initLoader(BASIC_LOADER_ID, null, this);
}

@Override
public Loader<Integer> onCreateLoader(int id, Bundle args) {
    return new BasicLoader(this);
}

@Override
public void onLoadFinished(Loader<Integer> loader, Integer data) {
    tvResult.setText(Integer.toString(data));
}

@Override
public void onLoaderReset(Loader<Integer> loader) {
    // Empty, the integer value is shown in a TextView
    // and should not be removed.
}
}
```

The BasicLoader executes the long task on the background thread and will be attached to the client lifecycle, but apart from that, it lacks most of the nice features expected from a loader. There is no data cache, for example, so the loader will reload the same data every time the client is recreated instead of returning a cached value.

Content Management

When the underlying data set changes, the loader should automatically initiate new background data loads. Consequently, the underlying data set has to be observable, in the same way as the CursorLoader utilizes a ContentObserver to get notified about updates in the content provider. The observer mechanism depends on the underlying data set, but typical mechanisms are:

Observable *and* Observer
> An in-memory data model of Java objects can be monitored by implementing the model as an Observable that reports changes to an Observer class. Both classes reside in the java.util-package.

Broadcasted intent to a BroadcastReceiver
> A content-independent content notifier, this can be used locally within an application or across process boundaries.

FileObserver
> Observes file system changes with an android.os.FileObserver that monitors a path in the file system and sends events when changes occur. The events that are reported can be configured with an event filter, which can limit the observations,

---

such as addition, deletion, and move. The usage of the `FileObserver` is shown in "Example: Custom File Loader" on page 238.

When the observer receives an update notification, it is up to the loader to load the new data asynchronously, which should be done either with `forceLoad` or `onContentChanged`. `forceLoad` triggers a background execution independent of the loader's state, whereas `onContentChanged` initiates data loading only if the state is `started`. Otherwise, it will mark the content as changed so that when the loader is restarted, it can check whether there is a content change that should be loaded and delivered to the client. A custom loader should check whether there is content to load with `takeContentChanged()` when the loader is started:

```
@Override
protected void onStartLoading() {
        super.onStartLoading();

        // Note: There are other interesting things to
        // implement here as well.

        if (takeContentChanged()) {
            forceLoad();
        }
    }
}
```

 Once `takeContentChanged()` is called, the content is no longer marked as changed, and consecutive calls will not return `true` until a new content change has been reported with `onContentChanged`.

Content observation should be active from the time the loader is `started` until it's `reset`, so that it can continue to do background loading even in the `stopped` state and deliver new data from the cache, as described in the next section.

Delivering Cached Results

When you subclass `AsyncTaskLoader`, it delivers results after new data has been returned from `loadInBackground()`. But triggering a new background task—i.e., calling `loadInBackground`—when there is no new data is a waste of resources. Instead, you should implement the loader so that it can speed up the result delivery to the clients. For example, if the loader has delivered a result and no content change has been reported, there is no point in starting a new background task. It's faster to return the previous result directly. Consequently, the loader should cache loaded data—i.e., keep the result of the last successful load. The delivery control is implemented with a result cache. You also override `Loader.deliverResult(<D>)`, which delivers data to the clients when it is invoked if the loader is started, as shown in the following example.

Example: Custom File Loader

The file system should be accessed asynchronously and the loader framework can be used to load new data as soon as any changes occur. In this example, we create a `File Loader` that delivers the names of the files in the application directory. It observes the directory for changes, and if a file is added or deleted, an asynchronous load will be initiated that will deliver a list of file names to the client on the UI thread.

The `FileLoader` uses the `AsyncTaskLoader` as background executor and it is configured to handle a data source of file names, like `List<String>`:

```java
public class FileLoader extends AsyncTaskLoader<List<String>> {

    // Cache the list of file names.
    private List<String> mFileNames;

    private class SdCardObserver extends FileObserver { ❶

        public SdCardObserver(String path) {
            super(path, FileObserver.CREATE|FileObserver.DELETE);
        }

        @Override
        public void onEvent(int event, String path) {
            // This call will force a new asynchronous data load
            // if the loader is started otherwise it will keep
            // a reference that the data has changed for future loads.
            onContentChanged();
        }
    }

    private SdCardObserver mSdCardObserver;

    public FileLoader(Context context) {
        super(context);
        String path = context.getFilesDir().getPath();
        mSdCardObserver = new SdCardObserver(path);
    }

    @Override
    protected void onStartLoading() {
        super.onStartLoading();
        // Start observing the content.
        mSdCardObserver.startWatching(); ❷

        if (mFileNames != null) { ❸
            // Return the cache
            deliverResult(mFileNames);
        }

        if (fileNames == null || takeContentChanged()) { ❹
```

```
            forceLoad();
        }
    }

    @Override
    public List<String> loadInBackground() {
        File directory = getContext().getFilesDir();
        return Arrays.asList(directory.list());
    }

    @Override
    public void deliverResult(List<String> data) {
        if (isReset()) {
            return;
        }

        // Cache the data
        mFileNames = data;

        // Only deliver result if the loader is started.
        if (isStarted()) {
            super.deliverResult(data);
        }
    }

    @Override
    protected void onStopLoading() {
        super.onStopLoading();
        cancelLoad(); ❺
    }

    @Override
    protected void onReset() {
        super.onReset();
        mSdCardObserver.stopWatching(); ❻
        clearResources(); ❼
    }

    private void clearResources() {
        mFileNames = null;
    }
}
```

❶ Define a filesystem observer for the addition and removal of files. The constructor of the FileLoader configures it to observe the application file directory—retrieved with getContext().getFilesDir(). When changes are detected, the onEvent method will be invoked. The file observation is handled by the android specific android.os.FileObserver class.

❷ The `FileLoader` is told to start loading data, typically when the `Activity` or `Fragment` is started and is ready to display the data. At this point, the loader is started and the `FileLoader` is expected to observe the underlying data set—i.e., the filesystem—so `startWatching` is invoked.

❸ If a previously delivered data set is cached in the loader, we deliver that to the client so that we don't need to do another asynchronous load.

❹ Force a data load if there is no previous data or if the content has been marked as changed earlier but not delivered.

❺ Try to cancel an ongoing load, because the result will not be delivered anyway.

❻ Stop content observation when the loader is reset, because content changes should not be loaded or cached.

❼ When the loader is reset, it is not expected to be used any more, so remove the reference to the cache.

The `FileLoader` is used to populate a list of file names that is displayed in a `Fragment`:

```
public class FileListFragment extends ListFragment implements
    LoaderManager.LoaderCallbacks<List<String>>{

    private static final int FILE_LOADER_ID = 1;

    private ArrayAdapter<String> mFileAdapter;
    private List<String> mFileNames = new ArrayList<String>();

    @Override
    public void onActivityCreated(Bundle savedInstanceState) {
        super.onActivityCreated(savedInstanceState);
        getLoaderManager().initLoader(FILE_LOADER_ID, null, this);
        setEmptyText("No files in directory");
        setListShown(false);

        mFileAdapter = new ArrayAdapter<String>(getActivity(),
            android.R.layout.simple_list_item_1, android.R.id.text1, mFileNames);
        mFileAdapter.setNotifyOnChange(true);
        setListAdapter(mFileAdapter);
    }

    @Override
    public Loader<List<String>> onCreateLoader(int i, Bundle bundle) {
        return new FileLoader(getActivity());
    }

    @Override
    public void onLoadFinished(Loader<List<String>> fileLoader,
        List<String> fileNames) {
        mFileAdapter.clear();
        mFileAdapter.addAll(fileNames); ❶
```

```
        setListShown(true);
    }

    @Override
    public void onLoaderReset(Loader<List<String>> fileLoader) {
        mFileNames = null;
        mFileAdapter.clear();
    }
}
```

❶   Add the loaded file names to the list and update the UI.

Handling Multiple Loaders

Most commonly, a LoaderManager only manages one loader, in which case the callbacks
are invoked from a known loader: only one exists. If you create multiple loaders, the
callbacks should check the identifier—i.e., invoke Loader.getId()—to verify which
loader has generated the callback. A code skeleton that serves as a template for multiple
loaders is:

```
public class SkeletonActivity extends Activity implements
LoaderManager.LoaderCallbacks<D> {

    private static final int LOADER_ID_ONE = 1;
    private static final int LOADER_ID_TWO = 2;

    public void onCreate(Bundle savedInstanceState) {
        getLoaderManager().initLoader(LOADER_ID_ONE, null, this);
        getLoaderManager().initLoader(LOADER_ID_TWO, null, this);
    }

    // LoaderCallback methods
    public Loader<D> onCreateLoader(int id, Bundle args) {
        switch(id) {
            case LOADER_ID_ONE:
                /* TODO: Create the loader. */
                return ...;
            case LOADER_ID_TWO:
                /* TODO: Create the loader. */
                return ...;
        }
    }

    public void onLoadFinished(Loader<D> loader, D data) {
        switch(loader.getId()) {
            case LOADER_ID_ONE:
                /* TODO: Use the delivered data. */
                break;
            case LOADER_ID_TWO:
                /* TODO: Use the delivered data. */
                break;
```

```
        }
    }
    public void onLoaderReset(Loader<D> loader) {
        switch(loader.getId()) {
            case LOADER_ID_ONE:
                /* TODO: The loader data is invalid, stop using it. */
                break;
            case LOADER_ID_TWO:
                /* TODO: The loader data is invalid, stop using it. */
                break;
        }
    }
}
```

Summary

The Loader framework is the latest asynchronous techniques to be added to the Android platform. It is a framework for asynchronous execution that shines when it comes to the CursorLoader, as it encapsulates the difficulties of a specific use case—i.e., content providers—and solves it efficiently. The framework also offers flexibility by allowing custom loader implementations, but that requires more effort from the application, and it may be better to consider other asynchronous techniques.

CHAPTER 15

Summary: Selecting an Asynchronous Technique

As we've seen, the Android platform provides us with many asynchronous techniques to help us run tasks both concurrently and off the UI thread. Without these techniques, it wouldn't be possible to implement a fast and responsive application, so they become part of the core functionality. The range of techniques are there to assist us and make life easier, but we always have to make choices about which techniques to use. Sometimes the choice is easy—e.g., `CursorLoader` when reading data from a provider—but often we face situations where several mechanisms could solve the problem. In those situations, it's a natural habit to fall back on a mechanism we know and have used before. This may, however, be a suboptimal choice, and we should aim for something better, based on a set of conditions about each technique:

- It uses the fewest system resources—i.e., CPU cycle and memory—as necessary.
- It provides the application with maximum performance and responsiveness.
- It allows low implementation effort.
- It provides a good code design, making it easy to understand and maintain.

This chapter summarizes the asynchronous techniques and how to choose between them. First, let's take a look at the relationships among the mechanisms, shown in Figure 15-1. The `Thread` is the fundamental entity of all mechanisms. Features supporting the asynchronous execution are added further up in the hierarchy, each invoking the following features.

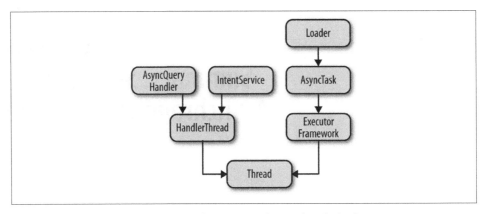

Figure 15-1. The asynchronous mechanisms in the Android platform

When selecting the proper asynchronous mechanism, the rule of thumb is to move as high up in the hierarchy as possible to utilize the added platform functionality. When you need to give more execution control to the application, you can move to a lower level, where that control is provided.

Keep It Simple

The Android platform contains a range of powerful asynchronous techniques that are all based on the `java.lang.Thread` class. The techniques are there to make life easier for us so that we don't have to manage all the threading ourselves. Nevertheless, the simplicity of a single thread can be a good choice for occassional one-shot tasks. For example:

- Initializing an `Activity` with data from a network resource
- Storing data on the file system when `Activity` is destroyed

However, execution with `Thread` doesn't scale well. If there are many tasks to execute, a thread-per-task pattern can cause equally as many threads as there are tasks to run simultaneously, which in turn can cause memory exhaustion and reduced performance. Instead, it's better to use a thread pool that easily can constrain the number of threads.

Thread and Resource Management

Thread pools are a part of Java's Executor framework that helps us with thread execution and resource management. Each pool holds and manages a set of worker threads, making their number of threads and dynamics configurable. Threads that have finished executing a task can remain idle in the pool, waiting for the next task to execute. Hence, the thread pool can keep required memory usage within bounds. The thread pool achieves this by queuing the tasks that are added while all threads in the pool are occupied by other tasks.

Thread pools are powerful asynchronous processors with a flexible setup. They are typically used when the application should execute multiple tasks concurrently while limiting the number of threads—for example, when the application uses multiple HTTP connections that should have an upper limit. In combination with a Service, the pool creates an asynchronous executor that can receive tasks from multiple clients and avoid system termination.

Message Communication for Responsiveness

Both the Thread and the Executor framework are Java mechanisms and have no built-in support for Android message passing, which has to be implemented in the application. The most common use cases for asynchronous execution involve message passing so that data can be passed between the UI thread and background threads.

The HandlerThread combines the execution of a Thread with the possibility of receiving and processing messages sequentially. Hence, you need somewhat less coding to use HandlerThread directly than to decorate a Thread with a Handler.

Messages are processed sequentially. This makes the HandlerThread a good alternative for thread-safe execution of dependent tasks, which would require synchronization in a concurrent environment. It's also a very flexible sequential environment that makes it easy to implement state-machine behavior, where the thread passes messages to itself to change state or chain background tasks, as we saw in "Task Chaining" on page 128.

The sequential execution limitation of the HandlerThread is solved by AsyncTask, a popular asynchronous technique. The AsyncTask allows background task execution in combination with thread communication, offering a generic and adaptable asynchronous technique that can be applied on many use cases—the AsyncTask itself does not impose any constraints. It has occasionally—and incorrectly—been given the epithet "Android's thread," as it hides the message passing between threads.

A fully utilized AsyncTask passes data to the background thread, reports progress updates, and sends the result back to the UI thread. That also serves as a good use case. However, as we saw in Chapter 10, it has a couple of concerns you need to consider:

- Global execution environment
- Differences between execution types depending on platform versions

The AsyncTask is often overused in applications due to its simplicity. It isn't a silver-bullet solution for asynchronous execution on Android. For many use cases, you should look into alternative techniques, for reasons of architecture, program design, or just because they are less error prone.

Avoid Unexpected Task Termination

The system doesn't take running threads into consideration when shutting down applications to reclaim system resources. Therefore, background tasks can be unexpectedly terminated when the application process is killed. The application termination is based on process rank, and a running `Service` raises the application process rank—e.g., how likely an `Activity` is to be stopped when the application isn't visible on the screen. Use of a `Service` helps by reducing the risk that the application and its threads are terminated when the system is low on resources.

There is no asynchronous executor in the `Service`; it's a collaborator rather than a competitor with other asynchronous mechanisms. By moving the asynchronous execution to a `Service`, you can achieve several advantages:

- Critical background tasks execute independently of the application's visibility on the screen—i.e., the user's interaction will be less likely to interfere with the lifetime of the tasks.
- The asynchronous execution can easily be shared between multiple clients, such as Activities.
- The asynchronous execution can be triggered both via `Intents` and through method calls, or even across processes via IPC.

For services that should execute tasks sequentially, you can use `IntentService`, an extension to `Service` containing a `HandlerThread`. It has the lifecycle and process rank advantages of a `Service` combined with a handoff mechanism. The strength of the `IntentService` is its simplicity: clients only have to send an `Intent` with data to be processed.

The `IntentService` is a great candidate for sequential background execution for multiple reasons:

- Simple usage.
- The process rank reduces the risk of background tasks being terminated prematurely.
- It is reachable from all other Android components.

When asynchronous execution is required from a `BroadcastReceiver`, the `IntentService` should be the first mechanism you consider.

Easy Access to ContentProviders

The `AsyncQueryHandler` is an asynchronous `ContentProvider` accessor with a built-in `HandlerThread`, which guarantees that the provider accesses the thread safely. It exists specifically to handle a full set of CRUD operations on a provider and isn't useful otherwise.

Another—more capable—reader of provider data is the `CursorLoader`. It is both simple and powerful, not requiring much effort to implement. It connects to a provider and observes the content so that new data can be loaded asynchronously to an `Activity` or `Fragment`, enabling it to easily update the UI.

For other data sources—where you have to implement a custom loader—a loader isn't necessarily the best choice. It's often more complex to implement a custom loader than to adopt another asynchronous mechanism. As a rule of thumb, custom loaders can be a good choice when the following conditions are fulfilled:

- The underlying content is easily observable.
- There should be an easy way to use a data cache.
- Started tasks don't need to be finished, because the tight coupling of the loader with the `Activity` and `Fragment` lifecycles will destroy the attached `Loader` objects and lose the result.

Thus, it isn't advisable, for example, to use loaders for network requests; they are not easily observed and they will be interrupted based on the client lifecycle. Data loading that should execute until completion should use a `Service` or `IntentService` instead.

The array of options in this book can be intimidating. One of the reasons for the variety of asynchronous options is the wide range of considerations that go into different applications: memory use, number of concurrent tasks, needs to access data stores, latency issues, and so on. By studying the issues I've presented in the book and how they pertain to your particular app, you can find the best technique to suit your needs.

Bibliography

Books

- Brian Goetz et al. *Java Concurrency in Practice.* Addison-Wesley, 2006.

Articles

- Schreiber, Thorsten. "Android Binder: Android Interprocess Communication." Thesis, Ruhr-Universitat Bochum, 2011. *http://bit.ly/1jgw0ui.*
- Pepperdine, Kirk. "Tuning the Size of Your Thread Pool," InfoQ. 2013. *http://bit.ly/1g5mefe.*

Presentations

- Morrill, Dan. "Inside the Android Application Framework." Google I/O, 2008.
- Bornstein, Dan. "Dalvik Virtual Machine Internals." Google I/O, 2008.
- Dubroy, Patrick. "Memory Management for Android Apps." Google I/O, 2011.

Index

Symbols

| (pipe operator), 39

A

activities
    Activity implementing LoaderManager.Loa-
      derCallbacks, 221
    Activity object, 3
    BluetoothActivity (example), 189
    BoundLocalActivity (example), 197
    configuration changes on Activity objects,
      114
    DownloadActivity (example), 191
    implementation of Activity displaying im-
      ages downloaded with AsyncTask, 164
    loaders working with, 220
    memory leaks from Activity objects, 96
    one-way communication between Service
      and Activity in different processes, 84
    retaining worker threads from old to new
      Activity components, 102
    thread retention in an Activity, 114
    two-way communication between Activity
      and Service in different processes, 86
Activity.runOnUiThread() method, 73
ActivityThread class, 60

Android Interface Definition Language (AIDL),
    76, 77
    asynchronous RPC, 81
    synchronous RPC, 79
Android platform, 1
    asynchronous mechanisms in, 243
    software stack, 1
android.os.FileObserver class, 236
anonymous inner class, 112
Application Framework, 2
Application Not Responding (ANR) dialog, 10
Application object, 3
application threads, 29
    background threads, 30
    binder threads, 30
    memory leaks from, 91
    UI thread, 29
applications, 2
    Activities, 3
    architecture, 2
      components, 3
    BroadcastReceiver, 5
    ContentProvider, 5
    execution, 5
      lifecycle, 6
      Linux process, 6
    execution of AsyncTask instances, 169
    Services, 5
    structuring for performance, 9

We'd like to hear your suggestions for improving our indexes. Send email to index@oreilly.com.

ArrayBlockingQueue class, 140
ART (Android Runtime), 2
asynchronous operations, 9
    asynchronous execution in BroadcastReceiver, 204–207
    Remote Procedure Calls (RPC), 81
    selecting an ansynchronous technique, 243
        avoiding unexpected task termination, 246
        easy access to ContentProviders, 247
        message communication for responsiveness, 245
        thread and resource management, 244
    using a Service for asynchronous execution, 177
asynchronous programming, 105–119
    choosing an asynchronous technique for Services, 197
    lifecycle of a thread, 107
    managing threads, 112
        definition and start, 112
        retention, 114
    thread basics, 107
    thread interruptions, 108
    uncaught exceptions during thread execution, 110
AsyncQueryHandler class, 209, 212–218
    asynchronous access to ContentProviders, 212
    example, expanding contact list, 214
    easy access to ContentProviders, 247
    limitations, 218
    methods wrapping provider operations of ContentResolver, 213
AsyncTask class, 157–175, 226, 245
    alternatives to, 173
        background tasks needing a Looper, 174
        local Service, 174
        using execute(Runnable), 174
        when AsyncTask is trivially implemented, 173
    background task execution, 167
        application global execution, 169
        custom execution, 172
        execution across platform versions, 170
    cancellation of the task, 161
    creating and starting implementations, 160
    data passing from execute() to doInBackground(), 158

    example, downloading images, 164
    example, limiting execution to one task at a time, 163
    execute() method, triggering callback to doInBackground(), 157
    executing task in background and delivering result to UI thread, 158
    implementing, 163
    Services and, 198
    states, 162
AsyncTask.getStatus() method, 162
AsyncTask.isCancelled, 161
AsyncTaskLoader class, 220, 225
    extension by custom loaders, 234
atomic regions, 19

B

background processes, 7
background task execution (AsyncTask), 167
    application global execution, 169
    custom execution, 172
    execution across platform versions, 170
background tasks, in Service restarts, 186
background threads, 30
binder class, 76
Binder class
    ServiceBinder subclass (example), 194
binder framework, 75
    message passing with, 83
        one-way communication, 84
        two-way communication, 86
binder threads, 30, 91
blocked threads, 20, 108
    causing memory leaks, 93
BlockingQueue class, 46
Bluetooth connection (user-controlled Service example), 187
bound services, 5, 182, 192
    local binding, 194
bounded task queues, 140
BroadcastReceiver, 5
    asynchronous execution in, 204–207
        example, periodical long operations, 205
    use in content management, 236
BroadcastReceiver.goAsync() method, 204
BroadcastReceiver.PendingResult, 205

C

cached thread pools, 137
Callable interface, 146
    retrieving a result, 148
CalledFromWrongThreadException, 29
cancellation points, 109
cancellation requests to AsyncTask, 161
CancellationSignal, 218
CFS (completely fair scheduler), 34
cgroups (see control groups)
completely fair scheduler (CFS), 34
components, 3
    independence of thread lifecycle from, 177
    lifecycle mismatch between components, objects, and threads, 96
    Service, creation of, 182
concurrent execution of tasks, 26
    AsyncTask implementations, 167
        across platform versions, 170
    concurrent file download executor running in a Service, 190
consumer-producer pattern (example), 24
ContentObserver, 236
ContentProvider, 5, 209–218
    asynchronous access with AsyncQueryHandler, 212–218
        examplel, expanding a contact list, 214
    easy access to, 247
    introduction to, 209
    justification for background processing of, 211
ContentProviderOperation class, 218
ContentResolver class, 210, 217
    AsyncQueryHandler methods wrapping provider operations, 213
context switch, 16
Context.bindService() method, 5, 182, 192
Context.startService() method, 5, 182
Context.stopService() method, 5, 185
Context.unbindService() method, 193
control groups (thread), 36
core threads, 140
critical sections (of code), 20
CursorLoader class, 220, 226
    adding CRUD support, 229
    reader of provider data, 247
    using, 227
        example, contact list, 227

D

Dalvik Debug Monitor Service (DDMS), 33
Dalvik runtime, 2
data inconsistency in multithreaded applications, 18
data messages
    processing, 66
    sending, memory leaks from, 98
DDMS (Dalvik Debug Monitor Service), 33
definition and start, threads, 112
    defining a thread as a public class, 112
    defining a thread as a static inner class, 113
    summary of options for thread definition, 113
    using anonymous inner class, 112
dispatch time for messages, 62
dispatched state (messages), 57
DownloadService (example), 191
dynamic-size thread pools, 137, 139

E

empty processes, 7
exceptions, uncaught, during thead execution, 110
ExecutionException, 147
Executor framework, 133–155
    custom Executor for AsyncTask implementations, 172
    execution behaviors controlled by, 134
    Executor interface, 133
        simple implementation, 134
    ExecutorCompletionService, 152
    SerialExecutor implementation (example), 134
    task management, 146
        rejecting tasks, 151
        submitting tasks, 147
        task representation, 146
    thread pools, 244
        advantages of using, 136
        custom, 137
        designing, 138
        predefined, 136
        use cases and pitfalls, 145
ExecutorCompletionService, 152
Executors class, 136
Executors.newCachedThreadPool() method, 137

Executors.newFixedThreadPool() method, 136, 141

Executors.newSingleThreadExecutor() method, 137

ExecutorService interface, 147

ExecutorService.invokeAll() method, 149

ExecutorService.invokeAny() method, 151

explicit intents, 3

explicit locks, 23

F

FileLoader class (example), 238

FileObserver class, 236, 239

fixed-size thread pools, 136

foreground processes, 7

Fragment
  FileListFragment (example), 240
  loaders working with, 220
  retaining a thread in, 117

Future interface, 147

G

garbage collection, 89
  garbage collection roots, 90
  stopped by retained threads, 116
  thread lifecycle and its GC roots, 92

garbage collector (GC), 89

global services, 180

grep command, 32

H

Handler class, 48, 60–68
  inserting messages in message queue, 62
  message creation, 61
  message processing, 66
  methods for managing the message queue, 69
  removing messages from the queue, 68
  setup of handlers, 60
  using Handler and Runnable in thread communication, memory leaks from, 98
  using with Messenger, 87

HandlerThread, 121–131, 245
  background task executor in IntentService, 199
  fundamentals, 121
  lifecycle, 123

limiting access to, 122

use cases, 124
  conditional task insertion, 131
  data persistence with SharedPreferences, 125
  related tasks, 125
  repeated task execution, 125
  task chaining, 128
  using instead of AsyncTask, 174

heap, 44, 89

HTTP requests, 201

I

IBinder interface, 193

IBinder.FLAG_ONEWAY, 77

idle time for threads in thead pool, 138

IdleHandler interface, 52
  using to terminate an unused thread, 53

implicit intents, 3

inner classes, 93
  anonymous, 112
  static, 94, 113
    using to avoid memory leaks, 101

IntentFilter, 3, 181

Intents, 3, 179
  identifying Service to bind to, 193
  terminated Services and, 185

IntentService class, 199–208, 246
  client creating start request, 200
  good ways to use, 201
    asynchronous execution in BroadcastReceiver, 204–207
    sequentially ordered tasks, 201
  overriding with application specific implementation, 200
  restoring IntentService if process is killed, 200
  Service class versus, 207

interfaces
  asynchronous RPC, 82
  remote communication, construction of, 77

interprocess communication (IPC), 75–87
  Android Interface Definition Language (AIDL), 77
    asynchronous RPC, 81
    synchronous RPC, 79
  Android RPC, 75
    binder class, 76

message passing using the binder, 83
    one-way communication, 84
    two-way communication, 86
InterruptedException, 109
interruptions, thread, 108, 161
intrinsic locks, 20
    in producer-consumer pattern example, 25
    using to synchronize access to shared re-
        sources, 22

J

Java
    core libraries used in Android applications, 2
    multithreading in, 15–27
    pipes, 39
    priority values for threads, 35
java.lang.Runnable interface, 16
java.lang.Thread class, 2, 15, 105, 244
java.util.concurrent package, 2
java.util.concurrent.BlockingQueue class, 46

K

keep alive time (thread pools), 140

L

lifecycle
    application, 6
    mismatch between components, objects, and
        threads, 95, 177
    of a HandlerThread, 123
    of a thread, 107
    of a thread pool, 142
    of Loaders, 233
    of messages in Android, 56
    of processes hosting threads, 177
    of Services, 181
LinkedBlockingQueue class, 140
Linux kernel, 2
    scheduling of application threads in An-
        droid, 34
Linux processes, 6
    (see also processes)
    and threads, 31–37
        finding application process information,
            32
    application execution in, 6

lifecycle of, and unexpected termination of
    background tasks, 177
Loader class, 220
Loader framework, 219–242
    asynchronous data management, 219
    AsyncTaskLoader class, 225
    cached data with, 220
    core classes, 220
    CursorLoader class, 226, 247
        example, contact list, 227
        example, using with AsyncQueryHan-
            dler, 229
    implementing custom loaders, 233, 247
        background loading, 234
        content management, 236
        delivering cached results, 237
        example, custom file loader, 238
        handling multiple loaders, 241
        Loader lifecycle, 233
    lifecycle management with, 219
    LoaderManager class, 221
        initLoader() versus restartLoader(), 222
        LoaderCallbacks interface, 224
LoaderManager class, 221
    (see also Loader framework)
    control of Loader lifecycle, 234
    typical setup with callbacks in an Activity,
        221
LoaderManager.LoaderCallbacks interface, 221,
    224
    sequence of loader callbacks, 224
local services, 179
    bound local service, 194
locks
    intrinsic lock and Java monitor, 20
    locking mechanisms in Android, 20
    using explicit locking mechanisms, 23
    using to synchronize access to shared re-
        sources, 22
long-running tasks, 10
Looper class, 48, 58
    background tasks that need a Looper, 174
    enabling message queue logging, 72
    in a HandlerThread, 121
    Looper for handlers, 60
    Looper for UI thread, 60, 73
    termination of the Looper, 59

M

mark and sweep, 90
marshalling, 76
memory management, 89–103
  avoiding memory leaks, 101
    cleaning up the message queue, 102
    in AsyncTask implementations, 163
    retaining worker threads, 102
    starting and stopping Services, 187
    stopping worker thread execution, 102
    using Services instead of threads for
      background tasks, 177
    using static inner classes, 101
    using weak references, 101
  garbage collection, 89
  memory leaks, defined, 89
  protection against memory leaks with Load-
    ers, 220
  thread definition and start, 112
  thread-related memory leaks, 91
    thread communication, 98
    thread execution, 92
memory, shared, passing information between
  threads, 44
Message class, 48, 55
  Handler class wrapper functions for message
    creation, 61
  memory leaks from Message objects, 100
  Message object insertion into queue by Han-
    dler, 62
  repeated task execution with Handler-
    Thread, 125
message insertion errors, 63
message passing in Android, 47–74
  API overview, 48
  AsyncQueryHandler and ContentResolver,
    217
  between producer threads and consumer
    thread, overview of, 48
  classes used, 51
  cleaning up the message queue, 102
  communicating with the UI thread, 73
  example, basic message passing, 49
  example, two-way message passing, 63
  Handler class, 60–68
  HandlerThread, 121–131
  Looper class, 58
  memory leaks from thread communication,
    98

Message class, 55
message communication for responsiveness,
  245
MessageQueue class, 51
  observing the message queue, 70
    tracing message queue processing, 72
  removing messages from the queue, 68
  using the binder framework, 83
    one-way communication, 84
    two-way communication, 86
MessageQueue class, 48, 51
  in a HandlerThread, 121
MessageQueue.IdleHandler interface, 52
Messenger class, 83
  using Handler with, 87
ModernAsyncTask class, 226
monitors, 20
multithreading in Java, 15–27
  task execution strategies, 26
  thread basics, 15
    execution, 15
    multithreaded applications, 17
    single-threaded applications, 17
  thread safety, 19–26
    example, consumer-producer pattern, 24
    intrinsic lock and Java monitor, 20
    synchronizing access to shared resources,
      22
mutually exclusive atomic regions in Java, 19

N

native libraries in Android platform, 2
network calls, chained, using HandlerThread,
  128
NetworkCheckerIntentService (example), 206
nice value (see niceness)
niceness, 34
  Java priority versus, 35

O

Object identifier (messages), 69
objects, 90
  (see also references, object)
  created in methods, garbage collection of, 93
  GC root, 91
  lifecycle mismatch between components, ob-
    jects, and threads, 95
  marked as unused, 90

object dependency tree with static inner class thread executing external Runnable, 95

removal from heap by GC, 90

Observable class, 236

Observer class, 236

oneway keyword, 82

operational modes, 185

P

Parcel object, 76

Parcelable interface, 77

parent process identifier (PPID), 31

pending state (messages), 57

PID (process identifier), 31

pipes, 39

basic use of, 40

example, text processing on a worker thread, 42

PPID (parent process identifier), 31

priority (threads), 16, 34

changing, 35

HandlerThread, 123

Java priority versus Linux niceness, 35

lowering with Process.setThreadPriority(), 37

PriorityBlockingQueue class, 140

process identifier (PID), 31

process rank, 4

Process.setThreadPriority() method, 37

processes

ranking for termination, 7

threads versus, 33

producer-consumer synchronization problem, 46

progress updates, using AsyncTask, 160

Proxy class, 78

ps (process status) command, 32

thread control group information from, 36

pthreads, 33

Q

queues

blocking queue, 46

bounded or unbounded task queues, 140

message queue (android.os.MessageQueue), 51

task queue type for thread pools, 138

thread pools handling preloaded task queues, 145

queuing, favoring thread creation over, 145

R

race conditions, 19

reachable and unreachable objects, 90

recycled state (messages), 58

ReentrantLock class, 23

ReentrantReadWriteLock class, 23

references, object, 90

inner and outer classes, 93

object reference tree when posting task message, 100

object reference tree when sending data message, 99

static inner classes, 101

threads defined in static inner classes, 94

weak references, 101

RejectedExecutionHandler interface, 151

Remote Procedure Calls (RPC), 75

asynchronous RPC, 81

binder class, 76

synchronous, 79

remote services, 180

resource consumption, increased, for multi-threaded applications, 18

responsive applications, creating through threads, 9

restarting services, 184

retaining threads, 114

in a Fragment, 117

in an Activity, 114

RPC (see Remote Procedure Calls)

Runnable interface, 16, 107

repeated task execution with Handler-Thread, 125

using execute(Runnable) with AsyncTask, 174

Runnable object, 92, 98

posting Runnable to execute on consumer Thread with a Looper, 99

static inner class thread executing external Runnable, 95

Runnable state (threads), 108

Runnable.run() method, 146

S

saturation policy, 140
schedulers, 16
    Linux kernel scheduler, 34
scheduling threads on Android, 34
sequential execution of tasks, 26
    AsyncTask implementations, 167
        across platform versions, 170
    for a task-controlled service, 198
    using IntentService, 201
        web service communication (example), 201
service processes, 7
Service.onBind() method, 182
Service.stopSelf() method, 185
ServiceConnection interface, 193
ServiceConnection.onServiceConnected() method, 195
ServiceListener class, 197
services, 177–198
    bound, 192
        local binding, 194
    choosing an asynchronous technique, 197
    creation and execution, 181
    IntentService, 199–208
        versus Service, 207
    lifecycle, 181
    local Service, alternatives to AsyncTask, 174
    local, remote, and global, 179
    one-way communication between Service and Activity in different processes, 84
    Service object, 5
    started, 183
        implementing onStartCommand(), 184
        onBind() method, 183
        options for restarting, 184
        task-controlled Service, 190
        user-controlled Service, 186
    two-way communication between Activity and Service in different processes, 86
    using a Service for asynchronous execution, 177
    using a Service to avoid unexpected task termination, 246
    using for data loading, 247
signaling, 45
single thread executor thread pools, 137
single-threaded applications, thread execution, 17

size of thread pools, 138
SQLite databases
    ContentProvider exposing data in, 210
    faster access by write-ahead logging, 211
stack property, 31
started services, 5, 182, 186
    (see also services)
    onStartCommand() method, 183
        implementing, 184
starting applications, 6
START_FLAG_REDELIVERY, 186
START_FLAG_RETRY, 186
START_NOT_STICKY (Services), 185
    IntentService, 200
START_REDELIVER_INTENT (Services), 185
    IntentService, 200
START_STICKY (Services), 185
starvation, 16
static inner classes, 94
    defining threads as, 113
    using to avoid memory leaks, 101
Stub class, 78
synchronization
    synchronized keyword in Java, 19
    synchronizing access to shared resources, 22
    thread signaling and, 45
synchronous operations, 9
    RPC (Remote Procedure Calls), 79

T

targetSdkVersion, manifest file, 170
task management with Executor framework, 146
    rejecting tasks, 151
    submitting tasks, 147
        individual submission, 148
    task representation, 146
    task submission
        invokeAll() method, 149
        invokeAny() method, 151
task messages
    posting, memory leaks from, 99
    processing, 66
task-controlled Services, 190
    concurrent download (example), 190
    sequential execution for, 198
tasks
    avoiding unexpected termination, 246

background task execution with AsyncTask, 167

chaining, using HandlerThread, 128
    example, chained network calls, 128

conditional task insertion using Handler-Thread, 131

custom thread pool tracking number of tasks currently executing, 142

defined, 15

execution behaviors controlled by Executor implementation, 134

execution strategies, 26

premature termination of, 177

queue type, 138
    bounded or unbounded, 140

related, executing with HandlerThread, 125

repeated execution with HandlerThread, 125

task messages, 56

terminated threads, 108
    HandlerThread, 124

terminating applications, 7

text processing on a worker thread (pipes example), 42

Thread class, 2, 15, 92, 105, 107, 244
    (see also threads)

thread pools, 30, 136, 244
    custom, creating using Executor framework, 137
    designing, 138
        dynamics, 139
        extending ThreadPoolExecutor, 141
        size, 138
        thread configuration, 140
    lifecycle, 142
    predefined, in Executor framework, 136
    shutting down, 143
    use cases and pitfalls, 145
        danger of zero core threads, 146
        favoring thread creation over queuing, 145
        handling preloaded task queues, 145

thread safety, 19–26
    example, consumer-producer pattern, 24
    intrinsic locks and Java monitor, 20
    synchronizing access to shared resources, 22

Thread.setPriority() method, 35

Thread.State class, 107

ThreadFactory interface, 141

threading, 15
    (see also multithreading in Java)
    creating responsive applications through threads, 9
    fundamental Java mechanisms, 2

ThreadPoolExecutor class, 137
    configuration of thread pool behavior, 137
    extending, 141
    predefined handlers for rejected tasks, 151
    thread configuration, 140

ThreadPoolExecutor.prestartAllCoreThreads() method, 145

ThreadPoolExecutor.prestartCoreThread() method, 145

threads
    basics of, 107
    communication, 39–74
        pipes, 39
        shared memory, 44
        signaling, 45
        using Android message passing, 47–74
        using BlockingQueue, 46
    defined, 15
    execution, controlling with Executor framework, 133–155
    interruptions, 108
    lifecycle, 107
    managing, 112
        definition and start, 112
        retention, 114
    memory leaks from, 91
        cleaning up the message queue, 102
        lifecycle mismatch, 95
        thread communication, 98
        thread execution, 92
    on Android, 29–37
        application threads, 29
        Linux process and threads, 31–37
    processes versus, 33
    thread creation and task execution strategies, 26
    uncaught exceptions, 110

tokens, 214

transactions, 76
    asynchronous, 77

U

UI thread, 10, 29, 91
    communicating with, 73

involving with pipes, caution with, 44
Looper, 60
problems with mechanisms using blocking
    behavior, 47
tying a background task to, using AsyncTask,
    157–175
uncaught exceptions on, 111
UID (user id), 31
unbounded task queues, 140
UncaughtExceptionHandler interface, 110
unmarshalling, 76
unreachable objects, 90
unused objects, 90
user id (UID), 31
user-controlled Services, 186
    Bluetooth connection (example), 187

V
virtual machines (VMs), 89
    application execution in, 6

virtual runtime of a thread, 34
visible processes, 7

W
waiting threads, 20
WAL (write-ahead logging), 211
weak references, 101
worker threads, 31, 91
    continuing to execute after component is de-
        stroyed, 97
    defining and starting, 112
    retaining from old to new Activity compo-
        nents, 102
    stopping execution to avoid memory leaks,
        102
write-ahead logging (WAL), 211

Z
Zygote process, 7

About the Author

Anders Göransson is a software architect, developer, trainer, and international speaker. Having earned a M.Sc. in Engineering Physics, he has spent his entire career in the software industry. Anders started with industrial automation systems, but since 2005, he has focused on software for handheld devices, specializing in the Android platform since 2009.

Colophon

The animal on the cover of *Efficient Android Threading* is mahi-mahi, or the common dolphinfish (*Coryphaena hippurus*). This ray-finned fish is a surface-dweller that is found in temperate, tropical, and subtropical waters. The name *mahi-mahi* translates to "very strong" in Hawaiian. Despite its alternate name of "dolphinfish," mahi-mahi are not related to the marine mammals. There are two species of dolphinfish: the common dolphinfish and the pompano dolphin. Along the English speaking coast of South Africa, these fish are often called by the Spanish name, Dorado.

Mahi-mahi can grow up to 15–29 lb, seldom exceeding 33 lb. They can live up to five years, but average around four years. The mahi-mahi's compressed bodies have long dorsal fins that extend almost the entire body length. Mahi-mahi are characterized by their brilliant colors: broad golden flank with bright blues and greens on the side and back, and three diagonal black stripes on each side of the fish. These colors change after the fish is caught; out of water, mahi-mahi cycle through several colors before fading to a yellow-grey when it dies.

Males and females are distinguished by their head shapes: males have prominent foreheads that stick out past the body, whereas females have rounded heads. Within the first year, both males and females are sexually mature, around 4–5 months. Females can spawn two to three times a year, producing 80,000–1,000,000 eggs per spawn.

Mahi-mahi is primarily consumed in the US and Caribbean countries, though many European countries are increasing their consumption. Organizations such as the Monterey Bay Aquarium discourages consuming mahi-mahi imported and harvested by long line, which can injure or kill seabirds, sea turtles, and sharks as a bycatch. Mahi-mahi caught in the US Atlantic is classed as "Eco-Best" by the Environmental Defense Fund (EDF).

The cover image is from *Braukhaus Lexicon*. The cover fonts are URW Typewriter and Guardian Sans. The text font is Adobe Minion Pro; the heading font is Adobe Myriad Condensed; and the code font is Dalton Maag's Ubuntu Mono.

Have it your way.

Get even more for your money.

Join the O'Reilly Community, and register the O'Reilly books you own. It's free, and you'll get:

- $4.99 ebook upgrade offer
- 40% upgrade offer on O'Reilly print books
- Membership discounts on books and events
- Free lifetime updates to ebooks and videos
- Multiple ebook formats, DRM FREE
- Participation in the O'Reilly community
- Newsletters
- Account management
- 100% Satisfaction Guarantee

Signing up is easy:

1. Go to: oreilly.com/go/register
2. Create an O'Reilly login.
3. Provide your address.
4. Register your books.

Note: English-language books only

To order books online:
oreilly.com/store

For questions about products or an order:
orders@oreilly.com

To sign up to get topic-specific email announcements and/or news about upcoming books, conferences, special offers, and new technologies:
elists@oreilly.com

For technical questions about book content:
booktech@oreilly.com

To submit new book proposals to our editors:
proposals@oreilly.com

O'Reilly books are available in multiple DRM-free ebook formats. For more information:
oreilly.com/ebooks

O'REILLY®

Lightning Source UK Ltd.
Milton Keynes UK
UKOW07f2129131015

260454UK00008B/39/P